FANTASTIC TELEVISION

FANTASTIC
TELEVISION

FANTASTIC
TELEVISION
FANTASTIC
TELEVISION
FANTASTIC
TELEVISION

FANTASTIC TELEVISION

By
GARY GERANI

With
PAUL H. SCHULMAN

H

HARMONY BOOKS
New York

Dedicated to Len Brown and John and Jean Gerani.

Acknowledgments

The author would like to thank the following for their help: Alan Armer, Allan Asherman, Larry Brill, Mark Carducci, Dave Carlin, Casey Cole, Jim Danforth, Doug Diamond, Bruce Fedow, Doug Johnson, Steve Mitchell, Richard & Peggy Morisis, Doug Murray, Jerry Ohlinger, Thomas Rogers, Stanley Simon, Joseph Stefano, Ronald Tilton and Buddy Weiss.

Special thanks to John McClelland Danley and Ian Colin Allan for the use of their *Star Trek* paraphernalia and to Joseph Curley for his help with the indexes.

Thanks to the B.B.C. for the use of their photographs in British Telefantasy. Unless otherwise indicated, all other stills are from the author's private collection.

Book and Cover Designed by Ken Sansone.

Publisher: Bruce Harris
Executive Editor: Linda Sunshine
Editor: Pamela Riddle
Production: Gene Conner, Murray Schwartz
Typography: B.P.E. Graphics, Spring Valley, New York

Harmony Books
A division of Crown Publishers, Inc.
One Park Avenue
New York, New York 10016

Published simultaneously in Canada by General Publishing Company Limited. Printed in the United States of America.

Library of Congress Cataloging in Publication Data

Gerani, Gary.
    Fantastic television.

    Includes index.
    1. Fantastic television programs.   I. Schulman, Paul, joint author.
II. Title.
PN1992.8.F35G4   791.45′5   76-56821
ISBN 0-517-52646-8
ISBN 0-517-52645-X pbk.

Second Printing

CONTENTS

INTRODUCTION

The worlds of fantasy and science fiction have always had a strong appeal for Gary Gerani. Unlike most of us, he has been able to turn his childhood passion into a profitable career. As a writer of science fiction articles and a collector of television art, Gary is recognized in New York science fiction circles as the last word on the subject. Working with him on this project has been fun for me, and being asked to write the introduction led me to think about my own connection to the subject.

When I entered high school, I was assaulted with batteries of tests—vocational, intelligence, mechanical ability, personality. One question was: How much television do you watch? I considered this question at great length. I calculated the time spent watching TV on an average weekday, multiplied by five, added in the weekend, divided by seven, and then glanced at the measly total on the paper of the girl next to me. Mortified, I divided again by three. Even this dishonest tally singled me out as the leading TV watcher in the class.

In those days I had two main interests, baseball and television—but these were passions, *manias,* when I was even younger. Then, if I didn't like what was on CBS, I'd turn to NBC, or to ABC, or Dumont, or the other local stations until I found a program I did like. If I couldn't find something I liked, I'd watch something I didn't like. It never occurred to me to turn the thing off, so I didn't and watched some abysmal shows. Series like the *Cisco Kid, Crunch and Des, Racket Squad,* and *Soldiers of Fortune* were dull beyond imagining, but the tube had me mesmerized. That spell has since been broken, but little on the tube has changed. Then, as now, shooting, fighting, chasing, and killing were the lifeblood of the television set, though the formula has since been updated. In the old days, when a cowboy got shot it was always "just a flesh wound, ma'am," but nowadays, when someone takes a bullet the bone is shattered and it's serious.

When not sitting in our basement watching television, I was in the corner lot playing baseball. The lot's edges were overgrown with tall weeds, and a path cut through it just behind home plate. The infield was as loose as beach sand. (When we got home we had to sit on the stoop and empty the sand from our sneakers before being allowed into the house.) Right field was a crater filled with trees, poison ivy, and automobile tires, and left field was a fenced-in backyard. Only center field was fair territory, extending on the flat, a few feet beyond the shirt or piece of cardboard that was second base and then up the hill of an abandoned spur of the Long Island Railroad. Between second and third was a patch of stickers. First base was a gray boulder about the size of an elephant's head and shoulders. Just to the left of first was a smaller, pointed boulder.

First base and its little brother had been left by a receding glacier, but my friends and I figured that the Nazis had put them there in preparation for their invasion. They put machine guns under first and tommy guns under the smaller rock. Actually, *I* may have put the tommy guns under the smaller rock, since I would not have bought the theory without them. Besides, tommy guns fascinated me—I liked the sound of the word and I liked the heft of the gun. I reasoned that if machine guns were under the large rock, then tommy guns *must* be under the small one. This extra data point made the theory seem so irrefutable, so thrilling, that my first great goal in life was to move these boulders, not to prove it, but to play with the guns.

My interest in Superman was kindled because these boulders were too heavy to move. I had envied his strength and ability to fly ever since we became acquainted in the barbershop where I read Superman comics. The Man of Steel was also my first TV favorite, and I remember running across our front lawn yelling to my brother "Supe's on!" A frivolous kid myself, I also admired Captain Video's seriousness of purpose in defending freedom—he even sold war bonds—and was itching to get my hands on his weapons, especially the Cosmic Vibrator.

Superman was essentially a crime series and *Captain Video* was a Cold War parable with cartoons. They jackhammered their lessons about crime and freedom into my brain day after day, half hour after half hour. I finally learned them, but I was getting older and my fascination with Superman's gifts and Captain Video's guns was waning. Yet as soon as I pushed the button to turn these shows off, my pupils dilated and my ears snapped to attention.

Our television set was in the basement. When it was on, casting its dim gray light on the paneled walls, I was safe, but the moment the tube went dead, the darkness came alive. Heavy, arhythmic breathing came from the furnace; creatures in the pantry began to nibble crackers; the small windows close to the ceiling rattled when something on the back porch pressed against them; faint thunder rumbled behind the metal shower stall. Suddenly, there was a movement on the stairs—but that was just me, darting toward the light above, toward the protective haze of cigar smoke from my father's pinochle game. Toward reality.

Adult reality fits childhood like a secondhand suit. Children inspect the pattern, feel the weave, and wave their arms to see how much the suit restricts movement. Though the suit appears perfect to a child, childhood is also spent searching for a loose seam, an exception, where imagination might wear a hole. Superman is a loose seam, and he piques their interest, opens their eyes to fantastic possibilities. I found other seams in the dark and under boulders and they aroused an adrenal thrill of terror and fascination.

Nevertheless I grew up and came to accept adult reality. My fear of the dark disappeared overnight and so did the boulders in the corner lot—a construction crew removed them to put up a row of two-family houses. No tommy guns, but by then I didn't expect any.

The exhilaration of mystery, of fear and discovery, isn't lost, however; it progresses. The occult and science fiction television shows of my adolescence, like *One Step Beyond, Thriller, Outer Limits,* and especially *Twilight Zone,* probed the seams of my adolescent reality. They frightened me and held me in awe.

As I was being pushed from behind into adulthood and, not incidentally, as space travel became reality, the Captain Videos and Flash Gordons became camp. But a younger generation was already waist deep into *Batman, Lost in Space,* and Vulcan lore. In time, of course, even the Star Ship *Enterprise* will become camp and another new crop of kids will become enthralled by new TV shows.

Fantastic Television highlights series that have probed the seams, the raveled cuffs, the loose threads of reality. "Fine Tuning," the first of its two sections, focuses on thirteen of the very best fantasy and sci-fi TV shows, from their birth and development to their inevitable demise. It describes the men who made them—the actors, producers, writers, directors, right down to the cameramen and makeup artists. It is also an appraisal of the final products that saw the light of the picture tube. At the end of each chapter, there is a chronological index of every episode aired. Each includes a capsule description and lists the writer, director, stars, and more. The second part, "The Full Picture," is an encyclopedia of all the other representatives of the genre from *Topper* to *Wonder Woman*. Special sections detail made-for-TV movies, British telefantasy, and the best in children's fantasy programming.

Fantastic Television is the most complete and detailed treatment of occult and science fiction TV shows existing anywhere. If you caught these shows the first time around, this book will be a visit from old friends. If you were too young to stay up that late, *Fantastic Television* will introduce you to a world of new friends.

—Paul H. Schulman

FANTASTIC
TELEVISION

FANTASTIC
TELEVISION

FANTASTIC
TELEVISION

FANTASTIC
TELEVISION

PART 1: FINE TUNING

Scores of science fiction series have been produced in TV's thirty-year history. The earliest were naive, even bumbling by today's standards, but recent shows are extraordinarily sophisticated. Superman could fly faster than a speeding bullet but the *Enterprise* can fly faster than the speed of light. Each of the thirteen shows selected for "Fine Tuning" were distinctive and memorable. Some were intelligent, some had incredible special effects, some were haunting or funny, and, of course, most were popular.

For instance, *The Prisoner* had a brief run and was probably too cerebral for a mass audience, yet it had the most captivating premise of the genre. Irwin Allen's series had little to recommend their plots, acting, and directing, but they harvested honors for special effects. *The Outer Limits* was fairly popular the first time around, but by virtue of excellent stories, acting, and cinematography, it still haunts the chill night air. A show like *Twilight Zone* was a success on all levels—except it wasn't that popular.

The character of each show, the conflict behind the scenes, and the reason for its success or failure are discussed in each chapter. How, for instance, has *Star Trek* managed to influence audiences for eight years after its cancellation—a phenomenon showing no signs of abating? Why did *Outer Limits* die in its second season? Why did Rod Serling have little, and want less, to do with *Rod Serling's Night Gallery?* Why was Batman considered a risky venture? The character of these shows is laid open in "Fine Tuning."

Each chapter is accompanied by a complete index of episodes which TV buffs will surely appreciate. Every episode ever aired is listed in chronological order along with the names of the writer, director, and guest cast. A brief plot synopsis is also included. "Fine Tuning," in short, is a detailed history of a TV genre.

THE ADVENTURES OF SUPERMAN

In all the shows that I made there was only one murder. Most of the time, rather than Superman beating up those guys, we'd shoot them running into each other or cracking their heads on the wall. We made the crooks comic so we wouldn't frighten our audience.

—Whitney Ellsworth
Producer

Though Superman was a Depression-era fantasy created by Jerome Siegal and Joe Shuster, it seems as if he has always existed, as if George Washington, too, were reared on him. He started out as a comic book hero—kids too young for the girlie magazines discovered him at the barber shop; later he fought crime on the radio, then crime in the movies, and finally, television crime. After all, he had dedicated his life to fighting crime wherever it may be. When *Superman* began to appear on TV—debuting February 9, 1953—everyone would gather at the home of the kid on the block who had a set and have this message carved forever into his cortex: "Faster than a speeding bullet, more powerful than a locomotive, able to leap tall buildings in a single bound. Look...up in the sky ...it's a bird...it's a plane...it's Superman!" What naughty fun everyone had tinkering with those lines!

The Man of Steel's first bout with movie crime was in 1941. Animator Dave Fleischer, of "Popeye" fame, produced 17 Superman cartoons in technicolor. These were followed by a pair of low-budget serials in the mid-forties that starred Kirk Alyn. But it wasn't until 1951 that the most famous Superman of all appeared on the screen. In "Superman and the Mole Men" the two star reporters of the Metropolis *Daily Planet*, Clark Kent and Lois Lane, covered the story of the deepest oil well ever drilled in a little town called Silsby. Mild-mannered Clark Kent, of course, was Superman's disguise. George Reeves and Phyllis Coates played Clark and Lois (Bud Collier was Superman on the radio). An interesting angle suddenly developed on the oil well story: two furry creatures—half man, half mole—crawled out of the well rubbing their eyes to adjust to the sunlight and ambled into town. Though friendly enough, they seemed to be radioactive, because everything they touched began to glow. The frightened townspeople of Silsby, led by hateful Luke Benson, hunted the mole men, cornered one of them—the other escaped— and were about to shoot it when Superman intervened to save its life. Before you could run to the lobby and return with popcorn, the little fellow who escaped was leading an army of mole men down the streets of Silsby, looking for their lost comrade. They didn't find him, but did find Luke Benson and were just about to kill him with their ray guns when once again Superman intervened, blocking the rays with his body. Superman returned the missing mole man and both creatures returned to their burrows beneath the ground, blowing up the well shaft to ensure their privacy. Lois summed it up: "It's almost as though they were saying 'You live your lives,' and we'll live 'ours.' "

Two years after this feature, Superman made a successful move to television. The first show concerned Superman's origins and the response was electric. In just a few weeks it became the most popular late afternoon show on television. A scientist on the planet Krypton rocketed his infant son to Earth just prior to Krypton's destruction. The

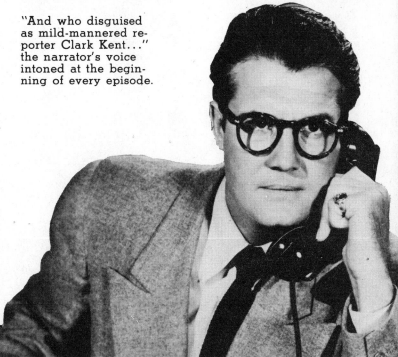

"And who disguised as mild-mannered reporter Clark Kent..." the narrator's voice intoned at the beginning of every episode.

The premiere episode was the only one to show Krypton, Superman's birthplace. Here, Jor-el, Superman's father, is wearing Flash Gordon's hand-me-down costume.

Joe Shuster (left) and Jerome Siegel, the artist and writer who created Superman for the comics.

boy landed and grew up just outside of Metropolis. He was reared by the Kent family and named Clark. Although he did not emerge as Superman until he was grown, it was clear from the first that Clark was an unusual child: He was super-strong, had X-ray vision enabling him to see through solid objects (except lead), and he was invulnerable, except to the element Kryptonite, which could severely weaken and even kill him.

As an adult Clark became a newspaper reporter, a profession which allowed him to keep abreast of crime; but to preserve his real identity as Superman, he pretended to be meek. Whenever something dangerous would come up, Clark would shrink away, chased by the contemptuous barbs of Lois Lane—only to return as Superman and be greeted by her adoring praise. Lois was of the every-column-as-tough-as-any-male's school of female reporting. George Reeves and Phyllis Coates continued in their now-familiar roles for the first TV season. Coates portrayed an abrasive Lois—when she called Clark a pantywaist, she meant it.

In the second season, she was replaced by Noel Neill, who, despite her blazing red hair, was less acidulous; when she called Clark a pantywaist, she didn't mean it. John Hamilton played the curmudgeonly editor-in-chief, Perry White, who was continually annoyed by naive, bumbling cub reporter Jimmy Olsen. "Don't call me Chief!" White would shout. "All right, all right, Chief. You don't have to get sore," Jimmy would say as he backed out of the office. Jack Larson, who played Jimmy, later became a playwright. Jimmy idolized Clark ("Golleee, Mr. Kent") and had a crush

ABOVE, John Hamilton as Perry White, editor-in-chief of the *Daily Planet;* Phyllis Coates as star reporter Lois Lane; and Robert Shayne as police Inspector Henderson. Phyllis Coates was replaced by Noel Neill after the first season. BELOW: Neill with Jack Larson who played cub reporter Jimmy Olsen.

"Faster than a speeding bullet" Superman "flew" over "Metropolis."

on Lois. Lois, of course, held Clark in contempt and doted on Jimmy in a big sister-like way. Clark was meek but level-headed and, except for Lois, respected by all. Out of the *Planet's* offices there was one other regular, Inspector Henderson, Chief of the Metropolis police force, played by Robert Shayne.

Though the movie was a morality play, the TV plots were essentially crime melodramas. Bob Maxwell, who produced Superman on radio and remained through the first year on TV, viewed the show as an adult adventure that should have just enough comic relief and heroics to keep the small fry clamoring for the breakfast cereal it pushed. As a result, his twenty-six *Adventures of Superman* were filled with corpses. National Comics, who had the copyright on Superman, ruled out this kind of rough stuff and put in Whitney Ellsworth as producer in the second season. The thugs became dis-dat-and-dose buffoons and Noel Neill played her less abrasive Lois. This milder approach was just as well-received as the earlier one and even sold more cereal. This was 1954, the third season, and the show was now shot in color. The first kids on the block to have color sets could catch Superman's red, yellow and blue costume and Noel Neill's brilliant red hair. Even today the early color work appears remarkably vivid.

The installments were shot at a rapid clip—four in ten days at a cost of $15,000 for each episode. Though the great majority of episodes were written with crime plots, there were some installments with science fiction plots, notably "Superman in Exile" and "Panic in the Sky," both shot for the second season. In the first, Superman is contaminated by radioactive isotopes. In the latter, he loses his memory after destroying a gigantic asteroid which had threatened earth's existence. The special effects in these shows were interesting, but in other episodes they were rarely used, except of course, the always necessary special effects which enabled George Reeves to "fly" and the padding inside his suits that gave him his "well-muscled" physique.

Thol (Si) Simonson was called in to make the Man of Steel leap tall buildings in a single bound without breaking his neck. At first, Reeves' take-offs were accomplished by a tricky pulley arrangement using a leather belt and wires. The results of this mechanism were spectacular but risky, so Simonson developed a safer hydraulic system. To enhance the illusion, Reeves would bounce off a spring-board—an idea which originated with staff director Tommy Carr—before the mechanism lifted him into the air. For Superman's famous "leap out of the window" shot, Reeves would jump onto the springs, sail through a mocked-up window and land gently—out of camera view—on a mattress. Making George Reeves appear to be in flight was cleverly solved. He would lie on a glass table, which was invisible to the camera, with his arms and legs outstretched as if he were gliding. This scene was matted over an aerial view of Metropolis—a disguised version of Hollywood.

Over time, Whitney Ellsworth's scripts became increasingly childish, and George Reeves, now getting gray, appeared tired of his role. *The Adventures of Superman* was canceled in 1957, though reruns have been aired ever since.

George Reeves' connection with the show tragically continued. It was so difficult for him to find acting jobs after his long Superman stint that he was planning to try professional wrestling. He loved acting—it had sustained him for 28 years—but had become so thoroughly typecast that he was no longer in demand for other roles. Though there were conflicting reports and though he left no note, this may have been the reason George Reeves committed suicide. On June 16, 1959, just two years after the show's cancellation, he shot himself in the head. Sadly, ironically, even in death he was cast as Superman: one newspaper headline screamed, "Superman Kills Self," and another ran a picture of him with the caption, "He blew his top"; cruel jokes had him bolting out the window or attempting to stop a locomotive. Maybe it was the only way he could escape his role.

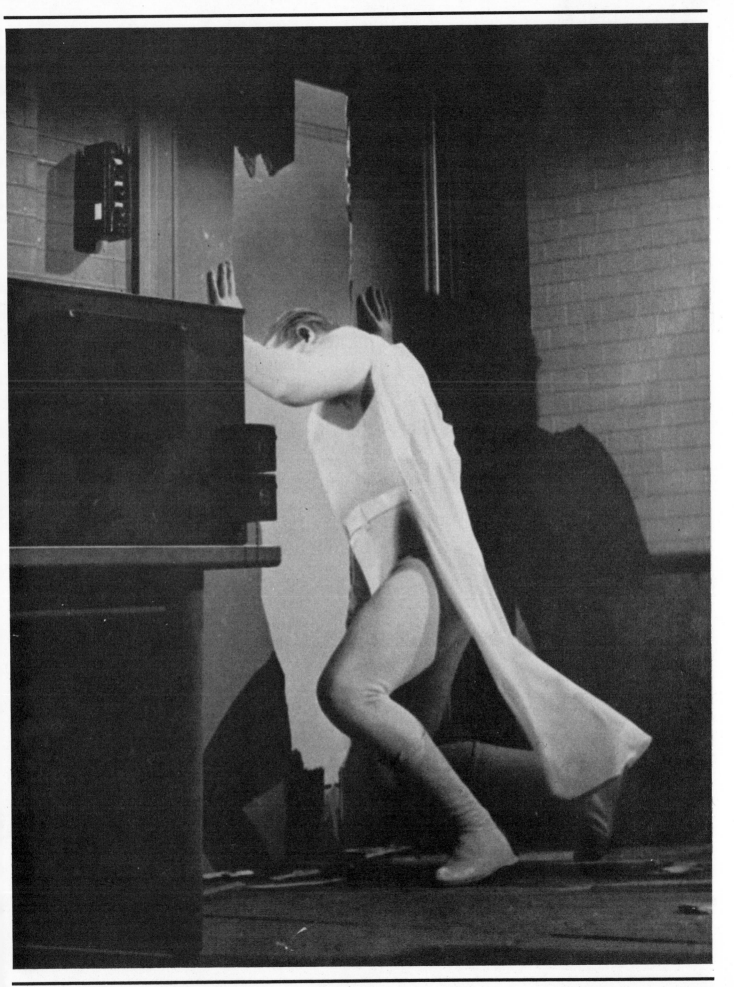

CLARK KENT

INDEX OF EPISODES

THE ADVENTURES OF SUPERMAN

1953-1957/104 episodes
ABC and syndication
30 minutes/black & white (first two seasons), color (from the third season)

Regular Cast: George Reeves (Superman/Clark Kent), Phyllis Coates (Lois Lane—first season), Noel Neill (Lois Lane from the second season), Jack Larson (Jimmy Olsen), John Hamilton (Perry White), Robert Shayne (Inspector Henderson).

Producers: Robert Maxwell and Bernard Luber (first season); Whitney Ellsworth (remaining seasons). **Creators:** Jerome Siegal and Joe Shuster (for the comics). **Directors of Photography:** Harold Stine, Harold Wellman, Joseph Biroc. **Special Effects:** Thol (Si) Simonson.

First Season: February 1953

SUPERMAN ON EARTH
Writer: Richard Fielding (pen name for Robert Maxwell, Whitney Ellsworth). **Director:** Thomas Carr. **Guest Cast:** Robert Rockwell, Herbert Rawlinson, Stuart Randall, Aline Towne, Tom Fadden, Frances Morris, Dani Nolan, Dabbs Greer.

Jor-El, a scientist from the planet Krypton, sends his infant son hurtling across space to the planet Earth as his own world is destroyed. The boy grows to maturity on Earth and uses his amazing powers in the fight against crime.

THE HAUNTED LIGHTHOUSE
Writer: Eugene Solow. **Director:** Thomas Carr. **Guest Cast:** Jimmy Ogg, Allene Roberts, Sarah Padden, Steve Carr.

Visiting his aunt's cabin, Jimmy faces danger when he investigates rumors of a haunted lighthouse, which is being used for smuggling.

THE CASE OF THE TALKATIVE DUMMY
Writers: Dennis Cooper, Lee Backman. **Director:** Thomas Carr. **Guest Cast:** Tristram Coffin, Syd Saylor, Pierre Watkin, Robert Keat.

A ventriloquist figures prominently in this mystery as Jimmy, trapped in a safe, is rescued from certain death by Superman.

THE MYSTERY OF THE BROKEN STATUES
Writer: William C. Joyce. **Director:** Thomas Carr. **Guest Cast:** Tristram Coffin, Michael Vallon, Maurice Cass, Phillip Pine, Joey Ray, Wayde Crosby, Steve Carr.

A gang of criminals destroys a collection of worthless plaster statues that contain the key to a great fortune.

THE MONKEY MYSTERY
Writers: Ben Peter Freeman, Doris Gilbert. **Director:** Thomas Carr. **Guest Cast:** Allene Roberts, Michael Vallon, Harry Lewis, William Challee.

An organ grinder's monkey holds a slip of paper with information concerning a nuclear scientist from an Iron Curtain country.

A NIGHT OF TERROR
Writer: Ben Peter Freeman. **Director:** Lee Sholem. **Guest Cast:** Frank Richards, John Kellog, Ann Doran, Almira Sessions, Joel Friedkin, Steve Carr, Richard Benedict.

Jimmy tries to rescue Lois, who is being held in a motel by gangsters.

THE BIRTHDAY LETTER
Writer: Dennis Cooper. **Director:** Lee Sholem. **Guest Cast:** Isa Ashdown, John Douchette, Virginia Carroll, Paul Marion.

Criminals kidnap a crippled girl when they realize that an important phone call meant for them reached her by mistake.

THE MIND MACHINE
Writers: Dennis Cooper, Lee Backman. **Director:** Lee Sholem. **Guest Cast:** Dan Seymour, Ben Weldon, Griff Barnett, James Seay.

A scientist is forced to use his invention to destroy witnesses at a federal hearing before they can give damaging testimony against a crime boss.

RESCUE
Writer: Monroe Manning. **Director:** Thomas Carr. **Guest Cast:** Houseley Stevenson, Sr., Fred E. Sherman, Ray Bennett, Edmund Coff.

Superman must save Lois and an old prospector, who are trapped in a coal mine.

THE SECRET OF SUPERMAN
Writer: Wells Root. **Director:** Thomas Carr. **Guest Cast:** Peter Brocco, Larry Blake, Helen Wallace, Joel Friedkin, Steve Carr.

Superman uses an amnesia act to capture a master scientist who has kidnapped Lois and Jimmy.

NO HOLDS BARRED
Writer: Peter Dixon. **Director:** Lee Sholem. **Guest Cast:** Malcolm Mealey, Richard Reeves, Richard Elliot, Herburt Vigran.

A college wrestler is used to expose a crippling grip employed by a crooked professional wrestler.

THE DESERTED VILLAGE
Writers: Dick Hamilton, Ben Peter Freeman. **Director:** Thomas Carr. **Guest Cast:** Fred E. Sherman, Maudie Prickett, Edmund Cobb, Malcolm Mealey.

The few remaining residents of Lois' hometown are apparently guarding a terrible secret, and Lois is determined to find out what it is.

THE STOLEN COSTUME
Writer: Ben Peter Freeman. **Director:** Lee Sholem. **Guest Cast:** Norman Budd, Frank Jenks, Veda Ann Borg, Dan Seymour, Bob Williams.

Superman must maroon two criminals on an icy peak in the Arctic when they discover his secret identity.

MYSTERY IN WAX
Writer: Ben Peter Freeman. **Director:** Lee Sholem. **Guest Cast:** Myra McKinney, Lester Sharpe.

A mad sculptress has added a suicide wing to her gallery through which she predicts the suicides of several major figures, including Perry White.

TREASURE OF THE INCAS
Writer: Howard Green. **Director:** Thomas Carr. **Guest Cast:** Leonard Penn, Martin Garralaga, Juan DuVal, Hal Gerard, Juan Rivero.

A damaged Peruvian tapestry leads Clark, Lois and Jimmy on a South American expedition that almost results in their destruction.

DOUBLE TROUBLE
Writer: Eugene Solow. **Director:** Thomas Carr. **Guest Cast:** Howard Chamberlin, Selmer Jackson, Rudolph Anders, Jimmy Dodd, Steve Carr.

Superman, flying to Europe to recover some stolen radium, must deal with a mystery involving identical twins.

THE RUNAWAY ROBOT
Writer: Dick Hamilton. **Director:** Thomas Carr. **Guest Cast:** Dan Seymour, John Harmon, Russell Johnson, Robert Easton, Lucien Littlefield, Herman Cantor.

An inventor's creation—a robot—is captured and used to commit robberies.

DRUMS OF DEATH
Writer: Dick Hamilton. **Director:** Lee Sholem. **Guest Cast:** Harry Corden, Leonard Mudie, Milton Wood, Mabel Albertson, George Hamilton, Smoki Whitfield.

While on assignment in Haiti the *Daily Planet* staff comes across some criminal activity linked to a voodoo cult.

THE EVIL THREE
Writer: Ben Peter Freeman. **Director:** Thomas Carr. **Guest Cast:** Rhys Williams, Jonathan Hale, Cecil Elliot.

While on a fishing trip, Perry and Jimmy are terrorized by an insane trio in an isolated hotel.

RIDDLE OF THE CHINESE JADE
Writer: Richard Fielding (pen name for Robert Maxwell). **Director:** Thomas Carr. **Guest Cast:** Paul Burns, Victor Sen Yung, Gloria Saunders, James Craven.

A young man helps steal a priceless Oriental jade figurine from his future father-in-law in Chinatown.

THE HUMAN BOMB
Writer: Richard Fielding (pen name for Whitney Ellsworth). **Director:** Lee Sholem. **Guest Cast:** Trevor Bardette, Dennis Moore, Marshall Reed, Lou Lubin.

To prevent Superman's interference with a robbery, a criminal abducts Lois and threatens to blow up both of them.

CZAR OF THE UNDERWORLD
Writer: Eugene Solow. **Director:** Thomas Carr. **Guest Cast:** Paul Fix, John Maxwell, Tony Caruso, Roy Gordon, Steve Carr.

Clark and Inspector Henderson are warned that their lives are in danger if they go to Hollywood to help make a crime expose film.

THE GHOST WOLF
Writer: Dick Hamilton. **Director:** Lee Sholem. **Guest Cast:** Stanley Andrews, Jane Adams, Lou Krugman, Harold Goodwin.

In the timberlands of Canada, Lois, Jimmy and Clark come across some strange doings involving arson and a mysterious, terrifying wolf.

THE UNKNOWN PEOPLE
Writer: Richard Fielding (pen name for Robert Maxwell). **Director:** Lee Sholem. **Guest Cast:** Jeff Corey, Walter Reed, J. Farrell MacDonald, Stanley Andrews, Ray Walker, Hal K. Dawson, Frank Reicher, Beverly Washburn, Steve Carr, Paul Burns, Margia Dean, Byron Foulger, Irene Martin, John Phillips, John Baer, Adrienne Marden, Billy Curtis, Jack Banbury, Jerry Marvin, Tony Baris.

This two-part show was an edited-for-TV version of the "Superman and the Mole Men" feature. In the first part, Clark and Lois arrive in Silsby to do their oil well story, but encounter the mole men instead. In the concluding half, Superman appears to rescue the captured mole man and return him to his fellow creatures.

CRIME WAVE
Writer: Ben Peter Freeman. **Director:** Thomas Carr. **Guest Cast:** John Eldredge, Phil Van Zandt, Al Eben, Joseph Mell, Barbara Fuller.

After Superman declares war on crime, a master criminal plots to destroy the Man of Steel.

Second Season: September 1953

FIVE MINUTES TO DOOM
Writer: Monroe Manning. **Director:** Thomas Carr. **Guest Cast:** Dabbs Greer, Sam Flint, Lois Hall, John Kellogg, Jean Willes, Lewis Russell, Dale Van Sickel, William E. Green.

Superman races the clock as he delivers a reprieve from the governor that will save an innocent man from the electric chair.

THE BIG SQUEEZE
Writer: David Chantler. **Director:** Thomas Carr. **Guest Cast:** Hugh Beaumont, John Kellogg, Aline Towne, Harry Cheshire, Bradley Mora, Ted Ryan, Reed Howes.

Superman must help an ex-con who's being blackmailed by gangsters.

THE MAN WHO COULD READ MINDS
Writer: Roy Hamilton. **Director:** Thomas Carr. **Guest Cast:** Larry Dobkin, Veola Vonn, Richard Karlan, Tom Bernard, Russell Custer.

The search for a phantom burglar leads Lois and Jimmy into serious danger.

"Able to bend steel with his bare hands." *Superman and the Mole Men,* the feature film that preceded the series was later re-edited into the two-part episode "The Unknown People."

JET ACE
Writer: David Chantler. **Director:** Thomas Carr. **Guest Cast:** Lane Bradford, Selmer Jackson, Richard Reeves, Jim Hayward, Larry Blake, Mauritz Hugo, Sam Balter, Bud Wolfe, Ric Roman.

Foreign agents try to capture an ace test pilot for their country.

SHOT IN THE DARK
Writer: David Chantler. **Director:** George Blair. **Guest Cast:** Vera Marshe, Billy Gray, John Eldredge, Frank Richards, Alan Lee.

A young amateur photographer accidentally turns up secret criminal activity.

THE DEFEAT OF SUPERMAN
Writer: Jackson Gillis. **Director:** Thomas Carr. **Guest Cast:** Maurice Cass, Peter Mamakos.

Lois and Jimmy must save Superman from Kryptonite, which has fallen into the hands of criminals.

SUPERMAN IN EXILE
Writer: Jackson Gillis. **Director:** Thomas Carr. **Guest Cast:** Leon Askin, Joe Forte, Robert S. Carson, Ph.' Van Zandt, John Harmon, Don Dillaway, Gregg Barton, Sam Balter.

Exposure to gamma rays leads Superman into self-imposed exile, to avoid contaminating Metropolis.

A GHOST FOR SCOTLAND YARD
Writer: Jackson Gillis. **Director:** George Blair. **Guest Cast:** Leonard Mudie, Colin Campbell, Norma Varden, Patrick Aherne, Evelyn Halpern, Clyde Cook.

Clark and Jimmy go to England to investigate a dead illusionist's supposed return from the grave.

THE DOG WHO KNEW SUPERMAN
Writer: David Chantler. **Director:** Thomas Carr. **Guest Cast:** Ben Welden, Billy Nelson, Dona Drake, John Daly, Lester Dorr.

A small dog's canine intuition almost reveals Superman's identity to his criminal owners.

THE FACE AND THE VOICE
Writer: Jackson Gillis. **Director:** George Blair. **Guest Cast:** Hayden Rorke, I. Stanford Jolley, George Chandler, Percy Helton, Carlton Young, William Newell, Nolan Leary, Sam Balter, George Reeves.

A thug has his appearance altered to resemble Superman.

THE MAN IN THE LEAD MASK
Writers: Leroy H. Zehren and Roy Hamilton. **Director:** George Blair. **Guest Cast:** Frank Scannell, John Crawford, Louis Jean Heydt, Paul Bryar, John Merton, Joey Ray, Lynn Thomas, Sam Balter.

A criminal has everyone baffled by an apparent change of fingerprints, until Superman enters the picture.

PANIC IN THE SKY
Writer: Jackson Gillis. **Director:** Thomas Carr. **Guest Cast:** Jonathan Hale, Jane Frazee, Clark Howat, Thomas Moore.

Superman loses his memory when he destroys a meteor that's loaded with Kryptonite.

THE MACHINE THAT COULD PLOT CRIMES
Writer: Jackson Gillis. **Director:** Thomas Carr. **Guest Cast:** Sterling Holloway, Billy Nelson, Ben Welden, Stan Jarman, Sherry Moreland, Sam Balter, Russell Custer.

A computer that can work out perfect crimes is taken over by criminals.

JUNGLE DEVIL
Writer: Peter Dixon. **Director:** Thomas Carr. **Guest Cast:** Doris Singleton, Damian O'Flynn, Nacho Galindo, James Seay, Al Kikume, Leon Lontoc, Steve Calvert, Henry A. Escalante, Bernard Gozier.

A jungle expedition is threatened by an angry tribe of natives when an idol's diamond eye is lost in quicksand.

MY FRIEND SUPERMAN
Writer: David Chantler. **Director:** Thomas Carr. **Guest Cast:** Tito Vivolo, Yvette Dugay, Paul Burke, Terry Frost, Ralph Sanford, Frederick Berest, Ruta Kilmonis, Edward Reider.

The owner of a diner gets into trouble when he brags that he is a friend of Superman's.

THE CLOWN WHO CRIED
Writer: David Chantler. **Director:** George Blair. **Guest Cast:** William Wayne, Peter Brocco, Mickey Simpson, Harry Mendoza, George Douglas, Charles Williams, Richard D. Crockett, Richard Lewis, Harvey Parry.

A petty crook disguises himself as a famous circus clown, to steal money from a telethon.

THE BOY WHO HATED SUPERMAN
Writer: David Chantler. **Director:** George Blair. **Guest Cast:** Roy Barcroft, Leonard Penn, Tyler McDuff, Charles Meredith, Richard Reeves.

A young thug vows revenge on Clark Kent for aiding in the arrest of a criminal he idolizes.

SEMI-PRIVATE EYE
Writer: David Chantler. **Director:** George Blair. **Guest Cast:** Elisha Cook, Jr., Paul Fix, Douglas Henderson, Richard Benedict, Alfred Linder.

Lois and Jimmy enlist the aid of a private detective to tail Clark Kent.

PERRY WHITE'S SCOOP
Writer: Roy Hamilton. **Director:** George Blair. **Guest Cast:** Steven Pendleton, Robert Wilke, Bibs Borman, Jan Arvan, Tom Monroe.

Perry White gets in over his head when he investigates a mysterious corpse.

BEWARE THE WRECKER
Writer: Royal Cole. **Director:** George Blair. **Guest Cast:** William Forrest, Pierre Watkin, Tom Powers, Denver Pyle, Renny McEvoy.

Police are baffled by an ingenious saboteur.

THE GOLDEN VULTURE
Writer: Jackson Gillis. **Director:** Thomas Carr. **Guest Cast:** Peter Whitney, Vic Perrin, Robert Rice, Murray Alper, Wes Hudman, Saul M. Gross, Carl H. Saxe, Dan Turner, William J. Vincent.

Lois, Jimmy and Clark are held captive by a deranged sea captain.

JIMMY OLSEN, BOY EDITOR
Writer: David Chantler. **Director:** Thomas Carr. **Guest Cast:** Herburt Vigran, Keith Richards, Dick Rich, Anthony Hughes, Ronald Hargrove, Bob Crosson, Jack Pepper.

Criminals are after Jimmy when he and Perry switch jobs for a day.

LADY IN BLACK
Writer: Jackson Gillis. **Director:** Thomas Carr. **Guest Cast:** Frank Ferguson, Virginia Christine, Mike Ragan, John Doucette, Rudolph Anders, Frank Marlowe.

Jimmy is haunted by weird noises and mysterious figures in an old house.

STAR OF FATE
Writers: Roy Hamilton and Leroy H. Zehren. **Director:** Thomas Carr. **Guest Cast:** Lawrence Ryle, Paul Burns, Jeanne Dean, Arthur Space, Ted Hecht, Tony deMario.

A scientist resorts to theft and murder, to gain possession of a poisonous sapphire.

THE WHISTLING BIRD
Writer: David Chantler. **Director:** Thomas Carr. **Guest Cast:** Sterling Holloway, Joseph Vitale, Otto Waldis, Toni Carroll, Allene Roberts, Marshall Reed, Jerry Hausner.

A scientist discovers a powerful explosive, but only his pet bird knows the formula.

AROUND THE WORLD
Writer: Jackson Gillis. **Director:** Thomas Carr. **Guest Cast:** Kay Morley, Judy Ann Nugent, Raymond Greenleaf, Patrick Aherne, Max Wagner, James Brown.

A blind girl enters a contest and wins a trip around the world.

Third Season: 1954

THROUGH THE TIME BARRIER
Writer: David Chantler. **Director:** Harry Gerstad. **Guest Cast:** Sterling Holloway, Jim Hyland, Florence Lake, Ed Hinton.

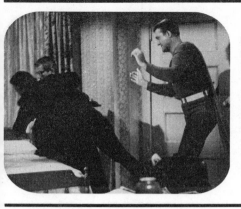

A scientist's time machine sends him, a gangster, Clark, Lois, Jimmy and Perry back to the Stone Age.

THE TALKING CLUE
Writer: David Chantler. **Director:** Harry Gerstad. **Guest Cast:** Billy Nelson, Julian Upton, Richard Shakleton, Brick Sullivan.

Inspector Henderson's son uses his tape recordings to help capture two wanted criminals.

THE LUCKY CAT
Writer: Jackson Gillis. **Director:** Harry Gerstad. **Guest Cast:** Harry Tyler, Carl Hubbard, Ted Stanhope, Charles Watts, John Phillips.

The members of an antisuperstition society are in danger of sabotage and attempted murder.

SUPERMAN WEEK
Writer: Peggy Chantler. **Director:** Harry Gerstad. **Guest Cast:** Herburt Vigran, Tamar Cooper, Paul Burke, Jack George, Buddy Mason.

During a week of festivities honoring Superman, a criminal gets hold of a block of Kryptonite.

GREAT CAESAR'S GHOST
Writer: Jackson Gillis. **Director:** Harry Gerstad. **Guest Cast:** Trevor Bardette, Jim Hayward, Olaf Hytten.

Perry White is slowly being driven mad by what appears to be the spirit of Julius Caesar.

TEST OF A WARRIOR
Writer: Leroy H. Zehren. **Director:** George Blair. **Guest Cast:** Ralph Moody, Maurice Jara, Francis McDonald, George Lewis, Lane Bradford.

Superman helps an Indian brave undergo a dangerous test of courage.

OLSEN'S MILLIONS
Writer: David Chantler. **Director:** George Blair. **Guest Cast:** Elizabeth Patterson, George E. Stone, Leonard Carey, Richard Reeves, Tyler McDuff.

A kindly old woman gives Jimmy one million dollars.

CLARK KENT, OUTLAW
Writer: Leroy H. Zehren. **Director:** George Blair. **Guest Cast:** John Doucette, Sid Tomack, Tristram Coffin, George Eldredge, Patrick O'Moore, Lyn Thomas.

Clark joins a gang of criminals after he's framed on a burglary rap.

THE MAGIC NECKLACE
Writer: Jackson Gillis. **Director:** George Blair. **Guest Cast:** Leonard Mudie, Lawrence Ryle, Frank Jenks, John Harmon, Paul Fierro, Ted Hecht, Cliff Ferre.

A scientist's discovery of a charmed necklace arouses the interest of an American gangster.

THE BULLY OF DRY GULCH
Writer: David Chantler. **Director:** George Blair. **Guest Cast:** Myron Healey, Martin Garralaga, Raymond Hatton, Eddie Baker.

While stranded in an old Western town, Jimmy rubs the town bully the wrong way.

FLIGHT TO THE NORTH
Writer: David Chantler. **Director:** George Blair. **Guest Cast:** Chuck Connors, Ben Welden, Richard Garland, Ralph Sanford, Marjorie Owens, George Chandler.

A backwoodsman named Superman agrees to fly a lemon meringue pie to Alaska—with a gangster in hot pursuit.

THE SEVEN SOUVENIRS
Writer: Jackson Gillis. **Director:** George Blair. **Guest Cast:** Phillips Tead, Arthur Space, Rick Vallin, Louise Lewis, Steve Calvert, Lennie Breman, Jack O'Shea.

The key to a series of mysterious thefts is contained in a set of matching daggers.

KING FOR A DAY
Writer: Dwight Babcock. **Director:** George Blair. **Guest Cast:** Peter Mamakos, Leon Askin, Phil Van Zandt, Chet Marshall, Jan Arvan, Carolyn Scott, Steven Bekassy.

Jimmy is caught up in political intrigues when he and a European prince switch places.

Fourth Season: 1955

JOEY
Writer: David Chantler. **Director:** Harry Gerstad. **Guest Cast:** Janine Perreau, Tom London, Billy Nelson, Mauritz Hugo, Jay Lawrence, Willard Kennedy.

A young girl's kindness inspires the *Daily Planet's* race horse to victory.

Lois and Jimmy frequently found themselves in this situation—all tied up with no place to go. This time in "The Jolly Roger."

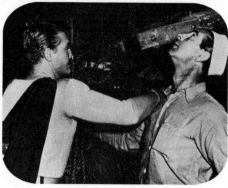

THE UNLUCKY NUMBER
Writer: David Chantler. **Director:** Harry Gerstad. **Guest Cast:** Henry Blair, Elizabeth Patterson, John Berardino, Russell Conklin, Jack Littlefield, Alan Reynolds, Tony deMario, Alfred Linder.

Clark helps an old woman win a contest that's been rigged by gangsters.

THE BIG FREEZE
Writer: David Chantler. **Director:** Harry Gerstad. **Guest Cast:** Richard Reeves, George E. Stone, John Phillips, Rolfe Sedan, Eddie Baker.

A scientist tries to keep Superman from interfering with a fixed city election by freezing him.

PERIL BY SEA
Writer: David Chantler. **Director:** Harry Gerstad. **Guest Cast:** Claude Aikens, Julian Upton, Ed Penny.

Perry's scientific research arouses the unhealthy interest of a pair of master criminals.

TOPSY TURVY
Writer: David Chantler. **Director:** Harry Gerstad. **Guest Cast:** Phillips Tead, Ben Welden, Mickey Knox, Charles Williams.

A professor's invention for making things appear upside down is being used for criminal purposes by a crooked carnival owner.

JIMMY THE KID
Writer: Leroy H. Zehren. **Director:** Phil Ford. **Guest Cast:** Damian O'Flynn, Diana Darrin, Florence Ravenel, Steven Conte, Rick Vallin, Jack Larson.

Jimmy is kidnapped by his lookalike, a young criminal who just escaped from prison.

THE GIRL WHO HIRED SUPERMAN
Writer: David Chantler. **Director:** Phil Ford. **Guest Cast:** Maurice Marsac, Gloria Talbott, John Eldredge, George Khoury, Lyn Guild.

A wealthy young woman who hires Superman to entertain at a party soon finds herself caught up in criminal activity.

THE WEDDING OF SUPERMAN
Writer: Jackson Gillis. **Director:** Phil Ford. **Guest Cast:** Milton Frome, Julie Bennet, Doyle Brooks, John Cliff, Dolores Fuller, Nolan Leary.

Lois dreams of the day when Superman will ask her to marry him.

DAGGER ISLAND
Writer: Robert Leslie Bellem. **Director:** Phil Ford. **Guest Cast:** Dean Cromer, Myron Healey, Ray Montgomery, Raymond Hatton.

The *Daily Planet* staff brings three brothers to a desert island to look for an inheritance.

BLACKMAIL
Writers: Oliver Drake and David Chantler. **Director:** Harry Gerstad. **Guest Cast:** Herburt Vigran, Sid Tomack, George Chandler, Selmer Jackson.

Superman must step in when Inspector Henderson is accused of taking a bribe.

THE DEADLY ROCK
Writer: Jackson Gillis. **Director:** Harry Gerstad. **Guest Cast:** Robert Lowery, Steven Geray, Lyn Thomas, Vincent G. Perry, Bob Foulk, Ric Roman, Jim Hayward, Sid Melton.

Through an unusual set of circumstances, a G-man becomes as susceptible to Kryptonite as Superman.

THE PHANTOM RING
Writer: David Chantler. **Director:** Phil Ford. **Guest Cast:** Paul Burke, Peter Brocco, Lane Bradford, Ed Hinton, Henry Rowland.

A gang of criminals has a machine that can make them invisible.

THE JOLLY ROGER
Writer: David Chantler. **Director:** Phil Ford. **Guest Cast:** Leonard Mudie, Myron Healey, Patrick Aherne, Jean Lewis, Eric Snowden, Ray Montgomery, Dean Cromer, Pierre Watkin, Chet Marshall.

Clark, Lois and Jimmy discover that a small island set for demolition by the Navy is inhabited by a crew of pirates.

Fifth Season: 1956

PERIL IN PARIS
Writers: Robert Drake and David Chantler. **Director:** George Blair. **Guest Cast:** Robert Shayne, Lilyan Chauvin, Peter Mamakos, Albert Carrier, Charles LaTorre, Franz Roehn.

In France, Superman helps a woman smuggle some family jewels from behind the Iron Curtain.

TIN HERO
Writer: Wilton Schiller. **Director:** George Blair. **Guest Cast:** Carl Ritchie, Sam Finn, Frank Richards, Jack Lomas, Paula Houston.

A timid bookkeeper fancies himself a great law enforcer when he accidentally foils a bank robbery.

MONEY TO BURN
Writer: David Chantler. **Director:** Harry Gerstad. **Guest Cast:** Mauritz Hugo, Dale Van Sickel, Richard Emory.

Two thieves rob the vaults of large corporations when the buildings that contain them catch fire.

THE TOWN THAT WASN'T
Writer: Wilton Schiller. **Director:** Harry Gerstad. **Guest Cast:** Frank Connor, Charles Gray, Richard Elliot, Terry Frost, Jack V. Littlefield, Michael Garrett, Phillip Barnes.

Lois and Jimmy are imprisoned in a phony town that's being used in an armored car hold-up.

THE TOMB OF ZAHARAN
Writer: David Chantler. **Director:** George Blair. **Guest Cast:** George Khoury, Jack Kruschen, Ted Hecht, Jack Reitzen, Gabriel Mooradian.

An ancient scarab convinces two Middle-Eastern dignitaries that Lois is really the reincarnated ruler of their country.

THE MAN WHO MADE DREAMS COME TRUE
Writer: David Chantler. **Director:** George Blair. **Guest Cast:** Keith Richards, Cyril Delevanti, Sandy Harrison, John Banner, Laurie Mitchell, Hal Hoover.

A con man relies on a European king's superstition in his plot to usurp the throne.

DISAPPEARING LOIS
Writers: David and Peggy Chantler. **Director:** Harry Gerstad. **Guest Cast:** Milton Frome, Ben Welden, Yvonne White.

In order to prevent Clark from beating her to a major story, Lois pretends she's disappeared.

CLOSE SHAVE
Writer: Benjamin B. Crocker. **Director:** Harry Gerstad. **Guest Cast:** Rick Vallin, Richard Benedict, Donald Diamond, John Ferry, Jack V. Littlefield, Harry Fleer.

A barber uses the power of suggestion to reform a major criminal.

THE PHONY ALIBI
Writer: Peggy Chantler. **Director:** George Blair. **Guest Cast:** Phillips Tead, John Cliff, William Challee, Frank Kreig, Harry Arnie.

A scientist invents a machine that can send people anywhere in the world by telephone.

THE PRINCE ALBERT COAT
Writer: Leroy H. Zehren. **Director:** Harry Gerstad. **Guest Cast:** Stephen Wooton, Raymond Hatton, Phil Arnold, Daniel White, Frank Fenton, Claire DuBrey, Ken Christy, Jack Finch.

A boy gives an old coat to charity, unaware that it contained his grandfather's life savings.

THE STOLEN ELEPHANT
Writer: David Chantler. **Director:** Harry Gerstad. **Guest Cast:** Gregory Moffet, Thomas Jackson, Eve McVeigh, Gregg Martell, I. Stanford Jolley.

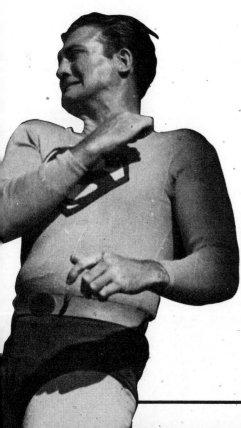

A kidnapped circus elephant is hidden in the garage of an old farm, but the boy who lives there believes the animal is a birthday present from his mother.

MR. ZERO
Writer: Peggy Chantler. **Director:** Harry Gerstad. **Guest Cast:** Billy Curtis, Herburt Vigran, George Barrows, Leon Altin, George Spotts.

A small visitor from outer space, who has the power to paralyze people by pointing at them, falls into the hands of criminals.

WHATEVER GOES UP
Writer: Wilton Schiller. **Director:** Harry Gerstad. **Guest Cast:** Tris Coffin, Milton Frome.

Amateur scientist Jimmy's discovery of anti-gravity fluid leads to political and criminal complications.

Sixth Season: 1957

THE LAST KNIGHT
Writer: David Chantler. **Director:** Thomas Carr. **Guest Cast:** Marshall Bradford, Paul Power, Pierre Watkin, Jason Johnson, Thomas P. Dillon, Ollie O'Toole, Ronald Foster.

Lois and Jimmy discover that the activities of a knighthood society are more treacherous than they seem.

THE MAGIC SECRET
Writers: Robert Leslie Bellem and Whitney Ellsworth. **Director:** Phil Ford. **Guest Cast:** Freeman Lusk, Buddy Lewis, George Selk, Jack Reynolds, Kenneth Alton.

Criminals use Lois and Jimmy to lure Superman into a Kryptonite trap.

DIVIDE AND CONQUER
Writers: Robert Leslie Bellem, Whitney Ellsworth. **Director:** Phil Ford. **Guest Cast:** Donald Lawton, Robert Tafur, Jack Reitsen, Jack V. Littlefield, Everett Glass.

Superman must divide himself in two, to prevent a political assassination in a European country.

THE MYSTERIOUS CUBE
Writers: Robert Leslie Bellem, Whitney Ellsworth. **Director:** George Blair. **Guest Cast:** Everett Glass, Ben Welden, Keith Richards, Bruce Wendell, Joel Riordin, John Ayres.

Superman is called on to apprehend a wanted criminal who has been hiding for seven years in an impenetrable cube.

THE ATOMIC CAPTIVE
Writers: Robert Leslie Bellem, Whitney Ellsworth. **Director:** George Blair. **Guest Cast:** Raskin Ben-Ari, Elaine Riley, Jan Arvan, Walter Reed, George Khoury, Mark Sheeler.

Foreign agents come after a famous nuclear scientist who has defected to America.

THE SUPERMAN SILVER MINE
Writer: Peggy Chantler. **Director:** George Blair. **Guest Cast:** Dabbs Greer, Charles Maxwell.

A prospector who strikes a vein of silver is kidnapped by his criminal lookalike.

THE BIG FORGET
Writer: David Chantler. **Director:** George Blair. **Guest Cast:** Phillips Tead, Herburt Vigran, Billy Nelson.

A scientist's antimemory vapor is stolen and used to commit perfect crimes.

THE GENTLE MONSTER
Writer: David Chantler. **Director:** Howard Bretherton. **Guest Cast:** Phillips Tead, Ben Welden, John Vivyan, Orville Sherman, Wilkie DeMartel.

A professor builds a robot that has super-strength, unaware that it also contains Kryptonite.

SUPERMAN'S WIFE
Writers: Robert Leslie Bellem, Whitney Ellsworth. **Director:** Lew Landers. **Guest Cast:** Joi Lansing, John Eldredge, John Bennes, Harry Arnie, Wayne Heffley.

Superman "marries" a woman police officer, to trap a gang of criminals.

THREE IN ONE
Writers: Wilton Schiller, Whitney Ellsworth. **Director:** Lew Landers. **Guest Cast:** Sid Tomack, Rick Vallin, Buddy Baer, Craig Duncan.

A trio of circus performers combine talents in order to commit crimes that look as though they could have been performed only by Superman.

THE BRAINY BURRO
Writer: David Chantler. **Director:** George Reeves. **Guest Cast:** Mark Cavell, Ken Mayer, Mauritz Hugo, Natividad Vacio, Edward LeVeque, Sid Cassell.

A clairvoyant donkey is forced to commit crimes by two crooks in a Mexican town.

THE PERILS OF SUPERMAN
Writers: Robert Leslie Bellem, Whitney Ellsworth. **Director:** George Reeves. **Guest Cast:** Michael Fox, Steve Mitchell, Yvonne White.

Superman must save the *Daily Planet* staff from a murderous gang of lead-masked criminals.

ALL THAT GLITTERS
Writers: Robert Leslie Bellem, Whitney Ellsworth. **Director:** George Reeves. **Guest Cast:** Phillips Tead, Len Hendry, Jack Littlefield, Richard Elliot, Myrna Fahey, George Eldredge, Paul Cavanagh.

Knocked unconscious by a professor's invention, Jimmy dreams that he and Lois have the powers of Superman.

ONE STEP BEYOND

I would say that approximately 30 percent of our mail is of the let-me-tell-you-what-happened-to-me variety and the other 70 percent is the usual fan mail except that most of it is highly literate. We hear from doctors, lawyers, engineers, students—that level. And I would say that perhaps only one letter out of 1000 is uncomplimentary.

—Merwin Gerard
Creator and associate producer

Sigmund Freud was once talking to Carl Jung, his protege, when Jung began to complain of a bizarre burning sensation in his diaphragm. All of a sudden, a loud sound from the direction of the bookcase startled both men. Jung believed that he had somehow "projected" this sound. Freud considered such an explanation preposterous, but Jung predicted that another sound would be heard shortly. Sure enough, a few moments later another loud crack came from the case. Neither man was able to find any physical cause for the sound.

Jung was an eminent psychologist, the very opposite of a crank, and he placed great significance on this and similar incidents. On another occasion, for example, a young woman patient was describing a dream to him in which she was given a golden scarab. Her description was interrupted by a gentle tapping at the window. Jung opened it, and in flew a common rose-chafer beetle, the closest relative to the golden scarab in those northern latitudes. Was it a mere coincidence that this insect, which prefers sunlight, would at that moment be attracted to Jung's darkened office? Or are we to believe, as Jung did, that the woman actually "caused" the bug to appear?

We have all had similar experiences. How often do we anticipate the ringing of a telephone? How often does the image of someone come to mind, to be followed almost immediately by a phone call or letter from that same person? Many people shrug off these occurrences as coincidences. Others, like Jung, however, believe that such events have profound significance, and carefully record them. As a result of his own records, Jung was certain that psychic phenomena were indications of an order that existed beyond scientific causality, that the

powers of the mind extended beyond rationality, beyond immediate perception.

This realm of the supernatural was the subject matter of *One Step Beyond*, which premiered in 1959. According to Merwin Gerard, the creator and associate producer of the show, the core of each story was true, and after each episode was aired, he got letters "corroborating" it. One especially notable example of this was the response to an entry titled "If You See Sally." It concerns a truck driver who discovers a little girl walking along a deserted back road. He takes her to her home, following the child's own directions. The goose pimples appear when we find out, along with the truck driver, that little Sally has been dead for several years. This broadcast elicited a spate of letters—forty-five in all—in which viewers described their own similar experiences. In one variation, the man lends the

ABOVE: John Newland who appeared each week as host, also acted in and directed the series. **OPPOSITE:** Cloris Leachman, in an early TV appearance, had her back against the wall in "The Dark Room."

child a sweater. When he is told that the child is dead, he cannot believe it and immediately asks what happened to his sweater. The garment is retrieved on the headstone of the child's grave. Gerard claimed that this incident in all its variations had been reported and documented many times.

Another episode concerned a man and a woman involved in an extramarital affair. In "Anniversary of a Murder," which starred Harry Townes, the guilty couple is driving home from one of their trysts when a small boy suddenly appears in front of their car. There is not enough time to swerve and, consequently, they smash right into him. Overwhelmed by the fear that aiding the boy will result in the discovery of their affair, they drive off, leaving him to die. The police are completely unable to solve the tragic hit-and-run murder. Then, exactly one year after the accident, the man hears the anguished moans and cries of the boy on his office dictaphone as he is playing back a business letter. Shaken, he calls his paramour only to discover that she, too, has heard the boy's cries, and was so unnerved that she turned herself in to the police. The man, now in a state of utter panic, feels compelled to retrace the route he drove that fatal night. As he approaches the scene of the accident, he sees a boy suddenly appear in the path of his car. The man is able to swerve just in time to avoid hitting him, but plows right into a tree, killing himself.

Harry Townes and Randy Stuart were the adulterers in "Anniversary of a Murder."

"The Sacred Mushroom" is of interest for a couple of reasons. First, it starred producer Collier Young and John Newland. Second, it demonstrated a bit of E.S.P. on their part, predating the sixties drug culture by several years. In the show, Young and Newland were seen searching for, then experimenting with, a certain "magic" mushroom which purportedly affects an individual's mental powers in bizarre ways.

John Newland, as host and director of each episode, Collier Young, Larry Marcus, as writer, and Merwin Gerard, as associate producer, were the men responsible for bringing the show to the air. Gerard, who was something of a supernatural enthusiast, said that there were fifteen basic psychic phenomenon stories. *One Step Beyond* juggled all of them for the two years it was on the air.

John Newland was fascinated by the subject. Born in Cincinnati, the son of a newspaper drama critic, he had established a distinguished reputation as an actor long before hosting and directing *One Step Beyond*. Though occasionally lackluster, his directing was always intelligent and often brilliant. It was not a simple task to make half-hour episodes about E.S.P. or other supernatural phenomena appear believable. He usually succeeded, thereby winning the respect of television critics.

The show was inevitably compared to *Twilight Zone*, which debuted the same year. Unlike *Twilight Zone*, *One Step Beyond* was based on fact, not fancy, and it took great pains to present psychic phenomena as realistically as possible. In fact, of all the episodes, only two ventured into monster-fantasy territory, and one of those was based on a real scientific possibility. "Ordeal on Locust Street" involved a human mutant—part human, part fish—who was kept prisoner in a house. He was never actually shown on the air except for a flash of his scaly hand at the end of the show. Even this monster, far out as it may seem, was based on the genetic fact that a fetus goes through levels of phylogenetic development. It was at least a possibility that a creature like this one, partially stuck at an early level, might be born, but it would be unlikely to survive. Aside from this offering, the show stayed strictly within the bounds of "reality."

One Step Beyond developed a small cult following and is still shown in syndication on local stations across the country. Like *Twilight Zone*, its audience was fairly sophisticated, something Gerard, in particular, was proud of. A great many of his letters were from highly educated people interested in the subject. He also liked to point out that people like Charles Steinmetz, the electrical engineer, believed that the serious study of psychic phenomena would soon lead to extraordinary scientific progress; that Albert Einstein and Thomas Edison were firm believers, and that some of the world's greatest universities, including Oxford and, of course, Duke, have entire departments established to study psychic phenomena. NASA has since supported research in this area.

Despite its integrity, reasonably favorable reviews and a devoted band of viewers, *One Step Beyond* received neither the critical acclaim nor the ratings that *Twilight Zone* did, and after two years, was canceled.

Warren Beatty was aged 20 years compliments of the makeup staff to play opposite Joan Fontaine in "The Visitor."

Host John Newland

INDEX OF EPISODES

"Emergency Only"

ONE STEP BEYOND

1959/94 episodes
ABC/a Collier Young Production
30 minutes/black & white

Host: John Newland.

Producer: Collier Young. **Creator:** Merwin Gerard. **Director:** John Newland. **Music:** Harry Lubin.

First Season: Spring 1959

THE BRIDE POSSESSED
Writer: Merwin Gerard and Larry Marcus. Director: John Newland. Guest Cast: Skip Homeier, Virginia Leith.

A newlywed finds herself becoming possessed by the spirit of a murdered woman.

EMERGENCY ONLY
Writer: Collier Young. Director: John Newland. Guest Cast: Lin McCarthy, Jocelyn Brando, Paula Raymond.

A skeptical man finds a woman's predictions of his future mysteriously coming true.

TWELVE HOURS TO LIVE
Writer: Merwin Gerard. Director: John Newland. Guest Cast: Paul Richards, Jean Allison.

When her husband leaves after a quarrel, a woman gets a terrifying premonition that he is in danger.

NIGHT OF APRIL 14
Writers: Collier Young, Larry Marcus. Director: John Newland. Guest Cast: Barbara Lord, Patrick MacNee.

A woman's nightmare of drowning in freezing ocean water is followed by her fiance's announcement that he's booked them on the maiden voyage of the Titanic.

PREMONITION
Writer: Paul David. Director: John Newland. Guest Cast: Beverly Washburn, Julie Payne, Pamela Lincoln, Clare Corelli, Thomas B. Henry.

A young girl's vision of being crushed by the giant chandelier in her family ballroom haunts her as she grows up, causing her to reject her father's suggestion that she hold her wedding party in the room.

THE DARK ROOM
Writer: Francis Cockrell. Director: John Newland. Guest Cast: Cloris Leachman, Marcel Calio, Ivan Triesault, Paul Dubov, Ann Codee.

An American photographer on assignment in France faces a mysterious strangler in her hotel room.

EPILOGUE
Writer: Don Mankiewicz. Director: John Newland. Guest Cast: Charles Aidman, Julie Adams, Charles Herbert, William Schallert.

When a woman and her son are trapped in a cave-in, her husband is alerted to the calamity by the insistence of a strange, disheveled woman.

THE DREAM
Writer: John Dunkel. Director: John Newland. Guest Cast: Reginald Owen, Molly Roden, Phillip Tonge, Jack Lynn, Peter Gordon.

A British Home Guardsman and his wife both have a curiously significant dream the night of the British evacuation of Dunkirk.

VISION
Writer: Larry Marcus. Director: John Newland. Guest Cast: Bruce Gordon, Pernell Roberts, Jerry Oddo.

The only explanation four French soldiers have for supposedly deserting under fire is that a strange light in the sky compelled them to do so.

THE DEAD PART OF THE HOUSE
Writer: Michael Plant. Director: John Newland. Guest Cast: Mimi Gibson, Philip Abbot, Joanne Linville, Philip Ahn.

A young girl's feeling for a strange, cold room in her aunt's house is linked to the fact that three other children met with terrible fates in that room years before.

THE DEVIL'S LAUGHTER
Writer: Alfred Brenner. Director: John Newland. Guest Cast: Alfred Ryder, Patrick Westwood, Ben Wright, Lester Mathews, Leslie Denison, Alma Lawton, John Ainsworth.

A condemned murderer has several supernatural experiences as he is about to be executed.

THE HAUNTED U-BOAT
Writer: Larry Marcus. Director: John Newland. Guest Cast: Eric Feldary, Werner Klemperer, Kort Flakenberg, Wesley Lau, Siegfried Speck, Paul Busch, Frank Obershall, Norberto Kerner.

The crew of a German U-Boat investigates a strange pounding that imperils their craft.

"The Bride Possessed," the show's premiere episode starred Skip Homeier and Virginia Leith.

"Night of April 14"

"Ordeal on Locust Street"

"The Vision"

THE NAVIGATOR
Writer: Don Mankiewicz. **Director:** John Newland. **Guest Cast:** Robert Ellenstein, Don Dubbins, Joel Fluellen, Stephen Roberts, Robert Osterloh, Don Womack, Olan Soule.

When a first mate navigates his ship according to the blackboard chart, he discovers that this course was not set by the captain.

THE RETURN OF MITCHELL CAMPION
Writer: Merwin Gerard. **Director:** John Newland. **Guest Cast:** Patrick O'Neal, Lilyan Chauvin, Richard Angarola.

A man goes to an island he's never visited before, and finds that he is known by name.

THE SECRET
Writer: Michael Plant. **Director:** John Newland. **Guest Cast:** Maria Palmer, Albert Carrier, Robert Douglas, Molly Glessing, Arthur Gould-Porter.

An old ouija board holds the key to a woman's past relationship with a mysterious man.

THE LOVERS
Writer: Joseph Petracca, Russell Beggs. **Director:** John Newland. **Guest Cast:** Vanessa Brown, John Beal, Rudolph Anders, Irene Tedrow, Sig Ruman, Lili Valenti.

A simple kiss between a retired postman and a waitress arouses some mischievous poltergeists.

THE AERIALIST
Writer: Larry Marcus. **Director:** John Newland. **Guest Cast:** Michael Connors, Robert Carricart, Yvette Vickers, Ruggero Romor, Penny Stanton, Charles Watts, Vernon Rice.

After a young aerialist has angrily threatened his father, strange events occur during his performance.

ECHO
Writer: Merwin Gerard. **Director:** John Newland. **Guest Cast:** Ross Martin, Leslie Barrett, Ed Kemmer, Rusty Lane.

While vacationing after being acquitted of the murder of his wife, a man sees a horrifying vision of his future.

IMAGE OF DEATH
Writer: Larry Marcus. **Director:** John Newland. **Guest Cast:** Max Adrian, Doris Dowling, John Wengraff, Gregory Gay, Deidre Owens.

When his second marriage closely follows the death of his first wife, a Marquis is haunted by an image appearing on the wall.

THE CAPTAIN'S GUESTS
Writer: Charles Beaumont. **Director:** John Newland. **Guest Cast:** Robert Webber, Nancy Hadley, Thomas Coley, John Lormer.

Against all advice, a young couple rent a strange house on the New England coast.

THE BURNING GIRL
Writer: Catherine Turney. **Director:** John Newland. **Guest Cast:** Luana Anders, Sandra Knight, Olive Deering, Ed Platt.

A young woman desperately searches for a rational explanation of a series of suspicious fires that start only when she's present.

ORDEAL ON LOCUST STREET
Writer: Michael Plant. **Director:** John Newland. **Guest Cast:** Suzanne Lloyd, Jack Kirkwood, Augusta Dabney, David Lewis.

A young man enters a supernatural world when he sees the strange prisoner in his fiancee's house.

THE RIDDLE
Writer: Larry Marcus. **Director:** John Newland. **Guest Cast:** Warren Stevens, Bethel Leslie, Patrick Westwood, Barry Atwater.

A tourist in India goes into an inexplicable frenzy when a man enters his train compartment carrying a chicken.

FRONT RUNNER
Writer: Don Mankiewicz. **Director:** John Newland. **Guest Cast:** Ben Cooper, Walter Burke, Sandy Kenyon.

A jockey receives supernatural retribution for committing a foul twenty years before against the man who helped him.

DELUSION
Writer: Larry Marcus. **Director:** John Newland. **Guest Cast:** Norman Lloyd, David White, Suzanne Pleshette, George Mitchell.

An accountant's explanation for refusing a dying girl a transfusion of rare blood leads to a series of supernatural occurrences.

FATHER IMAGE
Writers: Staff writers. **Director:** John Newland. **Guest Cast:** Jack Lord, Cee Cee Whitney, Ian Wolfe, Frank Scannel, George Selk.

A young man has a supernatural revelation about his late father's past when he visits the old burlesque house he's been bequeathed.

THE OPEN WINDOW
Writer: Larry Marcus. **Director:** John Newland. **Guest Cast:** Michael Harris, Louise Fletcher, Lori March, Charles Seel.

After nearly murdering a young model in a fit of anger, an artist looks out his studio window and sees the same thing taking place in the building next door.

BRAINWAVE
Writer: Charles Beaumont. **Director:** John Newland. **Guest Cast:** George Grizzard, Whit Bissell, Tod Andrews, Ray Bailey.

A grieving, gin-soaked seaman calls on his medical training and the supernatural to perform a delicate operation on his captain.

DOOMSDAY
Writers: Staff writers. **Director:** John Newland. **Guest Cast:** Torin Thatcher, Patricia Michon, Donald Harrons.

In 1682 an Earl breaks up his son's romance; the boy suddenly dies, and the Earl has the girl tried for witchcraft.

NIGHT OF THE KILL
Writers: Staff writers. **Director:** John Newland. **Guest Cast:** Dennis Holmes, Fred Bier.

A young boy's skeptical father investigates his story that, while lost in the woods, he was befriended by a giant creature.

Warren Stevens in "The Riddle."

Second Season 1959-1960

THE INHERITANCE
Writers: Staff writers. **Director:** John Newland. **Guest Cast:** Jan Miner, Sean McClory, Estelita, Iphigenie Castiglioni.

A series of weird incidents occurs when a contessa's maid refuses to call a doctor for her dying mistress.

REUNION
Writer: Larry Marcus. **Director:** John Newland. **Guest Cast:** Rory Harrity, Betsy Von Furstenberg, Paul Carr.

A post-W.W.II reunion for a group of glider enthusiasts leads to an unusual adventure.

FORKED LIGHTNING
Writer: Staff writers. **Director:** John Newland. **Guest Cast:** Ralph Nelson, Frank Maxwell.

Two complete strangers are drawn together by coinciding premonitions of death.

THE HAND
Writers: Staff writers. **Director:** John Newland. **Guest Cast:** Robert Loggia, Miriam Colon, Pete Candoli, Joe Sullivan.

A pianist is haunted by the circumstances of a murder he committed and that the police have already pinned on someone else.

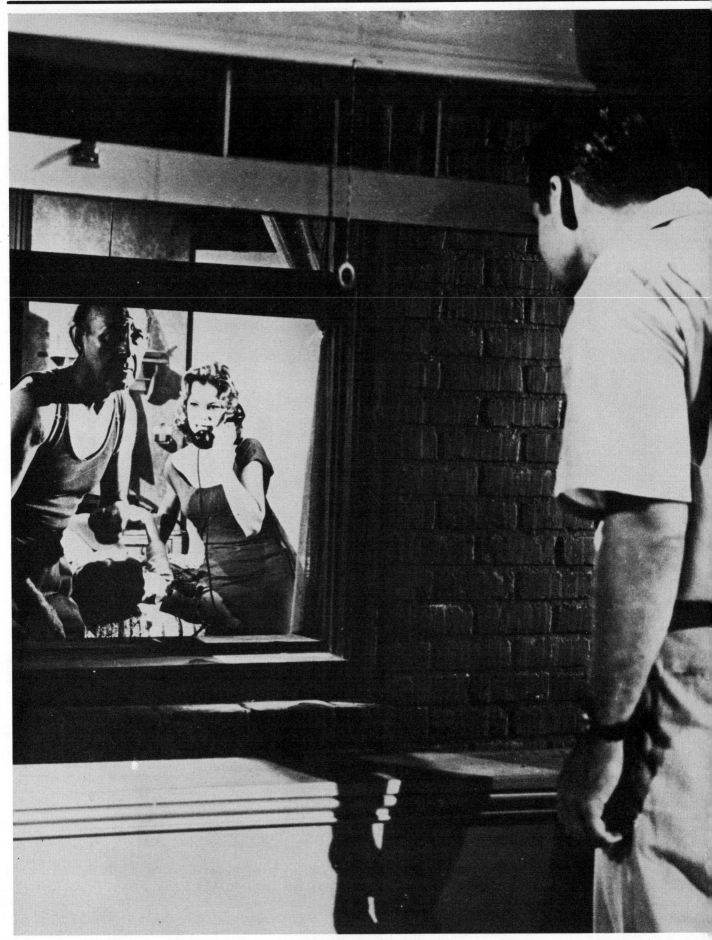

Louise Fletcher, Oscar's 1976 Best Actress, was seen on the phone through ''The Open Window.

"Make Me Not A Witch"

"Who Are You"

"Goodbye Grandpa"

MAKE ME NOT A WITCH
Writers: Staff writers. Director: John Newland. Guest Cast: Patty McCormick, Leo Penn, Eileen Ryan, Robert Emhardt.

When a young girl tells her parents of visions she's had, they accuse her of being a sorceress.

DEAD RINGER
Writer: Staff writers. Director: John Newland. Guest Cast: Norma Crane, Grant Williams, Ed Prentiss, Olive Blakeney.

A woman tells the police of a terrifying vision she's had of her sister burning down an orphanage.

MESSAGE FROM CLARA
Writers: Staff writers. Director: John Newland. Guest Cast: Barbara Baxley, Robert Ellenstein, Celia Lovsky, Oscar Beregi, Jr., Renata Vanna.

A teacher in a school for adults receives a gift of a brooch from one of her pupils, and soon after starts writing in a foreign language.

THE STONE CUTTER
Writers: Staff writers. Director: John Newland. Guest Cast: Joe Mantell, Arthur Shields, Walter Burke, Don Beddoes.

A tombstone cutter makes a fantastic prediction of death.

EARTHQUAKE
Writers: Staff writers. Director: John Newland. Guest Cast: David Opatoshu.

A middle-aged bellboy in a San Francisco hotel experiences metaphysical phenomena preceding the 1906 earthquake.

THE JUSTICE TREE
Writers: Staff writers. Director: John Newland. Guest Cast: Frank Overton, Sally Brosphy, Charles Herbert.

A convict manages an escape enroute to his execution, but is soon experiencing all sorts of weird occurrences.

THE DAY THE WORLD WEPT—THE LINCOLN STORY
Writer: Larry Marcus. Director: John Newland. Guest Cast: Barry Atwater, Jeanne Bates, Eric Sinclair.

This episode examines the many astounding supernatural events all over the country that accompanied the assassination of President Lincoln.

THE FORESTS OF THE NIGHT
Writers: Staff writers. Director: John Newland. Guest Cast: Alfred Ryder, Mark Roberts, Douglas Dick, Stacy Graham.

A man tests out the legend that a Chinese box possesses mystical powers.

WHO ARE YOU?
Writers: Staff writers. Director: John Newland. Guest Cast: Reba Waters, Anna Lee.

Shortly following her remarkable recovery from scarlet fever, a young girl's personality undergoes a startling, mysterious change.

CALL FROM TOMORROW
Writers: Staff writers. Director: John Newland. Guest Cast: Margaret Phillips, Arthur Franz.

Recovering from a nervous breakdown following the death of her child, an actress feels she's being haunted by the cries of a child.

VANISHING POINT
Writers: Larry Marcus, J.G. Ezra. Director: John Newland. Guest Cast: Edward Binns, Fredd Wayne, June Vincent.

A man frantically searches his house for his wife. She's disappeared, and he's charged with murder.

THE HAUNTING
Writer: Gabrielle Upton. Director: John Newland. Guest Cast: Ronald Howard, Keith McConnell, Christine White, Doris Lloyd.

A young man is made accountable when he lets his friend freeze to death following a skiing accident.

THE EXPLORER
Writer: Don Mankiewicz. Director: John Newland. Guest Cast: Gregory Morton, John Wenraf, Jeremy Slate, Rudolph Anders, Edith Evanson.

An explorer's explanation to his son's teacher of the boy's miraculous rescue of a desert expedition leads to an even more startling adventure.

GOODBYE GRANDPA
Writers: Staff writers. Director: John Newland. Guest Cast: Edgar Stehli, Anna Karen, Candy Moore, Donald Losby.

An old railroader's heartfelt promise to his young grandson leads to an unusual chain of events.

THE MASK
Writers: Joseph Petracca, Russell Beggs. Director: John Newland. Guest Cast: Wesley Lau, Luis Van Rooten, Joan Elam, Stephen Bekassy.

An Air Force lieutenant who recently survived a desert plane crash is astonished to discover that the spirit of an Egyptian prince has possessed his body.

THE VISITOR
Writer: Larry Marcus. Director: John Newland. Guest Cast: Joan Fontaine, Warren Beatty, Charles Webster.

When a man has an auto accident, his recently estranged wife rushes to his side, spurred on by a vision of what he had meant to her twenty years earlier.

Eddie Firestone, Bert Convy and Gregory Morton in "The Explorer."

"Gypsy"

"Night of Decision"

"The Death Waltz"

THE CLOWN
Writer: Gabrielle Upton. **Director:** John Newland. **Guest Cast:** Mickey Shaughnessy, Yvette Mimieux, Christopher Dark.

When a jealous husband misinterprets his wife's rendezvous with a mute clown and kills her, he must face bizarre consequences.

THE STORM
Writer: Jerome Gruskin. **Director:** John Newland. **Guest Cast:** Lee Bergere, Rebecca Welles, Danny Zaldivar.

A young woman is determined to discover how a brilliant painting, only half-completed at the time of the artist's death, came to be finished.

ENCOUNTER
Writer: Dewitt Copp. **Director:** John Newland. **Guest Cast:** Robert Douglas, Barbara Stuart.

A company executive cannot explain how his pilot could vanish for days and turn up a thousand miles from his last known location—without his plane.

THE PETER HURKOS STORY
Writers: Staff writers. **Director:** John Newland. **Guest Cast:** Andrew Prine, Albert Salmi, Betty Garde, Norbert Schiller, Alf Kjellin.

A two-part story about a man with psychic powers. In the first part his ESP experiences are chronicled, while in part two he offers to help the police solve a murder.

I SAW YOU TOMORROW
Writer: Merwin Gerard. **Director:** John Newland. **Guest Cast:** Rosemary Murphy, John Hudson.

Through a freak accident in time, a U.S. agent, who is visiting a wealthy American lady, witnesses a murder a day before it occurs.

CONTACT
Writer: Paul David. **Director:** John Newland. **Guest Cast:** Ron Randall, Catherine McLeod, Alexander Lockwood, Jason Johnson.

A man's attachment to a watch given him by his wife leads to a vision of death.

GYPSY
Writer: Gabrielle Upton. **Director:** John Newland. **Guest Cast:** John Seven, Robert Blake, John Kellogg, Murvyn Vye.

A young prisoner has a startling experience with clairvoyance and the supernatural when he's wounded in a jailbreak attempt.

THE LONELY ROOM
Writer: Larry Marcus. **Director:** John Newland. **Guest Cast:** Fabrizio Miomi, Letizia Noverese, Carl Esmond, Maurice Marsac, Peter Camlin.

A metaphysical phenomenon helps a shy young man find love with a woman he's always admired from afar.

HOUSE OF THE DEAD
Writer: Don Mankiewicz. **Director:** John Newland. **Guest Cast:** Mario Alcade, Laya Raki, Stephen Cheng, Hilda Plowright.

An English army lieutenant conducts a frantic search for an Oriental woman who consented to be his wife the day before, then mysteriously vanished.

DELIA
Writer: Merwin Gerard. **Director:** John Newland. **Guest Cast:** Lee Phillips, Barbara Lord, Murray Matheson, Maureen Leeds, Salvador Baquez, Peter Camlin.

A desolate man meets and falls in love with a strange woman while on vacation in Central America. She disappears, and the man's desperate search for her results in tragedy.

Third Season: 1960-1961

ANNIVERSARY OF A MURDER
Writer: Collier Young. **Director:** John Newland. **Guest Cast:** Harry Townes, Randy Stuart, Amzie Strickland, Alexander Lockwood.

A man and a woman are tormented by the memory of a hit-and-run auto accident in which they killed a boy.

MOMENT OF HATE
Writers: Staff writers. **Director:** John Newland. **Guest Cast:** Joanne Linville, John Kellogg, Joyce Chapman.

A woman seeks psychiatric help when she fears she has the power to kill people merely by wishing them dead.

NIGHT OF DECISION
Writers: Staff writers. **Director:** John Newland. **Guest Cast:** Robert Douglas, Donald Buka, Richard Tyler, Richard Hale.

A dream of an expansive and prosperous America causes General Washington to reverse a decision to surrender to the British.

LEGACY OF LOVE
Writers: Staff writers. **Director:** John Newland. **Guest Cast:** Norma Crane, Ollie O'Toole, Charles Aidman, Barbara Eiler, Olan Soule, Joe McGuinn.

A woman and a married couple are supernaturally drawn to a resort community called Seaside.

THE DEATH WALTZ
Writers: Staff writers. **Director:** John Newland. **Guest Cast:** Elizabeth Montgomery, Robert Sampson, Ed Prentiss, Joe Cronin, K.T. Stevens.

When a vicious woman persuades her father, an Army Colonel, to send a suitor on a scouting expedition so he'll be out of her way for a fancy ball, she receives a ghostly visitation.

THE EXECUTIONER
Writers: Bob and Wanda Duncan. **Director:** John Newland. **Guest Cast:** Tom Middleton, Will J. White.

When a Confederate soldier is caught by the Union Army, his dog is killed, but a supernatural event saves him from the firing squad.

THE RETURN
Writer: Larry Marcus. **Director:** John Newland. **Guest Cast:** Dick Davalos, Jack Mullaney, Chris Winters, Charles Gray.

A corporal is blinded while on mission in Korea, but, although totally lost and separated from his unit, finds his way back to camp.

TIDAL WAVE
Writers: Staff writers. **Director:** John Newland. **Guest Cast:** Jean Allison, Cliff Hall, Denny Patrick.

An isolated, invalid woman is saved from a Hawaiian tidal wave through a thought transference asking for help. (The woman who actually had the experience appeared at the end of the episode.)

IF YOU SEE SALLY
Writers: Staff writers. **Director:** John Newland. **Guest Cast:** Anne Whitefield, George Mitchel, Mary Lou Taylor, Pat McCaffrie.

Even though she's been dead seven years, a girl returns home and is seen by several people.

RENDEZVOUS
Writers: Staff writers. **Director:** John Newland. **Guest Cast:** Georgann Johnson, Donald Murphy, H.M. Wynant, Warren Kemmerling.

A woman who's never lost faith that her husband is alive screams for help against an attacker one night, and is astonished to see her husband rush to her aid.

TO KNOW THE END
Writers: Staff writers. **Director:** John Newland. **Guest Cast:** Ellen Willard, Sally Fraser, Alexander Davion, Noel Drayton, James Forrest, Anthony Eustrel, Jean Fenwick.

A woman vacationing in France has a vision of a stranger becoming her husband, then dying in battle.

THE PROMISE
Writer: Larry Marcus. **Director:** John Newland. **Guest Cast:** William Shatner, Deidre Owen, Ben Wright.

A woman has a supernatural experience when her husband breaks his promise not to deactivate any more bombs.

THE LAST ROUND
Writers: Staff writers. **Director:** John Newland. **Guest Cast:** Charles Bronson, Stewart Taylor, Felix DeBank, Ronald Long, Wally Cassell.

"The Promise"

"The Gift"

"Where Are They?"

An aging boxer has a vision of his dead colleague, whose presence reputedly foretells another death in the ring.

THE VOICE
Writers: Staff writers. Director: John Newland. Guest Cast: Robert Lansing, Paul Genge, Luana Anders, Carl Benton Reid, David Lewis, Harry Stang.

A reporter has a strange experience when he attends the trial of several members of a New England town who burned down a barn to try to kill a pet raccoon.

THE TRAP
Writer: Larry Marcus. Director: John Newland. Guest Cast: Mike Kellin, Alex Gerry, Ruth Story, Jeanne Bates.

A man inexplicably develops claustrophobia and then begins to have an unquenchable thirst for water that causes him to begin dehydrating. Fast and incisive action on the part of his doctor save both the man and another patient who is miles away.

BLOOD FLOWER
Writers: Staff writers. Director: John Newland. Guest Cast: Larry Gates, Eugene Iglesias, Marya Stevens.

A professor feels compelled to follow in the footsteps of a young patriot who died during an unsuccessful attempt to assassinate a dictator, and whose spilled blood has yielded an indestructible flower.

THE AVENGERS
Writers: Staff writers. Director: John Newland. Guest Cast: Andre Morell, Lisa Gastoni, Stanley Van Beers.

A general's party celebrating a similar one held by an ancient tyrant stirs up the spirits of that previous get-together.

TONIGHT AT 12:17
Writer: Larry Marcus. Director: John Newland. Guest Cast: Peggy Ann Garner, John Lasell, Jack Lester.

When a woman convinces her husband of the validity of a premonition of a plane crashing into her bedroom, an even more terrible calamity is avoided.

THE GIFT
Writer: Charles Larson. Director: John Newland. Guest Cast: Mary Sinclair, Betty Garde, Scott Marlowe.

A fraudulent fortune teller tries to avert a vision of a terrible future when she "sees" her son murdering her wealthy client.

WHERE ARE THEY
Writers: Staff writers. Director: John Newland. Guest Cast: Phil Pine, Joan Tompkins, Richard Devon.

A man's decision to sell a mysterious formula to Washington seems to cause a strange shower of boulders on a small California town.

PERSON UNKNOWN...
Writers: Staff writers. Director: John Newland. Guest Cast: David Stewart, Robert Carricut.

When a Mexican revolutionary takes refuge in a bewitched convent, his pursuer dies of strangulation at the hands of some unseen force. The person who had the actual experience appears at the end of the episode.

DEAD MAN'S TALE
Writers: Staff writers. Director: John Newland. Guest Cast: Lenny Chapman, Jean Engstrom, Walter Reed, Charles Steel.

A reporter's unusual mental image of two brothers named Barton leads him to search for them in order to determine if they are real or imaginary.

THE SACRED MUSHROOM
Writers: Staff writers. Director: John Newland. Guest Cast: John Newland, Collier Young, Dr. Andrija Puharich, M.D.

The episode concerns series producer Young and director Newland on a search for, and later experimenting with, a mushroom that supposedly affects an individual's powers of ESP.

THE ROOM UPSTAIRS
Writers: Staff writers. Director: John Newland. Guest Cast: Lois Maxwell, David Knight, Anthony Oliver, Gilda Emmanueli.

A childless couple rents a house in which the woman sees a spare room mysteriously converted into a nursery, while her husband hears voices arguing about a child.

THE STRANGER
Writer: Larry Marcus. Director: John Newland. Guest Cast: Peter Dyneley, Bill Nagy, Patrick McAlliney, Graham Stark.

The fingerprints of a man who miraculously saved seven people from an earthquake in which he died suggest a connection with a dead convict who has matching prints.

THE FACE
Writers: Staff writers. Director: John Newland. Guest Cast: Sean Kelly, John Brown, Gareth Tandy, Robin Summer.

A man sets out to find the person who he repeatedly dreams will murder him.

JUSTICE
Writers: Staff writers. Director: John Newland. Guest Cast: Meredith Edwards, Clifford Evans, Edward Evans, Barbara Mulle.

A man confesses to a murder and supplies absolute evidence of his guilt, but people from his church swear he was asleep in his pew at the time the crime was committed.

THE CONFESSION
Writers: Staff writers. Director: John Newland. Guest Cast: Donald Pleasance, Adrienne Corri.

A prosecutor is haunted when he allows a man to die for the murder of a woman he knows to be alive.

SIGNAL RECEIVED
Writers: Staff writers. Director: John Newland. Guest Cast: Mark Eden, Richard Gale, Terry Palmer.

A fortune teller predicts that a young sailor will have a long life, but he and two mates have a premonition that their ship will sink—until he's transferred to another vessel.

THE TIGER
Writers: Staff writers. Director: John Newland. Guest Cast: Pamela Brown, Pauline Challenor, Elspeth March.

A governess discovers that her charge is planning to dispose of her in a most unusual way.

THE PRISONER
Writers: Staff writers. Director: John Newland. Guest Cast: Anton Diffring, Catherine Feller, Faith Brook.

A woman kills a German soldier in retribution for Nazi atrocities, but when her doctor finds the soldier's body he insists the man has been dead for six years.

THE SORCERER
Writers: Staff writers. Director: John Newland. Guest Cast: Christopher Lee, Martin Benson, Gabrielli Licudi.

When a lieutenant is proved innocent of a murder he insists he committed, he plans another so he will be punished for the first.

THE VILLA
Writers: Staff writers. Director: John Newland. Guest Cast: Elizabeth Sellars, Ronald Lewis.

A woman envisions someone trapped in an elevator, and she and her husband investigate the villa where it is located.

NIGHTMARE
Writer: Martin Benson. Director: John Newland. Guest Cast: Peter Wyngarde, Mary Peach, Ambrosine Philpotts, Jean Cadell.

An artist tries to understand why he feels compelled to paint the same unknown woman in all his works.

EYEWITNESS
Writer: Derry Quinn. Director: John Newland. Guest Cast: John Meillon, Rose Alba, Anton Rodgers, Robin Hughes.

A reporter writes an eyewitness account of an explosion that occurred 15,000 miles away.

THE TWILIGHT ZONE

There is a sixth dimension beyond that which is known to man. It is a dimension as vast as space and as timeless as infinity. It is the middle ground between light and shadow—between science and superstition; between the pit of man's fears and the sunlight of his knowledge. It is the dimension of the imagination. It is an area that we call the Twilight Zone.

—Opening words of *Twilight Zone*

Rod Serling spoke the words above in his resonant, matter-of-fact, yet intimate voice. He was the creator, principal writer and co-producer of this fantasy-anthology series which debuted in 1959. His introduction gave an air of solid reality to the bizarre episodes which took place in the *Twilight Zone*. Loyal fans were transported to the sixth dimension each week for five years, and Serling became television's most celebrated writer.

His writing odyssey began after World War II. During the war he was an Army paratrooper in the Pacific, and in the course of his service he received the Purple Heart medal. He was also a boxer, winning all but his last bout—his nose was broken in that one. After the war Serling enrolled in Antioch College on the G.I. Bill and began to write, at first to exorcise himself of the war, later as a passion, a drive. He wrote forty scripts before selling one. The reason may have been that his own style had not yet developed. "Style is something you develop by copying the style of someone who writes well," Serling said years later. "For a while you're a cheap imitation. I was a Hemingway imitator. Everything I wrote began, 'It was hot.'" Nonetheless, by the time he was graduated in 1950, he had sold scripts to both radio and TV.

After graduation he worked for a while as a continuity writer for a local Cincinnati TV station, but soon turned freelance. In 1955, "Patterns," his play about ambition in big business, appeared on *Kraft Theater* and won him his first Emmy. Later he wrote the screenplay for the movie version. The next year *Playhouse 90* produced "Requiem for a Heavyweight," bringing him his second Emmy and a

OPPOSITE: Tracy Stratford was a "Little Girl Lost" in the third season. **RIGHT:** Creator and writer Rod Serling also served as host, introducing each episode in a matter-of-fact manner.

THE TWILIGHT ZONE

Peabody Award, the first ever for a creative writer. "Requiem" was later produced as a stage play and a movie. Serling won a third Emmy for his play "The Comedian" in 1957. He won more Emmys than any other person—six in all—including three for *Twilight Zone*.

Most of his early plays were serious and dealt with contemporary issues. As a result, Serling began a career-long struggle with the censors. All his plays were scrutinized, and demands for changes were frequent. "The Rank and File," which dealt with union corruption, had censor troubles, as did the earlier "Patterns." "Before the script goes before the cameras," Serling once said, "the networks, the sponsors, the ad agency men censor it so that by the time it's seen on the home screen, all the message has been squeezed out of it." It's almost as if a frozen food processor cultivated blandness to avoid complaints about the taste.

Sometimes the changes were astonishingly frivolous: a cigarette company wanted to snip the words "American" and "lucky" from one of his plays because they might make the viewers think of the competition. Sometimes, one doesn't know whether to laugh or to shudder: "One time we couldn't even mention Hitler's gas ovens," Serling recalled, "because a gas company sponsored the show." One script about racial prejudice was bought and paid for, but never produced, because of sponsor pressure; his other plays about prejudice were also heavily censored.

It was because he "simply got tired of battling" with censors, that Serling turned from serious TV drama to fantasy shows. In 1957 he wrote and produced "The Time Element" as a pilot for a science fiction series. In it, a man dreams of the Pearl Harbor bombing and tells the Army, only to be brushed off as a crackpot. Ironically, the sponsor, Westinghouse, demanded changes because they had many defense contracts and didn't want their client pictured in a bad light. The changes were made to show the man relating his dream to a newspaper instead of to the Army. When this show pulled more fan mail than any show of the season, CBS decided to take another look, and a second pilot, "Where is Everybody?" sold the series. *Twilight Zone* debuted in the fall of 1959 with this episode. In it a man played by Earl Holliman found himself in an uninhabited town; though coffee was perking, car engines and a lighted cigar were idling, there was no one around. After panicking and having other bizarre reactions to the barren town, it turned out that Holliman was an astronaut who had been locked into a five-foot box for two weeks to simulate a trip to the moon. His entire experience was an hallucination.

This was a good beginning and soon the show developed a fast following and extensive critical praise. Each installment had a single premise and was written in Serling's spare, plain words. There was nothing superfluous in his plays. You usually knew exactly where you stood until you slipped on the twist ending. The characters hardly mattered—at least in the half-hour versions, they were there just to advance the plot.

For instance, in "The Lonely" we see a shack with an old car beside it surrounded by a vast desert. A man named Corry (Jack Warden) is in the shack. A rocket lands, three men disembark, and walk toward the shack. Corry runs out to meet them; nervous, he asks them to stay a couple hours, have a beer, play a few hands of cards, talk. They have to leave in fifteen minutes. One man says, "Who knows what the next few years may bring? They may...imprison you on earth like the old days." Corry is a convict and has been imprisoned four years alone on this deserted asteroid; he is going crazy from loneliness. Four times a year these guards bring provisions, but this time they brought something additional, a large crate. Corry reads the attached instructions which say that he is now the proud owner of a female robot. Physiologically and psychologically she is a

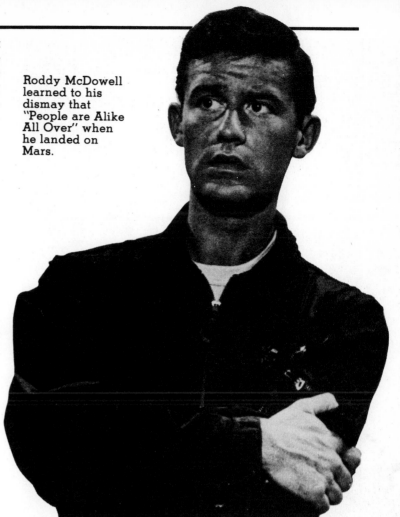

Roddy McDowell learned to his dismay that "People are Alike All Over" when he landed on Mars.

woman with a set of emotions, a memory track, the ability to reason, and to speak. Her name is Alicia.

Corry feels her arm, and she asks, "Not like flesh, Corry?"

"It *is* flesh. And underneath are veins and muscles. Tissue," he replies:

"It's plastic, you know, Corry," insists Alicia.

Corry and Alicia (Jean Marsh) talk to one another, read poetry, look at the stars. Corry is in heaven; he has a companion.

One day the rocket ship returns off schedule. The men have good news: Corry has been given a pardon. They have but a few minutes to leave and Corry is allowed fifteen pounds baggage. Corry laughs excitedly, joyously, but stops suddenly, realizing that Alicia can't come. He refuses to leave without her. She's a robot, they say. She's human! Corry shouts. There is a scuffle and one guard shoots Alicia—her face explodes into a clockwork of springs and gears. Corry is taken back—away from his loneliness—to Earth.

Shows like this one are the reason *Twilight Zone* won Rod Serling three Emmys. It has been perhaps the brightest series ever on American television.

In another episode, "People are Alike All Over," adapted by Serling from a story by Paul W. Fairman, the first Earthman (Roddy McDowall) to visit Mars finds that the Martians are much like us and treat him hospitably. They even build him a house just like the one he left behind on Earth. Alone inside, he discovers that the doors are locked. He pulls some curtains apart and sees a crowd of Martians gazing at him. Outside is a sign, "Earth Creature in His Native Habitat."

In the series' premiere episode, "Where is Everybody?" Earl Holliman discovered himself in a bustling, but uninhabited town.

Franchot Tone (left) appears shocked while Jonathan Harris (right) remains composed in "The Silence."

so quickly? A close associate said that Serling was an insomniac; he got his best ideas while trying to fall asleep. If *Twilight Zone* stories were going through his head, it's no wonder he couldn't sleep. He would keep a tape recorder beside the bed—the way other people might keep a glass of water—and whenever an idea frightened him awake, he would record it.

This wholesale butcher's son from Binghampton, New York, was a very intense, even driven, man. A day rarely went by that he didn't write something. He worked eighteen hours a day on *Twilight Zone* and smoked three to four packs of cigarettes daily. A friend said he set such a fierce pace because he was afraid his talent would atrophy. But it seems to be more than that. He celebrated his fortieth birthday by parachuting from a plane, perhaps to prove to himself he wasn't getting old.

Though he undoubtedly didn't need the money, he did TV commercials for beer, aspirin, luggage, banks and cars, among other products, capitalizing on his famous voice; he even did a magazine ad for socks, which showed him with his shoes off and feet up on his desk. He did these despite his frequent criticism of commercials: "How do you put on a meaningful drama or documentary that is adult, incisive, probing, when every fifteen minutes the proceedings are interrupted by twelve dancing rabbits with toilet paper?" He was a driven man, perhaps insecure and out to prove something.

From the start, *Twilight Zone* had problems with ratings, and sponsors would disappear overnight. But it was a critical success, reaching a sophisticated, enthusiastic audience, and so a new sponsor would usually materialize the next morning. CBS also liked airing what was recognized as a "prestige" show and did its best to keep it running.

However, after several years, audience interest began to wane further, and the series was canceled for half of a season. During this time, Serling returned to Antioch as a visiting professor and wrote the screenplay for *Seven Days in May*. In an attempt to breathe new life into it, the show returned the next semester in an hour-long format, but this did not win audiences over, as had been hoped. It returned to its original half-hour length the following season, its last. In the Spring of 1964, *Twilight Zone* was retired after a long and successful run.

Though the series never reached a very large audience, its influence was widespread. Perhaps the best measure of that influence is the way that the phrase "twilight zone" has found a permanent place in the American idiom. In the early 1960s, such diverse people as Archie Moore, the boxer reknowned for his long career in the ring and even longer boxer shorts, and Dean Rusk, then Secretary of State, used the phrase. Moore said of a punch that flattened him, "Man, I was in the 'twilight zone,'" and Rusk spoke of the " 'twilight zone' of international relations." Writing in *The New York Times* on the occasion of Mao Tse-tung's death in 1976, the American diplomat John S. Service referred to the "twilight zone" of Chinese-American relations. Commercials are still set up to imitate the style of the show, and an entire new generation of viewers casually uses the term without ever having seen even one episode. Long after the death of the show, and after Serling's own death, "twilight zone" survives.

In "The Silence," by Rod Serling, the incessant chatter of Jamie Tennyson (Liam Sullivan) inspires Colonel Archie Taylor (Franchot Tone) to bet $500,000 that Tennyson can't keep quiet for one full year. Tennyson accepts. Time passes and Taylor, becoming increasingly anxious, tries to call the bet off, but Tennyson won't have it. Finally when the year is up, a broken and broke Taylor confesses that he can't pay the wager. But Tennyson has a confession too: to win, he had his larynx removed. Alfred Hitchcock couldn't have done better.

For five years, Serling produced a top-notch teleplay a week, maintaining an extraordinarily rigorous schedule. Though many installments were written by others, principally Richard Matheson and Charles Beaumont, Rod Serling was the main writer. He would write an original *Twilight Zone* script in thirty-five to forty hours. He rarely used a typewriter, preferring to dictate a first draft into a tape recorder; a secretary would type it and he would then tighten it up. That was it. But these were not formula shows—no stock jokes, no chases, no fights, no monsters, just pure imagination.

The settings, ideas and situations were so various, it can truly be said that *Twilight Zone* was set in the quirky convolutions of Serling's mind. How was it possible for one man to produce so many different half-hour playlets, and

"The Invaders," in which Agnes Moorehead pantomimed a role as a farm woman besieged by exterrestial creatures, stands as one of the classics in the series

Rod Serling

INDEX
OF
EPISODES

"Third from the Sun"

THE TWILIGHT ZONE

1959-1964/151 episodes
CBS/a Cayuga Production (filmed at MGM Studios)
30 minutes (first, second, third and fifth seasons), 60 minutes (fourth season) black & white

Host: Rod Serling. **Producers:** Rod Serling and Buck Houghton. **Creator:** Rod Serling. **Makeup:** William Tuttle. **Music:** Bernard Herrmann, Jerry Goldsmith.

First Season: 1959-1960

WHERE IS EVERYBODY?
Writer: Rod Serling. **Director:** Robert Stevens. **Guest Cast:** Earl Holliman, James Gregory.
A terrified man searches a small town and discovers he is completely alone. The ordeal is finally revealed to be a test of his endurance under simulated conditions of loneliness.

ONE FOR THE ANGELS
Writer: Rod Serling. **Director:** Robert Parish. **Guest Cast:** Ed Wynn, Murray Hamilton, Dana Dillaway, Merritt Bohn.
In order to save a little girl's life, a sidewalk salesman makes the greatest pitch of his life to a mysterious stranger known as "Mr. Death."

MR. DENTON ON DOOMSDAY
Writer: Rod Serling. **Director:** Allen Reisner. **Guest Cast:** Dan Duryea, Malcolm Atterbury, Martin Landau, Jeanne Cooper, Ken Lynch, Arthur Batanides, Doug McClure.
A magic potion restores shooting skill to a broken-down gunslinger, but also ends his fast-draw career.

THE SIXTEEN-MILLIMETER SHRINE
Writer: Rod Serling. **Director:** Mitch Leisen. **Guest Cast:** Ida Lupino, Martin Balsam, Alice Frost, Jerome Cowan.
A forgotten movie star of the '30s tries to re-create the spirit of her heyday by viewing her old films—and living them.

WALKING DISTANCE
Writer: Rod Serling. **Director:** Robert Stevens. **Guest Cast:** Gig Young, Frank Overton, Michael Montgomery, Irene Tedrow.
Needing to escape the pressures of his advertising agency job, Martin Sloane visits his home town and slips thirty years into his own childhood.

ESCAPE CLAUSE
Writer: Rod Serling. **Director:** Mitch Leisen. **Guest Cast:** David Wayne, Virginia Christine, Wendell Holmes, Thomas Gomez, Raymond Bailey.

After making a pact with the devil for immortality, hypochondriac Walter Bedeker finds he doesn't get a kick out of living anymore.

THE LONELY
Writer: Rod Serling. **Director:** Jack Smight. **Guest Cast:** Jack Warden, Jean Marsh, John Dehner, Ted Knight, Jim Turley.
Convicted of murder and sentenced to spend forty years on an asteroid in outer space, James Corry is given a robot, which looks like a woman, for company.

TIME ENOUGH AT LAST
Writer: Rod Serling. **Director:** John Brahm. **Guest Cast:** Burgess Meredith, Jacqueline DeWit, Vaughn Taylor, Lela Bliss.
Nearsighted, meek bankteller Henry Bemis is the only survivor of an H-bomb attack. At last he has the time to pursue his sole interest in life: reading. Unfortunately, he breaks his glasses shortly after he has made his way to a library.

PERCHANCE TO DREAM
Writer: Charles Beaumont. **Director:** Robert Florey. **Guest Cast:** Richard Conte, John Larch, Suzanne Lloyd, Ted Stanhope, Eddie Marr.
Stumbling into a psychiatrist's office, Edward Hall claims he is terrified of falling asleep, fearing that a woman he meets in his dreams will murder him.

JUDGMENT NIGHT
Writer: Rod Serling. **Director:** John Brahm. **Guest Cast:** Nehemiah Persoff, Ben Wright, Patrick McNee, Hugh Sanders, Leslie Bradley, Deirdre Owen, James Franciscus.
A passenger on board a wartime freighter can't remember how he arrived there, but is certain the ship will be sunk at 1:15 A.M.

AND WHEN THE SKY WAS OPENED
Writer: Rod Serling. **Director:** Douglas Heyes. **Guest Cast:** Rod Taylor, Charles Aidman, James Hutton, Maxine Cooper.
After three men return from man's first space flight, each of them mysteriously disappears without a trace.

WHAT YOU NEED
Writer: Rod Serling. **Director:** Al Ganzer. **Guest Cast:** Steve Cochran, Ernest Truex, Read Morgan, William Edmonson, Arline Sax.
Broke and out of a job, Fred Renard tries to profit from another man's ability to tell the future.

THE FOUR OF US ARE DYING
Writer: Rod Serling. **Director:** John Brahm. **Guest Cast:** Harry Townes, Beverly Garland, Philip Pine, Ross Martin, Don Gordon.
Arch Hammer can change his face to make it look like anyone else's.

THIRD FROM THE SUN
Writer: Richard Matheson. **Director:** Richard

Bare. **Guest Cast:** Fritz Weaver, Joe Maross, Edward Andrews, Denise Alexander, Lori March.
Two families plan to steal a rocket ship and flee into outer space before an inevitable atomic war destroys their planet.

I SHOT AN ARROW INTO THE AIR
Writer: Rod Serling. **Director:** Stuart Rosenberg. **Guest Cast:** Edward Binns, Dewey Martin.
A space traveler kills his comrades, to prolong his own life, but later discovers the murders were unnecessary.

THE HITCH-HIKER
Writer: Rod Serling. **Director:** Alvin Ganzer. **Guest Cast:** Inger Stevens, Leonard Strong, Adam Williams, Lew Gallo, Dwight Townsend.
A woman, driving cross-country, keeps seeing the same ominous hitch-hiker on the road ahead.

THE FEVER
Writer: Rod Serling. **Director:** Alvin Ganzer. **Guest Cast:** Everett Sloane, Bibi Janiss, William Kendis, Lee Millar.
A man fanatically opposed to gambling battles a Las Vegas slot machine which has a malevolent mind of its own.

THE LAST FLIGHT
Writer: Richard Matheson. **Director:** William Claxton. **Guest Cast:** Kenneth Haigh, Alexander Scourby, Simon Scott, Robert Warwick.
A British World War I flyer lands at a modern air base, thinking the year is 1917, rather than 1959.

THE PURPLE TESTAMENT
Writer: Rod Serling. **Director:** Richard Bare. **Guest Cast:** William Reynolds, Dick York, Barney Phillips, William Phipps, Warren Oates, Marc Cavell, Ron Masak, Paul Mazursky.
A lieutenant finds he has the power to predict which men in his outfit will be killed in battle.

ELEGY
Writer: Charles Beaumont. **Director:** Douglas Heyes. **Guest Cast:** Cecil Kellaway, Jeff Morrow, Kevin Hagen, Don Dubbins.
A party of space travelers lands in a strange world where all the inhabitants seem to be in a trance.

MIRROR IMAGE
Writer: Rod Serling. **Director:** John Brahm. **Guest Cast:** Vera Miles, Martin Milner, Joe Hamilton.
A young woman thinks she's going mad when she's haunted by a strange lookalike in a bus depot.

THE MONSTERS ARE DUE ON MAPLE STREET
Writer: Rod Serling. **Director:** Ron Winston.

"The Hitch-Hiker"

"The Last Flight"

"The Big Tall Wish"

Guest Cast: Claude Akins, Jack Weston, Barry Atwater, Jan Handzlik, Burt Metcalfe, Mary Gregory, Anne Barton, Lea Waggner, Ben Erway, Lyn Guild, Sheldon Allman, William Walsh.

Hysteria engulfs a small town as residents suspect a power failure has been caused by invaders from space disguised as Earthmen.

A WORLD OF DIFFERENCE

Writer: Richard Matheson. Director: Ted Post. Guest Cast: Howard Duff, Eileen Ryan, Gail Kobe, Frank Maxwell, Peter Walker.

A businessman's normal working world suddenly and inexplicably becomes the set for a film in which he has become a character.

LONG LIVE WALTER JAMESON

Writer: Charles Beaumont. Director: Tony Leader. Guest Cast: Kevin McCarthy, Edgar Stehli, Estelle Winwood, Dody Heath.

A professor is astonished to learn that his colleague and future son-in-law is immortal and well over 2000 years old.

PEOPLE ARE ALIKE ALL OVER

Writer: Rod Serling. Director: Mitchell Leisen. Guest Cast: Roddy McDowall, Susan Oliver, Paul Comi, Byron Morrow, Vic Perrin, Vernon Gray.

A space party from Earth is pleased to discover that people on Mars act just like people at home.

EXECUTION

Writer: Rod Serling. Director: David Orrick McDearmon. Guest Cast: Albert Salmi, Russell Johnson, Than Wyenn, George Mitchell, Jon Lormer, Fay Roope, Richard Karlan.

An outlaw in the Old West is snatched from the hangman's noose by a modern day scientist and his time machine.

THE BIG, TALL WISH

Writer: Rod Serling. Director: Ron Winston. Guest Cast: Ivan Dixon, Steve Perry, Kim Hamilton.

A youngster's faith in miracles helps an aging boxer win an important match.

A NICE PLACE TO VISIT

Writer: Charles Beaumont. Director: J. Brahm. Guest Cast: Larry Blyden, Sebastian Cabot, Sandra Warner.

A third-rate thug gets killed while committing a crime and finds an afterlife in which all wishes are granted.

NIGHTMARE AS A CHILD

Writer: Rod Serling. Director: Alvin Ganzer. Guest Cast: Janice Rule, Terry Burnham, Shepperd Strudwick.

A young woman is haunted by the recurring image of herself as a child.

A STOP AT WILLOUGHBY

Writer: Rod Serling. Director: Robert Parrish. Guest Cast: James Daly, Howard Smith, Patricia Donahue, James Maloney.

An executive escapes from his harried world to the idyllic town of Willoughby—circa 1890.

THE CHASER

Writer: Robert Presnell, Jr. Director: Douglas Heyes. Guest Cast: George Grizzard, John McIntire, Patricia Barry.

A love-smitten man purchases a love potion from a strange doctor.

A PASSAGE FOR TRUMPET

Writer: Rod Serling. Director: D. Medford. Guest Cast: Jack Klugman, Mary Webster, John Anderson, Frank Wolff.

A down-and-out trumpet player is given a second crack at life—after he is struck and killed by a truck.

MR. BEVIS

Writer: Rod Serling. Director: R. Parrish. Guest Cast: Orson Bean, Henry Jones, Charles Lane, William Schallert, Horace McMahon.

A kindly man finds his life changed for the worse when he starts getting assistance from his guardian angel.

THE AFTER HOURS

Writer: Rod Serling. Director: Douglas Heyes. Guest Cast: Anne Francis, Elizabeth Allen, James Millhollin, John Conwell, Nancy Rennick.

A woman discovers that the floor of a department store on which she bought an item doesn't exist, and that the sales girl was, in reality, a mannequin.

THE MIGHTY CASEY

Writer: Rod Serling. Director: Douglas Heyes. Guest Cast: Jack Warden, Robert Sorrells, Don O'Kelly, Abraham Sofaer.

A manager banks his losing team's hopes on one star player, a robot named Casey.

A WORLD OF HIS OWN

Writer: Richard Matheson. Director: Ralph Nelson. Guest Cast: Keenan Wynn, Phyllis Kirk, Mary La Roche.

A playwright creates true-to-life characters, so true that he can make them appear in the room with him.

Second Season: 1960-1961

KING NINE WILL NOT RETURN

Writer: Rod Serling. Director: Buzz Kulik. Guest Cast: Bob Cummings, Paul Lambert, Gene Lyons, Seymour Green, Richard Lupino, Jenna MacMahon.

A downed bomber pilot cannot tell if the images of his crew that he sees in the desert are real or illusion.

THE MAN IN THE BOTTLE

Writer: Rod Serling. Director: Don Medford. Guest Cast: Luther Adler, Vivi Janiss, Lisa Golm, Joseph Ruskin, Olan Soule, Peter Coe, Albert Szabo.

A pawnbroker is granted four wishes by a genie in a bottle, but things don't turn out quite as planned.

NERVOUS MAN IN A FOUR DOLLAR ROOM

Writer: Rod Serling. Director: Douglas Heyes. Guest Cast: Joe Mantell, William D. Gordon.

A petty gangster is confronted by his conscience as he prepares to make a hit for the mob.

A THING ABOUT MACHINES

Writer: Rod Serling. Director: Dave McDearmon. Guest Cast: Richard Haydn, Barbara Stuart, Barney Phillips.

After a lifetime of abusing machines, a writer is convinced that the things are conspiring against him.

THE HOWLING MAN

Writer: Charles Beaumont. Director: Douglas Heyes. Guest Cast: H.M. Wynant, John Carradine, Robin Hughes, Ezelle Poule.

While taking refuge in a European monastery, a man is disturbed by the cries from a prisoner in the cellar who, he is told, is the Devil.

THE EYE OF THE BEHOLDER

Writer: Rod Serling. Director: Douglas Heyes. Guest Cast: William B. Gordon, Jennifer Howard, Joanna Hayes.

Plastic surgeons make a final desperate attempt to improve a young woman's face so she can live a normal life.

NICK OF TIME

Writer: Richard Matheson. Director: Richard L. Bare. Guest Cast: William Shatner, Patricia Breslin.

A newlywed husband finds a fortune-telling machine that makes uncanny predictions about his life.

THE LATENESS OF THE HOUR

Writer: Rod Serling. Director: Jack Smight. Guest Cast: Inger Stevens, John Hoyt,

A young woman is dissatisfied with the faultless precision which robot servants are providing in her and her family's lives.

THE TROUBLE WITH TEMPLETON

Writer: E. Jack Neuman. Director: Buzz Kulik. Guest Cast: Brian Aherne, Pippa Scott.

An aging actor is given a sobering glimpse at the past he holds so dear.

A MOST UNUSUAL CAMERA

Writer: Rod Serling. Director: John Rich. Guest Cast: Fred Clark, Jean Carson, Adam Williams.

"The After Hours"

"The Howling Man"

A pair of petty thieves find among their loot a camera that can predict the future.

NIGHT OF THE MEEK
Writer: Rod Serling. **Director:** Jack Smight. **Guest Cast:** Art Carney, John Fiedler, Meg Wyllie, Robert Lieb.

A department store Santa makes Christmas merry for some poor people with the help of a sack that produces whatever you ask for.

DUST
Writer: Rod Serling. **Director:** Douglas Heyes. **Guest Cast:** Thomas Gomez, Vladimir Sokoloff, John Alonso, John Larch.

On the day of his execution, a man is conned by a vicious traveling salesman.

BACK THERE
Writer: Rod Serling. **Director:** David Orrick McDearmon. **Guest Cast:** Russell Johnson, Paul Hartman.

A man tries to alter history when he is hurtled back in time to the moments preceding the assassination of President Lincoln.

THE WHOLE TRUTH
Writer: Rod Serling. **Director:** James Sheldon. **Guest Cast:** Jack Carson, Jack Ging, Nan Peterson, George Chandler.

The unscrupulous tactics of an obnoxious used-car salesman are altered by a haunted car.

THE INVADERS
Writer: Richard Matheson. **Director:** Douglas Heyes. **Guest Cast:** Agnes Moorehead.

A woman in an isolated farm house must battle two tiny extraterrestial beings who have crashed through the roof into her attic—but the tiny visitors are Earthmen. Particularly interesting episode in that there is no dialogue until the very end when the astronauts identify themselves.

A PENNY FOR YOUR THOUGHTS
Writer: George Clayton Johnson. **Director:** James Sheldon. **Guest Cast:** Dick York, Hayden Rorke, Dan Tobin, June Dayton.

A freak auto accident leaves a bank teller with the power to read minds.

TWENTY TWO
Writer: Rod Serling. **Director:** Jack Smight. **Guest Cast:** Barbara Nichols, Jonathan Harris, Fredd Wayne.

A woman's recurring nightmare always ends with her being escorted to hospital room number 22—the morgue.

THE ODYSSEY OF FLIGHT 33
Writer: Rod Serling. **Director:** J. Addiss. **Guest Cast:** John Anderson, Sandy Kenyon, Paul Comi, Harp McGuire, Wayne Heffley, Nancy Rennick, Beverly Brown, Jay Overholt.

A commercial airliner suddenly breaks the time barrier and flies into a prehistoric age.

MR. DINGLE, THE STRONG
Writer: Rod Serling. **Director:** John Brahm. **Guest Cast:** Burgess Meredith, Don Rickles.

A timid little man astonishes his cruel friends when an experimenting Martian gives him superpowers.

STATIC
Writer: Charles Beaumont. **Director:** Buzz Kulik. **Guest Cast:** Dean Jagger, Carmen Mathews, Robert Emhardt.

An old radio provides a valuable link with the past for two elderly lovers.

THE PRIME MOVER
Writer: Charles Beaumont. **Director:** Richard L. Bare. **Guest Cast:** Dane Clark, Buddy Ebsen.

Two men figure out a way to make a fortune from the ability one of them has to control inanimate objects.

LONG DISTANCE CALL
Writers: Charles Beaumont, William Idelson. **Director:** James Sheldon. **Guest Cast:** Billy Mumy, Philip Abbott, Patricia Smith, Lili Darvas.

A young boy has a toy telephone by which he mysteriously remains in contact with his dead grandmother.

A HUNDRED YARDS OVER THE RIM
Writer: Rod Serling. **Director:** Buzz Kulik. **Guest Cast:** Cliff Robertson, Miranda Jones.

A Western settler, circa 1850, is sent into the future when he needs medication to save his dying son.

THE RIP VAN WINKLE CAPER
Writer: Rod Serling. **Director:** Justus Addiss. **Guest Cast:** Oscar Beregi, Simon Oakland, Lew Gallo, John Mitchum.

Four thieves think they've planned the perfect crime when they cover a robbery of gold bullion by hiding out and "sleeping" for a hundred years.

THE SILENCE
Writer: Rod Serling. **Director:** Boris Sagal. **Guest Cast:** Franchot Tone, Liam Sullivan.

A half-million dollars rides on whether or not a loud-mouthed young man can keep silent for a full year.

SHADOW PLAY
Writer: Charles Beaumont. **Director:** John Brahm. **Guest Cast:** Dennis Weaver, Harry Townes, Wright King.

A hysterical young man tries to persuade the judge who sentenced him to death that he and the people around him are just part of a recurring nightmare.

THE MIND AND THE MATTER
Writer: Rod Serling. **Director:** Buzz Kulik. **Guest Cast:** Shelley Berman, Jack Grinnage, Jeanne Wood, Chet Stratton.

A book on the power of thought enables a meek clerk to create a world exactly as he would want it.

WILL THE REAL MARTIAN PLEASE STAND UP
Writer: Rod Serling. **Director:** Montgomery Pittman. **Guest Cast:** Morgan Jones, John Archer, Bill Kendis, John Hoyt, Jean Willes, Jack Elam, Barney Phillips.

Several strangers at a diner try to figure out which of them is really a Martian in disguise.

THE OBSOLETE MAN
Writer: Rod Serling. **Director:** E. Silverstein. **Guest Cast:** Burgess Meredith, Fritz Weaver.

A librarian plots revenge on the chancellor of a futuristic society when he's told he's obsolete and so must die.

Third Season: 1961-1962

TWO
Writer/Director: Montgomery Pittman. **Guest Cast:** Elizabeth Montgomery, Charles Bronson, Sharon Lucas.

A nuclear holocaust leaves two lone, scared survivors to start the world afresh.

THE ARRIVAL
Writer: Rod Serling. **Director:** Boris Sagal. **Guest Cast:** Harold J. Stone, Bing Russell, Robert Karnes, Noah Keen, Jim Boles, Robert Brubaker, Fredd Wayne.

An aviation administration examiner's theory that a mysterious airliner may be imaginary proves to be more sound than he realized.

THE SHELTER
Writer: Rod Serling. **Director:** Lamont Johnson. **Guest Cast:** Larry Gates, Peggy Stewart, Michael Burns, Jack Albertson, Jo Helton, Joseph Bernard, Moria Turner, Sandy Kenyon, Mary Gregory, John McLiam.

One family's bomb shelter turns a community of friends into vicious, selfish animals when a possible nuclear attack is announced.

THE PASSERBY
Writer: Rod Serling. **Director:** Elliot Silverstein. **Guest Cast:** Joanne Linville, James Gregory, Rex Holman, David Garcia, Warren Kemmerling, Austin Green.

A Civil War soldier slowly realizes that he and his company are not merely walking home from battle, they are dead.

A GAME OF POOL
Writer: George Clayton Johnson. **Director:** A.E. Houghton. **Guest Cast:** Jonathan Winters, Jack Klugman.

A eager young pool player plays a game with a master pool shark, who died years ago, for the highest stakes of his career—his life.

Many well-known comedians displayed their lesser-known dramatic talents on *Twilight Zone*. Among them were Carol Burnett, Wally Cox, Jack Weston, Orson Bean, Don Rickles, Buster Keaton and Mickey Rooney.

ABOVE LEFT:
Jonathan Winters (left) returns from the grave to face hustler Jack Klugman (right) in "A Game of Pool."

ABOVE:
The beloved Ed Wynn starred in "One for the Angels" as an old man forced to deal with Mr. Death in order to save a little girl's life.

RIGHT:
"Night of the Meek" starred Art Carney in a bedraggled beard playing a department store Santa whose sack could magically fulfill any wish.

"Nick of Time"

"Two"

THE MIRROR

Writer: Rod Serling. **Director:** Don Medford. **Guest Cast:** Peter Falk, Tony Carbone, Richard Karlan, Arthur Batanides, Rodolfo Hoyos, Will Kuluva, Vladimir Sokoloff, Val Ruffino.

When a revolutionary takes over the state offices, he sees a mirror that is reputed to show the viewer who will kill him.

THE GRAVE

Writer/Director: Montgomery Pittman. **Guest Cast:** Lee Marvin, James Best, Strother Martin, Ellen Willrad, Lee Van Cleef, William Challee, Stafford Repp, Larry Johns, Richard Geary.

A gunman ignores an outlaw's dying threats by defiling his grave.

IT'S A GOOD LIFE

Writer: Rod Serling. **Director:** Jim Sheldon. **Guest Cast:** Billy Mumy, John Larch, Cloris Leachman, Tom Hatcher, Alice Frost, Don Keefer, Jeanne Bates, Lenore Kingston, Casey Adams.

A young boy holds a community terrified with his mysterious, destructive powers.

DEATHS-HEAD REVISITED

Writer: Rod Serling. **Director:** Don Medford. **Guest Cast:** Joseph Schildkraut, Oscar Beregi, Chuck Fox, Karen Verne, Robert Boone, Ben Wright.

A former Nazi is haunted by the ghosts of his ghastly crimes when he visits the concentration camp at Dachau.

THE MIDNIGHT SUN

Writer: Rod Serling. **Director:** Anton Leader. **Guest Cast:** Lois Nettleton, Betty Garde, Jason Wingreen, Juney Ellis, Ned Glass, Robert J. Stevenson, John McLiam, Tom Reese, William Keene.

The Earth is experiencing a devastating heat wave and drought—it's being drawn into the sun.

STILL VALLEY

Writer: Rod Serling. **Director:** Jim Sheldon. **Guest Cast:** Gary Merrill, Ben Cooper, Vaughn Taylor, Addison Myers, Mark Tapscott, Jack Mann.

A magical book could ensure a Confederate victory during the Civil War—if they're willing to make a pact with the Devil.

THE JUNGLE

Writer: Charles Beaumont. **Director:** William Claxton. **Guest Cast:** John Dehner, Emily McLaughlin, Walter Brooke, Hugh Sanders, Howard Wright, Donald Foster, Jay Overholts, Jay Adler.

A prospector must face the wrath of a native conjurer when he threatens to violate African land.

ONCE UPON A TIME

Writer: Richard Matheson. **Director:** Norman Z. McLeod. **Guest Cast:** Buster Keaton, Stanley Adams, Gil Lamb, James Flavin, Michael Ross, Milton Parsons, George E. Stone, Warren Parker.

A nineteenth-century janitor experiments with a time machine invented by his employer and ends up in 1962.

FIVE CHARACTERS IN SEARCH OF AN EXIT

Writer: Rod Serling. **Director:** Lamont Johnson. **Guest Cast:** Bill Windom, Murray Matheson, Susan Harrison, Kelton Garwood, Clark Allen, Mona Houghton, Carol Hill.

Five people trying to escape from a cavernous prison soon realize they aren't human at all, but dolls being distributed to the poor.

A QUALITY OF MERCY

Writer: Rod Serling. **Director:** Buzz Kulik. **Guest Cast:** Dean Stockwell, Albert Salmi, Rayford Barnes, Ralph Votrian, Leonard Nimoy, Dale Ishimoto, Jerry Fujikawa, Michael Pataki.

A soldier sees the danger in his super-militaristic thinking when he mysteriously experiences the situation through the eyes of the enemy.

NOTHING IN THE DARK

Writer: George Clayton Johnson. **Director:** Lamont Johnson. **Guest Cast:** Gladys Cooper, Robert Redford, R.G. Armstrong.

An old woman locks herself into a room in a desolate building in order to escape confronting Death.

ONE MORE PALLBEARER

Writer: Rod Serling. **Director:** Lamont Johnson. **Guest Cast:** Joseph Wiseman, Trevor Bardette, Gage Clark, Katherine Squire, Josip Elic, Robert Snyder, Ray Galvin.

A wealthy old man devises an elaborate scheme to terrorize three people into apologizing for humiliating him at certain points in his life.

DEAD MAN'S SHOES

Writer: Charles Beaumont. **Director:** Montgomery Pittman. **Guest Cast:** Warren Stevens, Harry Swoger, Ben Wright, Joan Marshall, Eugene Borden, Richard Devon, Florence Marly, Ron Hagerthy, Joe Mell.

A dead gangster's fancy shoes enable a derelict to continue in the footsteps of the gangster's life.

THE HUNT

Writer: Earl Hamner. **Director:** Harold Schuster. **Guest Cast:** Arthur Hunnicutt, Jeanette Nolan, Titus Moede, Orville Sherman, Charles Seel, Robert Foulk, Dexter DuPont.

A hunter and his dog are killed while chasing

their prey and soon confront St. Peter at the gate of Heaven.

SHOWDOWN WITH RANCE MCGREW

Writer: Rod Serling. **Director:** C. Nyby. **Guest Cast:** Larry Blyden, William McLean, Troy Melton, Jay Overholts, Robert J. Stevenson, Robert Cornthwaite, Arch Johnson, Robert Kline, Hal K. Dawson.

An insufferable cowboy star is suddenly face to face with a spokesman for the outlaws who've been poorly portrayed and whom he's treated badly in his films.

KICK THE CAN

Writer: George Clayton Johnson. **Director:** Lamont Johnson. **Guest Cast:** Ernest Truex, Russell Collins, Hank Patterson, Earle Hodgins, Burt Mustin, Gregory McCabe, Marjorie Bennett, Lenore Shanewise, Anne O'Neal, John Marley, Barry Truex, Eve McVeagh, Marc Stevens.

An old man discovers miraculous rejuvenative powers in a simple children's game.

A PIANO IN THE HOUSE

Writer: Earl Hamner. **Director:** David Greene. **Guest Cast:** Barry Morse, Joan Hackett, Don Durant, Phil Coolidge, Cyril Delevanti, Muriel Landers.

When anyone hears the right music on a strange player piano, his true nature is revealed.

TO SERVE MAN

Writer: Rod Serling. **Director:** Richard Bare. **Guest Cast:** Richard Kiel, Hardie Albright, Robert Tafur, Lomax Study, Theodore Marcuse, Susan Cummings, Nelson Olmstead, Lloyd Bochner.

A scientist is skeptical of some alien visitors' gifts to Earth, which are a utopian existence and a book entitled "To Serve Man."

THE LAST RITES OF JEFF MYRTLEBANK

Writer/Director: Montgomery Pittman. **Guest Cast:** James Best, Ralph Moody, Ezelle Pouley, Vickie Barnes, Sherry Jackson, Helen Wallace, Lance Fuller, Bill Fawcett, Edgar Buchanan, Mabel Forrest, Dub Taylor, Jon Lormer, Pat Hector.

When a young man suddenly "awakens" from the dead, townspeople begin to suspect that the Devil has taken possession of his body.

THE FUGITIVE

Writer: Charles Beaumont. **Director:** Richard L. Bare. **Guest Cast:** J. Pat O'Malley, Susan Gordon, Nancy Kulp, Wesley Lau, Paul Tripp, Stephen Talbot, Johnny Eiman, Russ Bender.

A magical old man risks being taken back to his home planet in order to help a sick little girl.

LITTLE GIRL LOST

Writer: Richard Matheson. **Director:** Paul Stewart. **Guest Cast:** Sarah Marshall, Robert

"Little Girl Lost"

"The Dummy"

Sampson, Charles Aidman, Tracy Stratford.

A man and a woman are awakened by the desperate cries of their small daughter, who has disappeared into the fourth dimension.

PERSON OR PERSONS UNKNOWN
Writer: Charles Beaumont. **Director:** John Brahm. **Guest Cast:** Richard Long, Frank Silvera, Shirley Ballard, Julie Van Zandt, Betty Harford, Ed Glover, Michael Kelp, Joe Higgins, John Newton.

A man wakes up one morning to find that no one knows who he is.

THE GIFT
Writer: Rod Serling. **Director:** Allan Parker. **Guest Cast:** Geoffrey Horne, Nico Minardos, Cliff Osmond, Edmund Vargas, Carmen D'-Antonio, Paul Mazursky, Vladimir Sokoloff, Vito Scotti, Henry Corden.

A downed flyer is taken for an invader from outer space by the inhabitants of a small Mexican village.

THE LITTLE PEOPLE
Writer: Rod Serling. **Director:** Bill Claxton. **Guest Cast:** Joe Maross, Claude Akins, Michael Ford.

A space traveler takes advantage of his size to become the absolute ruler of the tiny inhabitants of a space station.

FOUR O'CLOCK
Writer: Rod Serling. **Director:** Lamont Johnson. **Guest Cast:** Theodore Bikel, Moyna MacGill, Phyllis Love.

A mad old man sets out to exact a strange revenge on all the evil people of the world.

THE TRADE-INS
Writer: Rod Serling. **Director:** Elliot Silverstein. **Guest Cast:** Joseph Schildkraut, Noah Keen, Alma Platt, Ted Marcuse, Edson Stroll, Terrence De Marney, Billy Vincent, Mary McMahon, David Armstrong.

An old man faces a lonely new life when he has his mind and personality transplanted into a young body.

HOCUS POCUS AND FRISBY
Writer: Rod Serling. **Director:** Lamont Johnson. **Guest Cast:** Andy Devine, Milton Selzer, Howard McNear, Dabbs Greer, Clem Bevans, Larry Breitman, Peter Brocco.

A bumpkin's tall tales impress a group of aliens so much that they take him to their planet as a prime specimen of Earthmen.

THE DUMMY
Writer: Rod Serling. **Director:** Abner Bibberman. **Guest Cast:** Cliff Robertson, Frank Sutton, George Murdock, John Harmon, Sandra Warner, Ralph Manza, Rudy Dolan, Bethelynn Grey.

A second-rate ventriloquist becomes in-creasingly convinced that his dummy has a mind and a will of its own.

THE CHANGING OF THE GUARD
Writer: Rod Serling. **Director:** Robert Ellis Miller. **Guest Cast:** Donald Pleasance, Liam Sullivan, Philippa Bevans, Kevin O'Neal, Jimmy Baird, Kevin Jones, Tom Lowell, Russell Horton, Buddy Hart, Darryl Richard, James Browning, Pat Close, Dennis Kerlee, Bob Biheller.

A popular teacher at a boys' school feels he will no longer be able to make a contribution to life when he is asked to retire from teaching.

YOUNG MAN'S FANCY
Writer: Richard Matheson. **Director:** John Brahm. **Guest Cast:** Phyllis Thaxter, Alex Nicol, Wallace Rooney, Ricky Kelman, Helen Brown.

A young man's ardent yearning for the days of his youth becomes so strong that the past actually reappears.

I SING THE BODY ELECTRIC
Writer: Ray Bradbury. **Director:** James Sheldon. **Guest Cast:** Josephine Hutchinson, David White, June Vincent, Vaughn Taylor, Charles Herbert, Dana Dillaway, Veronica Cartwright, Paul Nesbitt, Susan Crane, Judy Morton.

A young girl realizes that an electronic grandmother can also be a tender, loving woman.

CAVENDER IS COMING
Writer: Rod Serling. **Director:** Chris Nyby. **Guest Cast:** Carol Burnett, Jesse White, Howard Smith, William O'Connell, Pitt Herbert, John Fiedler, Stanley Jones, Frank Behrens, Albert Carrier, Roy Sickner, Norma Shattuc, Rory O'Brien, Sandra Gould, Adrienne Marden, Jack Younger, Danny Kulick, Donna Douglas, Maurice Dallimore, Barbara Morrison.

A bumbling guardian angel's attempts to make a klutzy woman happy don't work out quite as expected.

Fourth Season: (1 hour) 1/63-5/63

IN HIS IMAGE
Writer: Charles Beaumont. **Director:** Perry Lafferty. **Guest Cast:** George Grizzard, Gail Kobe, Katharine Squire, Wallace Rooney, Sherry Granato, James Seay, Joseph Sargent, Jamie Forster.

Following his compulsive murder of an old woman, a man realizes that there have been some unnatural changes in his home town.

THE THIRTY-FATHOM GRAVE
Writer: Rod Serling. **Director:** Perry Lafferty. **Guest Cast:** Mike Kellin, Simon Oakland, David Sheiner, John Considine, Bill Bixby, Tony Call, Derrick Lewis, Conlan Carter, Charles Kuenstle.

The crew of a Navy destroyer can't figure out the strange tapping noises coming from a submarine that sank twenty years before.

MUTE
Writer: Richard Matheson. **Director:** Stuart Rosenberg. **Guest Cast:** Frank Overton, Barbara Baxley, Ann Jilliann, Irene Dailey, Hal Riddle, Percy Helton, Oscar Beregi, Eva Soreny.

A child who was raised on telepathic communication is taught to adjust to the spoken word.

JESS-BELLE
Writer: Earl Hamner. **Director:** Buzz Kulik. **Guest Cast:** Anne Francis, James Best, Laura Devon, Jeanette Nolan, Virginia Gregg, George Mitchell, Helen Kleeb, Jim Boles, Jon Lormer.

A jealous woman goes to a witch for help in regaining her former suitor's love.

DEATH SHIP
Writer: Richard Matheson. **Director:** Dan Medford. **Guest Cast:** Jack Klugman, Ross Martin, Fredrick Beir, Sara Taft, Ross Elliott, Mary Webster, Tammy Marihugh.

The image of themselves as the victims of a fatal crash leads a space party to suspect they've been given a glimpse of the future.

VALLEY OF THE SHADOW
Writer: Charles Beaumont. **Director:** Perry Lafferty. **Guest Cast:** Ed Nelson, Natalie Trundy, David Opatoshu, James Doohan, Suzanne Cupito, Dabbs Greer, Jacques Aubuchon, Sandy Kenyon.

A reporter stumbles onto a backwoods town that houses a secret so awesome its revelation could mean the end of the world.

HE'S ALIVE
Writer: Rod Serling. **Director:** Stuart Rosenberg. **Guest Cast:** Dennis Hopper, Ludwig Donath, Curt Conway, Howard Caine, Barnaby Hale, Paul Mazursky, Bernard Fein, Jay Adler, Wolfe Brazell.

An ominous, shadowy figure advises a young reactionary on methods to mesmerize and control the populace.

MINIATURE
Writer: Charles Beaumont. **Director:** Walter Grauman. **Guest Cast:** Robert Duvall, Pert Kelton, Barbara Barrie, Len Weinrib, William Windom, Claire Griswold, Nina Roman, Richard Angarola, John McLiam.

A misfit escapes into a dream world by visiting a museum's miniature replica of life in the 1890s.

PRINTER'S DEVIL
Writer: Charles Beaumont. **Director:** Ralph Senensky. **Guest Cast:** Burgess Meredith, Robert Sterling, Patricia Crowley, Charles Thompson, Ray Teal, Ryan Hayes, Doris Kemper.

"The Thirty-Fathom Grave"

"Probe 7—Over and Out"

A community newspaper is saved from folding by a mysterious man whose printing machines can predict and dictate the news.

NO TIME LIKE THE PAST
Writer: Rod Serling. Director: Justus Addiss. Guest Cast: Dana Andrews, Patricia Breslin, Robert F. Simon, Violet Rensing, James Yagi, Tudor Owen, Lindsay Workman, Malcolm Atterbury, Reta Shaw.

A frustrated man travels further and further back in time to try to rid the world of its ills.

THE PARALLEL
Writer: Rod Serling. Director: Alan Crosland. Guest Cast: Steve Forrest, Jacqueline Scott, Frank Aletter, Shari Lee Bernath, Philip Abbott, Pete Madsen, Robert Johnson, Morgan Jones, William Sargent.

A routine seven-day space flight sends an astronaut into a strange parallel world.

I DREAM OF GENIE
Writer: John Furia. Director: Robert Gist. Guest Cast: Howard Morris, Patricia Barry, Loring Smith, Mark Miller, Robert Ball, James Millhollin, Bob Hastings, Jack Albertson, Joyce Jameson.

Limited to one wish instead of the usual three by a genie from an old brass lamp, a timid clerk must consider all the possibilities very carefully.

THE NEW EXHIBIT
Writer: Charles Beaumont. Director: John Brahm. Guest Cast: Martin Balsam, Will Kuluva, Maggie Mahoney, William Mims, Billy Beck, Robert L. McCord, Bob Mitchell, David Bond, Milton Parsons.

A museum custodian's fond attachment to the wax images of five murderers leads to tragedy when the figures come to life.

OF LATE I THINK OF CLIFFORDVILLE
Writer: Rod Serling. Director: David Rich. Guest Cast: Albert Salmi, Julie Newmar, John Anderson, Mary Jackson, Wright King, Jamie Forster, Guy Raymond, Pat O'Hara, John Harmon.

A heartless, wealthy man is given the chance to experience the thrill of achieving even greater success by a cunning female demon.

THE INCREDIBLE WORLD OF HORACE FORD
Writer: Reginald Rose. Director: Abner Biberman. Guest Cast: Pat Hingle, Nan Martin, Phillip Pine, Ruth White, Vaughn Taylor, Mary Carver, Anthony Jochim, George Spicer, Bernadette Hale, Bella Bruck, Jerry Davis, Lester Maxwell, Billy Hughes, Harry Short, Jim E. Titus.

A toy manufacturer, who has always yearned for his youth, gets a clear look at his past days when he visits his old neighborhood, which has remained miraculously the same.

ON THURSDAY WE LEAVE FOR HOME
Writer: Rod Serling. Director: Buzz Kulik. Guest Cast: James Whitmore, Tim O'Connor, James Broderick, Russ Bender, Paul Langton, Jo Helton, Mercedes Shirley, John Ward, Daniel Kulick.

A man tries to discourage his band of space explorers from returning to Earth, since it would destroy his position as absolute leader of the group.

PASSAGE ON THE LADY ANNE
Writer: Charles Beaumont. Director: Lamont Johnson. Guest Cast: Joyce Van Patten, Lee Philips, Wilfrid Hyde-White, Gladys Cooper, Cecil Kellaway, Cyril Delevanti, Jack Raine, Alan Napier, Colin Campbell.

To try to rekindle their fading romance, a young couple books passage on the final voyage of an ancient cruise ship that is inhabited by elderly couples.

THE BARD
Writer: Rod Serling. Director: David Butler. Guest Cast: Jack Weston, Henry Lascoe, John Williams, Marge Redmond, Doro Merande, Clegg Hoyt, Judy Strangis, Claude Stroud, George Ives, William Lanteau, Paul Dubov, Howard McNear, John Newton.

A hack writer conjures up William Shakespeare to help him write a television script, but the finished product is not to the liking of network executives.

Fifth Season: (½ hour) 63-64

IN PRAISE OF PIP
Writer: Rod Serling. Director: Joseph M. Newman. Guest Cast: Jack Klugman, Connie Gilchrist, Billy Mumy, Bob Diamond, John Launer, Ross Elliott, Gerald Gordon, Stuart Nisbet, Russell Horton, Kreg Martin.

A bookie tries to make up for the way he raised his son when he learns that the boy has been seriously wounded in Vietnam.

STEEL
Writer: Richard Matheson. Director: Don Weis. Guest Cast: Lee Marvin, Joe Mantell, Merritt Bohn, Frank London, Tipp McClure, Chuck Hicks, Larry Barton.

A small-time promoter is so determined not to throw a robot prize fight that he enters the bout when his robot gets damaged.

NIGHTMARE AT 20,000 FEET
Writer: Richard Matheson. Director: Dick Donner. Guest Cast: William Shatner, Christine White, Edward Kemmer, Asa Maynor, Nick Cravat.

A newly-recovered mental patient can't convince anyone that he sees a gremlin destroying the wing of their airliner.

A KIND OF STOP WATCH
Writer: Rod Serling. Director: John Rich. Guest Cast: Richard Erdman, Herbie Faye, Leon Belasco, Doris Singleton, Roy Roberts, Richard Wessel, Ken Drake, Ray Kellogg, Sam Balter.

In an attempt to become popular, a talkative man uses a watch that can stop and start all action in the world.

THE LAST NIGHT OF A JOCKEY
Writer: Rod Serling. Director: Joseph Newman. Guest Cast: Mickey Rooney.

A down-on-his-luck jockey thinks being taller would solve the problems of his life.

LIVING DOLL
Writer: Charles Beaumont. Director: Richard Sarafian. Guest Cast: Telly Savalas, Tracy Stratford, Mary LaRoche.

A man is threatened with revenge by an expensive doll he plans to get rid of.

THE OLD MAN IN THE CAVE
Writer: Rod Serling. Director: Alan Crosland, Jr. Guest Cast: James Coburn, John Anderson, Josie Lloyd, John Craven, Natalie Masters, John Marley, Frank Watkins, Don Wilbanks, Lenny Geer.

A small band of people are saved from a nuclear holocaust by following the guidance of "The Old Man in the Cave."

UNCLE SIMON
Writer: Rod Serling. Director: Don Siegel. Guest Cast: Sir Cedrick Hardwicke, Constance Ford, Ian Wolfe, John McLiam.

The spirit of an old inventor avenges himself on his greedy niece when he dies at her hands.

NIGHT CALL
Writer: Richard Matheson. Director: Jacques Tourneau. Guest Cast: Gladys Cooper, Nora Marlowe, Martine Bartlett.

A lonely, invalid spinster starts receiving mysterious phone calls from a long-dead lover.

PROBE 7—OVER AND OUT
Writer: Rod Serling. Director: Ted Post. Guest Cast: Richard Basehart, Antoinette Bower, Frank Cooper, Barton Heyman.

The lone survivors of two annihilated planets must start new lives together on a planet called Earth.

THE 7TH IS MADE UP OF PHANTOMS
Writer: Rod Serling. Director: Alan Crosland, Jr. Guest Cast: Ron Foster, Warren Oates, Randy Boone, Robert Bray, Wayne Mallory, Greg Morris, Jeffrey Morris, Jacque Shelton, Lew Brown.

Modern-day war maneuvers on the site of Custer's Last Stand lead to an encounter with the warring spirits of the 7th Cavalry and the Sioux nation.

"Mr. Dingle the Strong"

"The Brain Center at Whipple's"

NINETY YEARS WITHOUT SLUMBERING
Writer: George C. Johnson. **Director:** Roger Kay. **Guest Cast:** Ed Wynn, Carolyn Kearney, James Callahan, Carol Byron, John Pickard, Dick Wilson, Chuck Hicks, William Sargent.

An old man is convinced that his life will end the moment his grandfather's clock runs down.

RING-A-DING GIRL
Writer: Earl Hamner, Jr. **Director:** Alan Crosland, Jr. **Guest Cast:** Maggie McNamara, Mary Munday, David Macklin, George Mitchell, Bing Russell, Betty Lou Gerson, Hank Patterson, Bill Hickman, Vic Perrin.

A film star receives an opal ring that gives her visions of the future.

YOU DRIVE
Writer: Earl Hamner, Jr. **Director:** John Brahm. **Guest Cast:** Edward Andrews, Hellena Westcott, Kevin Hagen, Totty Ames, John Hanek.

A businessman's automobile will not let its owner shirk responsibility for killing a cyclist and fleeing the scene of the accident.

NUMBER 12 LOOKS JUST LIKE YOU
Writer: Charles Beaumont. **Director:** Abner Biberman. **Guest Cast:** Suzy Parker, Richard Long, Pam Austin, Collin Wilcox.

A young woman causes some eyebrows to be raised when she rejects treatments that will make her physically flawless.

THE LONG MORROW
Writer: Rod Serling. **Director:** Robert Flevry. **Guest Cast:** Robert Lansing, Mariette Hartley, George MacReady, Edward Binns,

A scientist hopes that by refusing to use a suspended animation apparatus on a thirty-year space probe he will remain in the same age ratio with the woman he loves.

THE SELF-IMPROVEMENT OF SALVATORE ROSS
Writers: Henry Selsar, Jerry McNeeley. **Director:** Don Siegel. **Guest Cast:** Don Gordon, Gail Kobe, Vaughn Taylor, Douglass Dumbrille, Doug Lambert, J. Pat O'Malley, Ted Jacques, Kathleen O'Malley, Seymour Cassel.

A man tries to parlay his strange ability to trade traits with other people into a perfect life.

BLACK LEATHER JACKETS
Writer: Earl Hamner. **Director:** Joseph Newman. **Guest Cast:** Lee Kinsolving, Shelley Fabares, Michael Forest, Tom Gilleran, Denver Pyle, Irene Hervey, Michael Conrad, Wayne Heffley.

A delegation of three aliens plans to conquer Earth, but one of them falls in love with an Earth woman.

FROM AGNES—WITH LOVE
Writer: Barney Scofield. **Director:** Dick Donner.

Guest Cast: Wally Cox, Ralph Taeger, Sue Randall, Raymond Bailey, Don Keefer, Byron Kane, Nan Peterson.

A computer technician gradually realizes that the advanced computer he's working with is so complex it registers feelings, including love and jealousy.

SPUR OF THE MOMENT
Writer: Richard Matheson. **Director:** Elliott Silverstein. **Guest Cast:** Diana Hyland, Marsha Hunt, Roger Davis, Robert Hogan, Jack Raine, Philip Ober.

A young woman unwittingly meets her future self and is so frightened by the experience that she does not comprehend the meaning of the encounter.

STOPOVER IN A QUIET TOWN
Writer: Earl Hamner, Jr. **Director:** Ron Winston. **Guest Cast:** Barry Nelson, Nancy Malone, Denise Lynn, Karen Norris.

A married couple wakes up one morning in a strange town where everything is artificial, and the air is filled with a child's laughter.

QUEEN OF THE NILE
Writer: Charles Beaumont. **Director:** John Brahm. **Guest Cast:** Ann Blyth, Lee Philips, Celia Lovsky, Ruth Phillips, Frank Ferguson, James Tyler.

An inquisitive interviewer tries to find the key to the apparent immortality of a glamorous film star.

WHAT'S IN THE BOX
Writer: Martin Goldsmith. **Director:** Dick Baer. **Guest Cast:** Joan Blondell, William Demarest, Sterling Holloway, Herbert Lytton, Howard Wright, Ron Stokes, John L. Sullivan, Sandra Gould, Ted Christy, Douglas Bank, Tony Miller.

A henpecked cab driver tries to warn his nagging wife of the portent of her death he's just seen on their television.

THE MASKS
Writer: Rod Serling. **Director:** Abner Biberman. **Guest Cast:** Robert Keith, Milton Selzer, Virginia Gregg, Brooke Hayward, Alan Sues, Bill Walker, Willis Bouchey.

An old millionaire tricks his ghastly family into donning grotesque masks that match their individual personalities.

I AM THE NIGHT—COLOR ME BLACK
Writer: Rod Serling. **Director:** Abner Biberman. **Guest Cast:** Michael Constantine, Paul Fix, George Lindsey, Terry Becker, Douglas Bank, Ward Wood, Eve McVeagh, Elizabeth Harrower, Ivan Dixon.

An idealistic young man is about to be executed for the willfull murder of one of the town's bigots.

CAESAR AND ME
Writer: A.T. Strassfield. **Director:** Robert Butler. **Guest Cast:** Jackie Cooper, Susanne Cupito, Stafford Repp, Sarah Selby, Don Gazzaniga, Sidney Marion, Ken Konopka, Olan Soule.

A dummy tempts a desperately unsuccessful ventriloquist to commit several small crimes.

THE JEOPARDY ROOM
Writer: Rod Serling. **Director:** Dick Donner. **Guest Cast:** Martin Landau, John Vandreelen, Robert Kelljan.

A defector is captured by a hired assassin and given three hours to earn his freedom.

MR. GARRITY AND THE GRAVES
Writer: Rod Serling. **Director:** Ted Post. **Guest Cast:** John Dehner, Stanley Adams, J. Pat O'Malley, Norman Leavitt, Percy Helton, John Cliff.

A con man's claim that he can restore the dead to life suddenly doesn't seem as far-fetched as it sounds.

THE BRAIN CENTER AT WHIPPLE'S
Writer: Rod Serling. **Director:** Dick Donner. **Guest Cast:** Richard Deacon, Paul Newlan, Ted DeCorsia, Burt Conroy, Jack Crowder.

A callous executive hopes to improve his corporation by replacing all the employees with robots and computers.

COME WANDER WITH ME
Writer: Tony Wilson. **Director:** Dick Donner. **Guest Cast:** Gary Crosby, Bonnie Beecher, Hank Patterson, John Bolt.

A fraudulent folk singer persuades a backwoods girl to sing him an authentic folk song, but her melody predicts an ominous future.

THE FEAR
Writer: Rod Serling. **Director:** Ted Post. **Guest Cast:** Hazel Court, Mark Richman.

An unstable woman and a state trooper sight a giant alien in a California park.

THE BEWITCHIN' POOL
Writer: Earl Hamner Jr. **Director:** Joseph Newman. **Guest Cast:** Mary Badham, Tim Stafford, Kim Hector, Tod Andrews, Dee Hartford, Georgia Simmons, Harold Gould.

The unloved children of bickering parents seek solace in a mysterious world in which lives a kindly, loving woman.

THRILLER

The show simply did not have enough time to find its identity.

—Hubbell Robinson
Executive Producer

With such prestigious triumphs as *Studio One, Climax!* and *Playhouse 90* to his credit, executive producer Hubbel Robinson easily sold *Thriller* to NBC as the "*Studio One* of mystery, a quality anthology drawing on the whole rich field of suspense literature..."

The new show was expected to be in a league with *Twilight Zone* and *Alfred Hitchcock Presents*. Robinson gave his word that the show would be his personal project, convincing everyone involved that the mystery-suspense anthology would be a success. So assured were they, that the deal was confirmed without benefit of a pilot film. This was the first of several big mistakes.

Robinson's description of *Thriller,* though high-sounding, was actually vague. Consequently there developed between Robinson, producer Fletcher Markle and associate producer/story editor James P. Cavanagh a running ideological battle over the nature of the series. Where, for example, does a thriller end and a horror tale begin? What about black comedy? Is graphic violence necessary to a crime story? There were many differences in taste and concept and, as the production deadline drew nearer, tensions escalated. Ready or not, *Thriller* was billed as a major fall entrant in NBC's '60 to '61 schedule.

The inaugural installment, "Twisted Image," was blasted by the critics as repulsive and heavy-handed. "A preposterous mystery—silly in its narrative construction, unpleasant in its production," snarled one. The next show was called "Worse Than Murder," and it was. Robinson blamed the poor quality of the first few scripts on a TV writers' strike that was raging at the time, but the network executives suspected a deeper problem. After some checking, their worst fears were confirmed: the TV pres-

sure cooker *behind* the cameras was creating more excitement and suspense than the *Thriller* scriptwriters.

Robinson, Markle and Cavanagh simply could not agree on what it is that makes a thriller thrilling, and NBC was not going to let its promised prestige program continue through a developmental crisis. With ratings low, critics increasingly hostile and a sponsor hopping mad, the network pushed the panic button and demanded that *Thriller* be made to live up to its name—or else. After the first eight installments, new producers were brought in and a rebirth was underway.

Robinson diagnosed the show's problem as its hazy, uncertain image. Under the direction of Revue (the parent studio), the whole field of mystery was whittled down to two specific types: the bone-chilling horror story with supernatural overtones and the violent, fast-paced crime melodrama. To carry out these story concepts, Revue recruited Maxwell Shane as producer of the crime shows and

OPPOSITE: With his famous voice and chiller image Boris Karloff as host set just the right mood at the beginning of each episode. **RIGHT:** "Twisted Image," the series' premiere episode, starred George Grizzard.

William Frye to handle the horrors. Both were veteran Revue workhorses, and after a few months on the job, the studio's extreme measures began to pay off.

Robinson, embarrassed by the whole affair, welcomed the changes: "Our new formula immediately eliminated a whole vast area of material...we now had a narrower... interpretation of the word 'thriller.'" Celebrated fright master Boris Karloff's presence as host and occasional star added to the atmosphere of mystery and intrigue. Replacing Pete Rugolo's loud, jazzy music scores were the subtle, spine-tingling compositions by Morton Stevens and Jerry Goldsmith.

The new stories also differed considerably from the original *Thriller.* Frye wanted to film only classic horror tales, set in gothic mansions laced with cobwebs, where creatures returning from the dead and others on their way often meet in passage. Short-story writer Robert Bloch—a Hitchcock regular—helped to evoke the proper ghoulish mood with such episodes as "Waxworks," "Yours Truly," "Jack the Ripper," "The Devil's Ticket" and "The Weird Tailor."

LEFT: Veteran character actor Oscar Homolka in "Waxworks." **BELOW:** Executive producer Hubbell Robinson looks "thrilled" to be on the set with Boris Karloff.

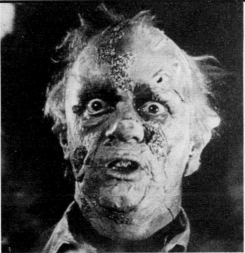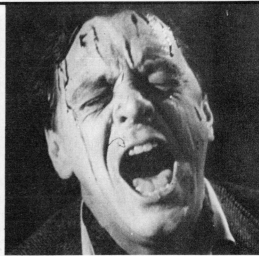

In "The Cheaters" actor Harry Townes, the last to don the mystical eyeglasses, looks into a mirror, sees his grotesque reflection, rips the cheaters from his face and smashes them.

Bloch also wrote "The Cheaters," the story on which one of Frye's earliest and most noteworthy successes is based. It was adapted for TV by Donald S. Sanford and beautifully directed by John ("Hangover Square," "The Lodger") Brahm. Boris Karloff's eerie narration sets the tone for this episodic horror tale with a most unusual star, a pair of glasses:

When a man shuts himself off from his neighbors, when he conducts mysterious experiments behind locked doors, there's bound to be talk. There were those who whispered that old Dierke Van Prinn was a sorcerer and worse. He might never have been remembered at all had not his research led him to the discovery of a most unusual formula for making glass....

Dierke Van Prinn (Henry Daniell) hangs himself after gazing into a mirror while wearing a pair of yellow-tinted spectacles he had developed in his experiments. Though he did not spare himself, he took care to preserve his devilish invention and concealed the glasses in a desk drawer. Some two hundred years later junkman Joe Henshaw (Paul Newlan) buys the decaying Van Prinn estate and happens upon the spectacles. Trying them on, he discovers that he can read people's minds and learns that his wife (Linda Watkins) and his assistant (Ed Nelson) plan to junk him—fatally. Henshaw beats them to the punch and murders them. Their plan was at least partially successful, however, for a policeman then kills Henshaw. The glasses, of course, survive with hardly a scratch and soon fall into the lap of old Miriam Alcott (Mildred Dunnock), who, like Henshaw, "hears" of a plot by her friend and physician to shorten her lifespan. However, fate—in the guise of an accidental fire—intervenes to preserve the doctor's reputation, but not his or Miriam's life.

The glasses remain in the family as Miriam's scheming, greedy nephew Edward Dean (Jack Weston) inherits them. Dean wears them during a poker game and discovers that he knows not only what cards the others are holding, but also that one of the players—in addition to himself—is cheating. He accuses the man, and is accidentally killed in the ensuing scuffle.

Another card player, Sebastian Grimm (Harry Townes), takes the glasses. He quickly learns the power of the lenses, but unlike all the previous owners, concludes that their purpose is not to read the minds of others, but rather one's own mind. He dons the spectacles and gazes into the mirror at his own reflection, just as Van Prinn had done over two hundred years before, and watches his features become hideously distorted into those of a loathsome monster. Terrified, he snatches the glasses from his eyes and smashes them, ending their curse forever.

"The Cheaters" is one of the finest horror tales ever aired. Its final terror—Grimm's hideous inner self—is conveyed by Jack Barron's makeup, which took two weeks of planning and work to reach its wretched magnificence. Another interesting note is the number of uses the writers find for the word "cheaters": the junkman's wife was cheating on him; Miriam Alcott's physician wanted to cheat her out of some years of her life; a man was cheating at cards; and, of course, eyeglasses are commonly called cheaters.

"Pigeons from Hell" was adapted from a story by Robert E. Howard and first appeared in the 1930s in *Weird Tales* magazine. Directed by John Newland, it stands as another notable entry in the series. In it, the car driven by

The ghoulish makeups created by Jack Barron made a significant contribution to the show's thrills. Here a horrifying old hag from "The Hungry Glass."

two brothers, Johnny and Tim Branner (David Walton and Brandon de Wilde), goes out of control near an abandoned plantation house in southern Louisiana. The boys have no choice but to stay the night in the old house. Soon after they fall asleep, an eerie wailing pierces the night, awakening Johnny. He arises and ascends the stairs in a trance. Next a terrified scream jolts Tim awake and sends him running in its direction. At the stairs Tim encounters Johnny awash with blood, his head split wide open, rushing at him with upraised axe in hand. Tim flees and when he is safely away, collapses into unconsciousness.

Tim awakens to discover himself in the presence of Sheriff Buckner (Crane Benton), to whom he relates his strange story. They reenter the house and find Johnny's dead body on the floor with axe in hand, the blade implanted in Tim's empty bedroll. As they search the house, the sheriff recollects its history. It had belonged to the Blassenvilles, a family so cruel that all their servants—except old Jacob Blout—ran away. Finally, only three Blassenville sisters remained and the house was believed abandoned when the last of them, Elizabeth, left to be married. In the course of their search, they discover Elizabeth's diary in which the last entry tells that she fears that she is not alone in the mansion—that it is inhabited by some inhuman presence.

Next, Buckner and Tim call on Jacob Blout. Though he fears for his life, he reveals that he was a maker of "zuvembies"—a kind of mongrel monster, predominantly zombie but also of witch, werewolf and vampire extraction. The creature has a wail that is capable of hypnotizing humans. Its only pleasure comes from slaughtering human beings, whereupon it controls the corpses until the flesh grows cold. Blout also tells them that only lead or steel can kill a zuvembie. He continues by telling them of a Blassenville servant who had begged him to make her a zuvembie in order for her to take revenge on her wicked employers. At that moment pigeons outside begin to coo, and the old man refuses to go on with his story. As he is reaching for a piece of wood to throw on the fire, he is struck dead by a snake.

Tim and the sheriff return to the house and discover that the car is covered with hundreds of pigeons. Told to wait in the car while the sheriff goes into the house, Tim dozes, but is later awakened by a nightmare. He goes to look for the sheriff and as he enters the house, the strange wailing begins and Tim, powerless to resist, is tugged up the stairs and along the darkened corridor. With a sudden flash of movement, a carrion-faced old hag brandishing an axe charges him. At the same moment shots ring out and the creature retreats, with the sheriff, his gun drawn, and Tim, now shaken out of his trance, in hot pursuit. Behind a hole in a wall, they find a room. Chained to the wall are three skeletons, their heads split open: the remains of Blassenville sisters. On the couch the zuvembie lies dead. The pigeons—former Blassenvilles all—are finally released.

Despite such individual successes, *Thriller* was an uneven series. The mixing of horror and crime episodes was an unsuccessful formula. A realistic little heist could not chill the blood of a horror fan and crime lovers simply did not find fantastic horror tales credible. Consequently, the show failed to project a consistent image and could not keep its audience from week to week. Ratings suffered and the show was canceled at the end of the 1962 season.

Brandon DeWilde discovers that the abandoned house where he and his brother spent a terrifying night is inhabited by a strange member of the undead called a zuvembie.

"The Purple Room"

INDEX
OF
EPISODES

"The Cheaters"

THRILLER

1960-1962/67 episodes
NBC/a Hubbell Robinson Production for
    Revue (Universal)
60 minutes/black & white

Host: Boris Karloff

Executive Producer: Hubbell Robinson.
Producers: Fletcher Markle (earliest
shows); William Frye and Maxwell Shane
(later shows). **Story Consultant:** James P.
Cavanagh. **Director of Photography:**
John L. Warren. **Makeup:** Jack Barron.
Music: Pete Rugolo, Jerry Goldsmith, Morton Stevens.

First Season 1960-1961

THE TWISTED IMAGE
Writer: James P. Cavanaugh. **Director:** Arthur
Hiller. **Guest Cast:** Leslie Nielson, Natalie
Trundy, George Grizzard.

An advertising man unwittingly antagonizes
a disturbed office boy, setting off his psychopathic tendencies.

CHILD'S PLAY
Writer: Robert Dozier. **Director:** Arthur Hiller.
Guest Cast: Frank Overton, Bethel Leslie,
Tommy Nolan.

An imaginative and neglected child, armed
with a rifle and live ammunition, takes off on an
afternoon excursion.

WORSE THAN MURDER
Writer: Mel Goldberg. **Director:** Mitchel Leisen. **Guest Cast:** Constance Ford, John Baragrey, Christine White.

After her husband and his uncle die intestate,
leaving her penniless, a woman discovers an
old diary suggesting murder.

THE MARK OF THE HAND
Writer: Maxwell Shane. **Director:** Maxwell
Shane. **Guest Cast:** Mona Freeman, Berry
Kroeger, Judson Platt, Shepperd Strudwick,
Terry Burnham.

A man is killed—shot through the heart—and
an eight-year-old girl is found holding the murder weapon.

ROSE'S LAST SUMMER
Writer: Maxwell Shane. **Director:** Maxwell
Shane. **Guest Cast:** Mary Astor, Al Donahue.

A former movie queen is found dead in the
Goodfields' garden, and a clause in her will
requires Mrs. Goodfield to impersonate her so
that the deceased's son can inherit the estate.
But who is impersonating whom?

THE GUILTY MEN
Writer: Maxwell Shane. **Director:** Ray Nazarro.

Guest Cast: Everett Sloane, Jay C. Flippen,
Frank Dana.

After turning legitimate, the leader of one of
the nation's major crime syndicates is opposed
by his associates.

THE PURPLE ROOM
Writer: Douglas Heyes. **Director:** Douglas
Heyes. **Guest Cast:** Rip Torn, Richard Anderson, Patricia Barry, Alan Napier.

The conniving cousins of a man who has just
inherited remote Black Oak mansion tell him
the place is haunted.

THE WATCHER
Writer: Donald S. Sanford. **Director:** John
Brahm. **Guest Cast:** Martin Gabel, Richard
Chamberlain, Olive Sturgess.

A psychopath drowns a seventeen-year-old
girl, then turns his killer's instinct on two young
lovers.

GIRL WITH A SECRET
Writer: Charles Beaumont. **Director:** Mitchell
Leisen. **Guest Cast:** Myrna Fahey, Rhodes
Reason, Cloris Leachman.

A woman learns that her husband's real job is
to ferret out men who are selling U.S. secrets to
enemy agents.

THE PREDICTION
Writer: Donald S. Sanford. **Director:** John
Brahm. **Guest Cast:** Boris Karloff, Alex Davion,
Audrey Dalton.

A mentalist warns the fiance of his assistant
that he must not take the trip he has planned, for
it will end up in death.

THE FATAL IMPULSE
Writer: Philip MacDonald. **Director:** Gerald
Mayer. **Guest Cast:** Conrad Nagel, Elisha
Cook, Mary Tyler Moore, Robert Lansing.

A psychopath slips a bomb into a woman's
handbag, and the police work desperately to
find her before it goes off.

THE BIG BLACKOUT
Writer: Oscar Millard. **Director:** Maurice Geraghty. **Guest Cast:** Jack Carson, Nan Leslie,
George Mitchell.

A man fears that he may have commited
murder during an alcoholic blackout.

KNOCK THREE-ONE-TWO
Writer: John Kneubuhl. **Director:** Herman
Hoffman. **Guest Cast:** Joe Maross, Beverly Garland, Charles Aidman, Warren Oates.

A man sees a way of getting out of gambling
debts by setting up his wife as the victim of a
compulsive woman-killer.

MAN IN THE MIDDLE
Writer: Howard Rodman. **Director:** Fletcher
Markle. **Guest Cast:** Mort Sahl, Sue Randall.

A TV writer overhears two criminals discussing the kidnapping and possible murder of
an attractive young socialite.

THE CHEATERS
Writer: Donald S. Sanford. **Director:** John
Brahm. **Guest Cast:** Paul Newlan, Mildred
Dunnock, Harry Townes, Henry Daniell, Jack
Weston.

Five people meet violent deaths after wearing
an unusual pair of eyeglasses.

THE HUNGRY GLASS
Writer: Douglas Heyes. **Director:** Douglas
Heyes. **Guest Cast:** William Shatner, Joanna
Heyes, Elizabeth Allen, Russell Johnson.

A photographer and his wife see haunting
images in the windows of their new home.

THE POISONER
Writer: Robert H. Andrews. **Director:** Herschel
Daugherty. **Guest Cast:** Murray Matheson,
Sarah Marshall, Brenda Forbes.

Thomas Griffith murders his wife's mother
and crippled sister, then turns his thoughts to
his unsuspecting spouse.

MAN IN THE CAGE
Writers: Maxwell Shane, Stuart Jerome. **Director:** Gerald Mayer. **Guest Cast:** Philip Carey,
Guy Stockwell, Barry Gordon, Eduardo Ciannelli.

A man traces his missing brother to Tangier,
where he becomes involved with murder and
drug smuggling.

CHOOSE A VICTIM
Writer: George Bellak. **Director:** Richard Carlson. **Guest Cast:** Larry Blyden, Susan Oliver.

A mercenary beach bum is framed for a murder he was planning to commit.

HAY-FORK AND BILL-HOOK
Writer: Allan Caillou. **Director:** Herschel
Daugherty. **Guest Cast:** Kenneth Haigh, Audrey Dalton.

Murder and the ritual exorcising of a witch
cast a spell of evil over a little English village.

THE MERRIWEATHER FILE
Writer: John Kneubuhl. **Director:** John Brahm.
Guest Cast: Bethel Leslie, James Gregory, Ross
Elliot, Edward Binns.

A complicated investigation of an attempted
murder reveals an actual murder committed
years earlier.

THE FINGERS OF FEAR
Writer: Robert H. Andrews. **Director:** Jules
Bricken. **Guest Cast:** Nehemiah Persoff, Robert
Middleton, Thayer Roberts.

A grotesque, mentally ill man fears he may
be incriminated as the mad-dog slayer of little
girls.

"Well of Doom"

"The Premature Burial"

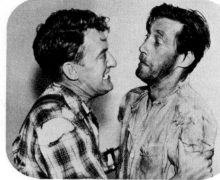
"Masquerade"

WELL OF DOOM
Writer: Donald S. Sanford. **Director:** John Brahm. **Guest Cast:** Ronald Howard, Torin Thatcher, Fintan Meyler, Henry Daniell.

Robert Penrose, wealthy master of Hardwick Castle, is captured and imprisoned by a monstrous hulk.

THE ORDEAL OF DR. CORDELL
Writer: Donald S. Sanford. **Director:** Lazlo Benedak. **Guest Cast:** Robert Vaughn, Kathleen Crowley, Marlo Thomas.

After an accident in a college chemistry laboratory, a strange gas sends a scientist into fits of madness, during which he commits brutal murders.

TRIO FOR TERROR
Writer: Barre Lyndon. **Director:** Ida Lupino. **Guest Cast:** Richard Lupino, Terence deMarney, Iris Bristol, Robin Hughes, Michael Pate.

Three chillers. In the first, a man murders his uncle, an experimentor in the occult. The second traces the good and bad luck of a young gambler forced to spend the night in a very peculiar bed. In the third, a murder suspect eludes the police by hiding in a museum.

PAPA BENJAMIN
Writer: John Kneubuhl. **Director:** Ted Post. **Guest Cast:** John Ireland, Jeanne Bal.

A famous bandleader discovers a secret voodoo melody, but is warned that death will follow if he ever tries to play it.

LATE DATE
Writer: Donald S. Sanford. **Director:** Herschel Daugherty. **Guest Cast:** Larry Pennell, Edward Platt, Steve Mitchell.

A man is framed for his lover's murder.

YOURS TRULY, JACK THE RIPPER
Writer: Robert Bloch. **Director:** Ray Milland. **Guest Cast:** John Williams, Donald Woods, Edmon Ryan, Ransom Sherman.

Sir Guy believes a current string of murders was commited by the original Jack the Ripper, who maintains his youth by taking the lives of others.

THE DEVIL'S TICKET
Writer: Robert Bloch. **Director:** Jules Bricken. **Guest Cast:** MacDonald Carey, Joan Tetzel, John Emery, Patricia Medina.

An artist tries to pawn one of his paintings and discovers that the pawnbroker is the Devil, who agrees to give him wealth and fame for three months if he pawns his soul.

PARASITE MANSION
Writer: Donald S. Sanford. **Director:** Herschel Daugherty. **Guest Cast:** Pippa Scott, James Griffith, Jeanette Nolan, Tommy Nolan.

After an auto accident, a girl is held prisoner in a strange house.

A GOOD IMAGINATION
Writer: Robert Bloch. **Director:** John Brahm. **Guest Cast:** Edward Andrews, Patricia Barry, Ed Nelson.

A man murders his wife's lover and gets away with it, then finds he must use his "good imagination" to polish off her new beau and fix things once and for all.

MR. GEORGE
Writer: Donald S. Sanford. **Director:** Ida Lupino. **Guest Cast:** Gina Gillespie, Virginia Gregg.

Her greedy guardians plot to murder a little girl for her inheritance, but each attempt is thwarted by a strange, invisible companion named Mr. George.

TERROR IN TEAKWOOD
Writer: Alan Caillou. **Director:** Paul Henreid. **Guest Cast:** Guy Rolfe, Hazel Court, Charles Aidman, Reggie Nalder.

A pianist desecrates the grave of his former rival and steals his hands, with which he can play the rival's greatest composition.

THE PRISONER IN THE MIRROR
Writer: Robert Arthur. **Director:** Herschel Daugherty. **Guest Cast:** Lloyd Bochner, Henry Daniell, Pat Michon, Jack Mullaney.

Evil magician, Count Cagliostro, imprisons a researcher in an enchanted mirror, while his own soul enters the researcher's body.

DARK LEGACY
Writer: John Tomerlin. **Director:** John Brahm. **Guest Cast:** Harry Townes, Ilka Windish, Henry Silva.

A small-time nightclub magician inherits a book that enables him to summon up demonic forces.

PIGEONS FROM HELL
Writer: John Kneubuhl. **Director:** John Newland. **Guest Cast:** Brandon de Wilde, David Whorf.

Two brothers spend a terrifying night in an abandoned Southern mansion which is haunted by the zombie sister of two earlier inhabitants.

THE GRIM REAPER
Writer: Robert Bloch. **Director:** Herschel Daugherty. **Guest Cast:** William Shatner, Natalie Schafer, Scott Merrill, Elizabeth Allen, Henry Daniell.

Owners of a macabre painting of the Grim Reaper meet violent deaths.

Second Season 1961-1962

WHAT BECKONING GHOST?
Writer: Donald S. Sanford. **Director:** Ida Lupino. **Guest Cast:** Judith Evelyn, Tom Helmore.

A woman, home to convalesce from a heart ailment, begins to have strange visions of a casket and a funeral wreath and hears the ominous sounds of a dirge.

GUILLOTINE
Writer: Cornell Woolrich. **Director:** Ida Lupino. **Guest Cast:** Robert Middleton, Alejandro Rey, Danielle de Metz.

If the official executioner should die before Robert Lamont's execution can take place, Lamont will be freed.

THE PREMATURE BURIAL
Writer: William D. Gordon. **Director:** Douglas Heyes. **Guest Cast:** Boris Karloff, Sidney Blackmer, Patricia Medina, Scott Marlowe.

A victim of a cataleptic seizure is buried alive, and his wife and her lover plan to make sure he remains "dead."

THE WEIRD TAILOR
Writer: Robert Bloch. **Director:** Herschel Daugherty. **Guest Cast:** Henry Jones, Sandra Kerr, George Macready, Gary Clarke.

A dabbler in black magic has a special tailor make a suit that will bring his dead son back to life.

GOD GRANT THAT SHE LYE STILLE
Writer: Robert H. Andrews. **Director:** Herschel Daugherty. **Guest Cast:** Henry Daniell.

Returning to her ancestral home, a young woman is haunted by the spirit of an evil ancestor who was buried as a witch in 1661.

MASQUERADE
Writer: Donald S. Sanford. **Director:** Herschel Daugherty. **Guest Cast:** Tom Poston, Elizabeth Montgomery, John Carradine.

A young honeymooning couple seeks shelter in a sinister old house run by vampires.

THE LAST OF THE SOMMERVILLES
Writer: R.M.H. Lupino. **Director:** Ida Lupino. **Guest Cast:** Boris Karloff, Phyllis Thaxter, Martita Hunt, Peter Walker.

A tour-de-force performance by Karloff highlights this murder yarn about a man and his cousin-by-marriage who scheme to get their Aunt Celia's money and sink to a horrible end.

LETTER TO A LOVER
Writer: Donald S. Sanford. **Director:** Herschel Daugherty. **Guest Cast:** Ann Todd, Murray Matheson, Avis Scott.

A doctor's murder lays bare a tangled web of jealous passions.

A THIRD FOR PINOCHLE
Writer: Mark Ranna. **Director:** Boris Sobelman. **Guest Cast:** Edward Andrews, Doro Merande, June Walker.

A man murders his wife and gets away with it by using a pair of nosey neighbors as witnesses on his side.

"The Remarkable Mrs. Hawks"

"Waxworks"

"The Incredible Dr. Markesan"

THE CLOSED CABINET

Writer: Kay Lenard. **Director:** Jess Carneol. **Guest Cast:** Olive Sturgess, David Frankham, Jennifer Raine, Peter Forster.

A pretty American visits Merwyn Castle and encounters a three-hundred-year-old curse.

DIALOGUES WITH DEATH

Writer: Robert Arthur. **Director:** Herschel Daugherty. **Guest Cast:** Boris Karloff, Ed Nelson.

Two terror-filled stories. In the first, Karloff plays a morgue attendant who talks with the dead and learns their sometimes dangerous secrets. The second casts him as Colonel Jackson of the bayou country, who outwits his money-hungry nephew.

THE RETURN OF ANDREW BENTLEY

Writer: Richard Matheson. **Director:** John Newland. **Guest Cast:** John Newland, Antoinette Bower, Reggie Nalder, Philip Bourneuf, Terence deMarney.

Ellis and Sheila Corbett are urgently summoned to the home of his uncle, who fears death and the possession of his soul by an evil sorcerer and his accomplice.

THE REMARKABLE MRS. HAWKS

Writer: Donald S. Sanford. **Director:** John Brahm. **Guest Cast:** Jo Van Fleet, John Carradine, Paul Newlan.

A woman raises the best pigs in the county, and for good reason—she is the reincarnation of Circe, the Greek goddess who turned men into swine.

PORTRAIT WITHOUT A FACE

Writer: Jason Wingreen. **Director:** John Newland. **Guest Cast:** John Newland, Jane Green, Robert Webber, George Mitchell.

After an artist is killed by a bow and arrow, his unfinished painting starts completing itself until only the murderer's face remains to be painted.

AN ATTRACTIVE FAMILY

Writer: Robert Arthur. **Director:** John Brahm. **Guest Cast:** Joan Tetzel, Richard Long, Otto Kruger, Joyce Bouliphant.

The three Farringtons are always in need of money—so they keep murdering their relatives to get it.

WAXWORKS

Writer: Robert Bloch. **Director:** John Brahm. **Guest Cast:** Oscar Homolka, Antoinette Bower, Booth Colman, Ron Ely.

The figures in a traveling waxworks exhibit are molded after real murderers and, through black magic, can be brought to life.

LA STREGA

Writer: Alan Caillou. **Director:** Ida Lupino. **Guest Cast:** Jeanette Nolan, Ursula Andress, Alejandro Rey.

An impoverished painter rescues a beautiful girl from drowning, only to fall under the terrifying curse of her grandmother, "La Strega"—the witch.

THE STORM

Writer: McNight Malmar. **Director:** Herschel Daugherty. **Guest Cast:** Nancy Kelly, David McLean, James Griffith, Jean Carroll.

To her horror, a woman discovers the body of a murdered girl.

A WIG FOR MISS DEVORE

Writer: Donald S. Sanford. **Director:** John Brahm. **Guest Cast:** Linda Watkins, John Fielder, John Baragrey, Patricia Barry.

The wig of a nineteenth-century witch becomes the property of an aging Hollywood film star, and her dwindling career suddenly receives a tremendous lift.

THE HOLLOW WATCHER

Writer: Jay Simms. **Director:** William Claxton. **Guest Cast:** Audrey Dalton, Sean McClory, Warren Oates, Denver Pyle.

A woman murders her father-in-law and sews him up in a scarecrow that stands on a hill overlooking her home. Soon after, the scarecrow adopts a malevolent life of its own and begins stalking its killer.

COUSIN TUNDIFER

Writer: Boris Sobelman. **Director:** John Brahm. **Guest Cast:** Edward Andrews, Vaughn Taylor.

All people who enter a mansion which has been restored to its 1890 condition enter that year as well. A man then plots an ingenious murder eighty years before the victim was even born.

THE INCREDIBLE DOCTOR MARKESAN

Writer: Donald S. Sanford. **Director:** Robert Florey. **Guest Cast:** Boris Karloff, Dick York, Carolyn Kearney.

A doctor who has been dead for more than a year has discovered a horrible way to bring the dead back to life. Forced to stay at his uncle's eerie mansion are his nephew and his wife, who undergo a terrifying experience.

FLOWERS OF EVIL

Writer: Hugh Walpole. **Director:** John Brahm. **Guest Cast:** Luciana Paluzzi, Kevin Hagen, Jack Weston.

The skeleton of a murdered man begins to shriek, raising problems for those responsible for his death.

TILL DEATH DO US PART

Writer: Robert Bloch. **Director:** Herschel Daugherty. **Guest Cast:** Henry Jones, Reta Shaw, Edgar Buchanan, Philip Ober.

A woman-happy undertaker gets rid of his successive wives by burying each of them in a casket that already contains one legitimate corpse.

THE BRIDE WHO DIED TWICE

Writer: Robert H. Andrews. **Director:** Ida Lupino. **Guest Cast:** Joe de Santis, Mala Powers, Robert Colbert, Eduardo Ciannelli.

In Mexico, 1914, an evil colonel, known as the Frog, desires the lovely fiancee of his captain. The colonel's wickedness results in the girl's death.

KILL MY LOVE

Writer: Donald S. Sanford. **Director:** Herschel Daugherty. **Guest Cast:** Richard Carlson, David Kent, K.T. Stevens.

The murder of a man's mistress first leads to his wife's death, and finally, the man's own son is nearly killed.

MAN OF MYSTERY

Writer: Robert Bloch. **Director:** John Newland. **Guest Cast:** John Van Dreelen, Mary Tyler Moore, William Windom.

An attempted biography of a mysterious financier sets a murderous chain of events in motion.

THE INNOCENT BYSTANDERS

Writer: Hardy Andrews. **Director:** John English. **Guest Cast:** John Anderson, George Kennedy, Steve Terrell, Janet Lake.

Body snatching, though forbidden by law, is a profitable business in New England in 1830. Part of the strange trade includes murdering specific body types on order.

THE LETHAL LADIES

Writer: Boris Sobelman. **Director:** Ida Lupino. **Guest Cast:** Rosemary Murphy, Howard Morris.

In "Murder On The Rocks," husband-and-wife hatred leads to various murder attempts committed by and for both parties. In "Goodbye Dr. Bliss," a new librarian tries to fire a woman who really knows the job, but he loses out—completely.

THE SPECIALISTS

Writer: John Kneubuhl. **Director:** Ted Post. **Guest Cast:** Lin McCarthy, David Frankham, Ronald Howard, Suzanne Lloyd.

A group of specially-trained experts become involved with breaking an international ring of jewel thieves.

OVERLEAF: Boris Karloff made frequent tour-de-force appearances as a guest star in addition to his role as host. LEFT: "The Last of the Summervilles." RIGHT: "The Incredible Dr. Markesan."

THE OUTER LIMITS

There must be no apology, no smirk; each drama, no matter how worldless or timeless, must be spoken with the seriousness and sincerity and suspension-of-disbelief that a caring and intelligent parent employs in the spinning of a magic-wonderful tale to a child at bedtime. Humor and wit are honorable; the tongue in the cheek is most often condescending and gratuitous. When the tongue is in the cheek it is almost impossible to speak in anything but a garbled, foolish, fashion.

—Joseph Stefano
Producer

On a Monday evening early in the Fall of 1963, somnolent TV viewers tuned to ABC were jolted alert when the image on the tube went haywire and an impassive voice instructed them:

There is nothing wrong with your television set. Do not attempt to adjust the picture. We are controlling transmission. We will control the horizontal, we will control the vertical. For the next hour, sit quietly and we will control all you see and hear. You are about to experience the awe and mystery that leads you from the inner mind to...*The Outer Limits.*

With an opening reminiscent of Orson Welles' radio production of "The War of the Worlds," *Outer Limits* signed on the air for the first time. This similarity was not accidental. The man responsible was Leslie Stevens who, when he had been a high school student, had sold a play to Welles's Mercury Theatre Company and talked himself into a job with them. Truant officers who tracked him down—presumably after checking all the fishing holes on the east coast—raised compelling objections to his employment and took him home. But Welles' flamboyance and love of theater had already rubbed off on the kid and after his school days were over, Stevens seized the opportunity to starve to death in Greenwich Village as half of a song-and-dance team. The other half was Joseph Stefano, who had wanted to be a song writer and performer

Every episode of *Outer Limits* featured a specially-created monster, "the bear," this one from "Children of Spider County."

since winning a Charleston contest in South Philadelphia at the age of three. Eventually, the pair gave up this dream and wound their separate paths to California and drama.

By 1963, Stevens, now an established writer, was working on the *Stoney Burke* television series, which he had created, written and directed, when he sold ABC a science fiction series called *Please Stand By*. Too busy with *Stoney Burke* to produce it, he tapped his old friend Stefano, who, since writing the screenplay for Alfred Hitchcock's *Psycho*, had become a hot property.

The change from Stevens to Stefano was followed by a change of title from *Please Stand By* to *Outer Limits*. Once he took over, Stefano set up strict editorial guideposts to the high and low roads of the series. The high road explored the human situation. Each drama had to be consistent with scientific knowledge; the episodes were not to be *about* science, but were to focus instead on the character and condition of man. And as for the low road: "The viewer must know the delicious and consciously desired element of terror"; each show was to have a blood-blanching monster, what Stefano called "the bear." It is widely believed that

ABOVE: Producer Joseph Stefano relaxes on the set of "Tourist Attraction" with the episode's bear Icthyosaurus Mercurius. BELOW: "The Zanti Misfits"

ABC demanded the bear, but actually it had been Stefano himself who insisted on it. To him, terror without a bear was a whiff without a bite.

And it couldn't be a teddy bear. Rod Serling's *Twilight Zone* was *Outer Limits'* big brother and, as the younger sibling, it was eager to establish a separate identity. Serling's shows elicited a shudder but also a smile—they were more clever than frightening. Stefano was deadly earnest about terrifying people, but creating a scarifying monster to do the job was a task demanding the extraordinary in both imagination and sums of money. No *Outer Limits* episode was filmed for less than $150,000, of which $40,000 was devoted to the bears. The Ray Mercer Company was hired for special effects. Jim Danforth, Ralph Rodine and Tim Barr founded a unique production company called Projects Unlimited which, with help from the sculptor of some of the monster heads, Wah Chang, worked full time to produce such bears as "The Zanti Misfits," a race of alien, bearded insects with huge rolling eyes and quizzical expressions who were propelled by stop-motion animation. "The Galaxy Being" was a cathode-ray-fulgurating creature played by William O. Douglas, Jr., son of the former great libertarian Supreme Court Justice. Its shimmering appearance was created by filming a specially treated rubber suit through polarized filters. Also memorable was an army of plastic and rubber amphibeasts—creatures as alien at sea as on land. Other special effects people included Fred Phillips and, occasionally, John Chambers, who did special make-up; Forrest T. Butler and Sabine Manela, who provided costumes for humans and bears alike and John Poplin, who headed the art department.

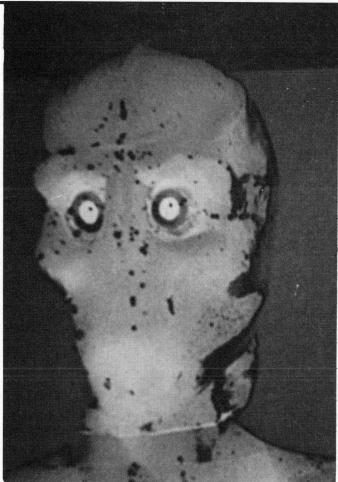

ABOVE: David McCallum, the guest bear in "The Sixth Finger," shows Jill Haworth a few tricks of the trade.
RIGHT: "The Galaxy Being" seen in the show (above) was actually the negative of a special effects shooting (below).

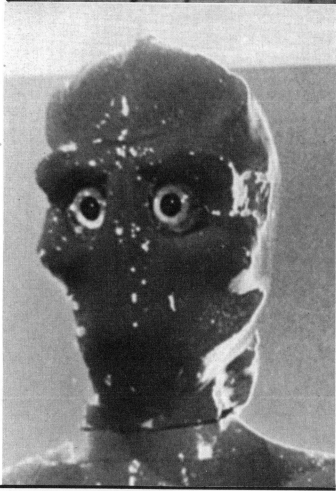

Stefano genuinely wanted excellent productions, and his concern is best indicated, perhaps, by his encouragement of imaginative cinematography. Long an admirer of Bergman and Fellini, he wanted *Outer Limits* to capture the exciting look of foreign films. Consequently, he allowed his cinematographers—they hardly needed incentive—freedom to experiment. One of them was Conrad Hall, then an alumnus of Stevens' *Stoney Burke,* but today one of the most highly acclaimed cinematographers in the business; Hall won an Oscar in 1968 for cinematography in *Butch Cassidy and the Sundance Kid,* and was nominated for his work in *In Cold Blood* and *The Day of the Locust,* among other films. In *Outer Limits* Hall used low shots, angled to catch the ceiling, which lent the sets for rooms an enclosed feeling; he used wide-angled lenses and panned, dollied and tracked—camera techniques rarely used on TV. However, the visual signature of *Outer Limits* was its frequent use of dim lighting—so dim that faces were often difficult to make out—enhancing the impact of tense scenes. In distinction, to produce clear, good-contrast home reception, most commercial TV shows used brilliant, almost incendiary, lighting; the only concern these shows had in their cinematography was in keeping the fire buckets full.

In addition to his capacity for visual innovation, Stefano also possessed a knack for discovering talented, young actors, such as Robert Culp, later of *I Spy,* David McCallum, who made his mark in *The Man From U.N.C.L.E.,* and Martin Landau, who was to star in *Mission: Impossible* and *Space: 1999.* Each played several roles for Stefano, with at least one go as the bear.

Stefano demonstrated an ear for detail by choosing Dominic Frontiere to compose the series' dramatic scores.

ABC liked the music so much that it turned up later as background for *The Invaders* and, still later, for *The Fugitive*, without so much as a single note changed.

Stefano's domain also extended to scripting; much of the best writing was done by him. One of his screenplays, "The Invisibles," was directed by Gerd Oswald and starred George Macready as the main strategist of a group of extraterrestrial parasites who sought to conquer the Earth. These super-intelligent creatures, resembling slugs, attached themselves to human spinal cords and dominated their hosts' wills. The attachment procedure—filmed in tender detail—showed a slug puncturing the flesh and oozing into the body of its screaming, writhing host. Very creepy.

Another one of Stefano's scripts, "The Forms of Things Unknown," was filmed twice. In the version shown on TV, David McCallum played a scientist brought back to life by a "time-tilting" machine he had invented. The last scene shows McCallum re-entering the device and fading away as he returns to death by slipping back into his own past. The second version of this story was changed slightly and was the pilot for a never-launched anthology called The Unknown. ABC wanted no fantastic elements, so Stefano added new scenes that made McCallum a madman who only thinks he has conquered death and time. The ending, of course, was changed completely. Instead of entering his machine and fading into the past, McCallum is shot to death by guest star Vera Miles.

Some concepts for *Outer Limits* never even reached the filming stage. One concerned a scientist who miniaturizes himself and enters the body of an evil dictator. The scientist tries to remove his war-mongering tendencies by "correcting" the dictator's criminal brain. The show's budget simply could not accommodate so fantastic a voyage, and the idea was scrapped.

Another story, "The Cats," was killed for a very different reason. The plot concerned a takeover by aliens that resembled ordinary housecats. Realizing that his show reached young viewers and that many of them had pet pussycats, Stefano axed the potentially traumatic concept and substituted rocks instead. The result was "Corpu

The bear in "Nightmare" was aptly named.

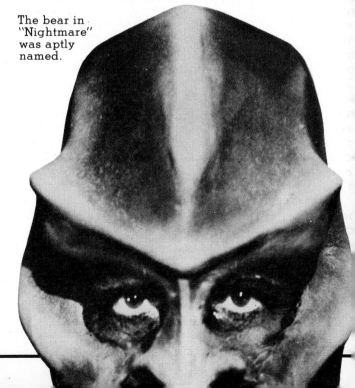

Special double exposure positive-negative photography helped to create the bears in "Special One."

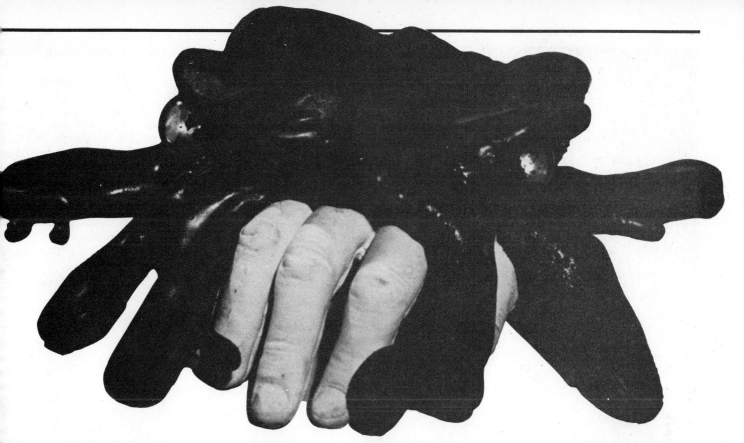

ABOVE: A prop from "Corpus Earthling." This "glove" was used by the actor to simulate attack by a space rock. BELOW: On the set of "Fun and Games" the episode's bear and scriptgirl enjoy a laugh together.

Earthling" starring Robert Culp as Paul Cameron, a doctor with a metal plate in his head. The plate enables him to hear the alien rocks' plan to take over the Earth by entering our (by now sore) bodies and controlling our minds. It is left unclear until the end whether this plot is real or imagined by Cameron; the focus is on his fears and doubts. Dr. Jonas Temple (Barry Atwater), an associate of Cameron's, corners him and it is a fight to the death (of Temple) as Cameron kills him to destroy the alien within. This play was written by Orin Borstein and it is the sort of human science fiction drama Stefano had in mind.

Though critics groused or even laughed at the bears, Outer Limits quickly attained high ratings, which seemed to indicate that they had produced their intended effect and the show was renewed for another season. But for the second season, ABC programming wizards decided to switch it to Saturday night, opposite the indomitable The Jackie Gleason Show. Irwin Allen's first TV entry, Voyage to the Bottom of the Sea, was to play in the time slot in which Outer Limits had originally been. Stefano was furious, believing that the early Monday night slot was especially receptive to science fiction, and, unable to change the network's decision, he resigned. (Stefano then went to CBS and tried—unsuccessfully—to sell them The Haunted, an occult-horror series starring Martin Landau.) Ben Brady, earlier of Perry Mason, was hired to replace him and began to put his own stamp on the show.

Perhaps as a response to derisive critics, Brady did in the bears and switched the emphasis from horror to science. He brought in writer Harlan Ellison whose contributions, "Demon With A Glass Hand" and "Soldier," were to win two Hugo awards. Brady also thought that the cinematography was too confusing for the audience and sent Hall the way of the bears—a move that cost the show its visual distinction. In the Fall of 1964, the different—though not worse—Outer Limits appeared on Saturdays, only to be crushed by Jackie Gleason and canceled in mid-season.

CLOCKWISE FROM TOP LEFT: June Havoc, Eddie Albert, Barbara Rush, Robert Culp and Harry Guardino were all victims of fear in episodes of *Outer Limits*.

"O.B.I.T."

INDEX OF EPISODES

"The Human Factor"

THE OUTER LIMITS
1963-1965/49 episodes
ABC/a Daystar-Villa di Stefano Production for United Artists Television.
60 minutes/black & white

Executive Producer: Leslie Stevens. **Producers:** Joseph Stefano (first season); Ben Brady (second season). **Creator:** Leslie Stevens. **Story Consultant:** Lou Morheim. **Director of Photography:** Conrad Hall; John Nickolaus; Kenneth Peach. **Special Effects:** Ray Mercer Company; Projects Unlimited. **Makeup:** Fred Phillips; John Chambers; Wah Chang. **Music:** Dominic Frontiere (first season); Harry Lubin (second season).

First Season: 1963-1964

THE GALAXY BEING
Writer: Leslie Stevens. **Director:** Leslie Stevens. **Guest Cast:** Cliff Robertson, Jacqueline Scott, Lee Phillips, William O. Douglas, Jr.

A radio engineer experimenting with a three-dimensional television receiver tunes in a being from the constellation Andromeda.

THE ONE HUNDRED DAYS OF THE DRAGON
Writer: Albert Balter. **Director:** Byron Haskin. **Guest Cast:** Sidney Blackmer, Phil Pine, Richard Loo, James Hong, James Yagi.

A winning Presidential candidate is being impersonated by the agent of an Oriental despot who can alter skin structure and change his appearance.

THE ARCHITECTS OF FEAR
Writer: Meyer Dolinsky. **Director:** Byron Haskin. **Guest Cast:** Robert Culp, Geraldine Brooks, Leonard Stone, Hal Bokar.

A group of scientists creates a creature that they pass off as being from another planet in order to frighten nations into peaceful co-existence.

THE MAN WITH THE POWER
Writer: Jerome Ross. **Director:** Laslo Benedek. **Guest Cast:** Donald Pleasance, Priscilla Morrill, Edward C. Platt.

A meek college professor acquires incredible mental powers after a unique scientific experiment.

THE SIXTH FINGER
Writer: Ellis St. Joseph. **Director:** James Goldstone. **Guest Cast:** David McCallum, Edward Mulhare, Jill Haworth, Constance Cavendish, Robert Doyle, Nora Marlowe, Janos Prohaska.

A geneticist uses an uneducated miner in his experiments with evolution and thrusts the unsuspecting subject into the biological future.

THE MAN WHO WAS NEVER BORN
Writer: Anthony Lawrence. **Director:** Leonard Horn. **Guest Cast:** Martin Landau, Shirley Knight, Bob Constantine, Karl Held.

An astronaut passes through a time warp into the year 2148, where he finds a barren Earth inhabited by grotesque humanoids.

O.B.I.T.
Writer: Meyer Dolinsky. **Director:** Gerd Oswald. **Guest Cast:** Peter Breck, Jeff Corey, Harry Townes, Jeanne Gilbert.

A Senatorial investigation reveals the existence of an electronic surveillance device invented by beings from another world.

THE HUMAN FACTOR
Writer: David Duncan. **Director:** Abe Biberman. **Guest Cast:** Gary Merrill, Harry Guardino, Sally Kellerman.

At a military base in Greenland, the brains of two men are accidentally exchanged during an experiment.

CORPUS EARTHLING
Writer: Orin Borstein. **Director:** Gerd Oswald. **Guest Cast:** Robert Culp, Salome Jens, Barry Atwater, David Garner, Ken Renard.

A doctor with a metal plate in his head is able to overhear an unusual conversation: two black crystalline rocks planning to take over the Earth by possessing the bodies of humans.

NIGHTMARE
Writer: Joseph Stefano. **Director:** John Erman. **Guest Cast:** Ed Nelson, James Shigeta, Martin Sheen, David Frankham.

Aliens from planet Ebon attack Earth and capture some humans. As prisoners of war, the Earthpeople undergo an intensive interrogation.

"The Zanti Misfits"

"Second Chance"

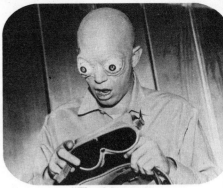

"The Mutant"

IT CRAWLED OUT OF THE WOODWORK
Writer: Joseph Stefano. **Director:** Gerd Oswald. **Guest Cast:** Scott Marlowe, Michael Forest, Barbara Luna, Joan Camden, Edward Asner, Kent Smith.

A ball of dust sucked into a vacuum cleaner feeds on the motor and grows to uncontrollable proportions.

THE BORDERLAND
Writer: Leslie Stevens. **Director:** Leslie Stevens. **Guest Cast:** Mark Richman, Nina Foch, Phillip Abbott.

Financed by a wealthy man hoping to contact his dead son, a team of scientists propels itself into a fourth dimension, where everything is a mirror image of itself.

TOURIST ATTRACTION
Writer: Dean Riesner. **Director:** Laslo Benedek. **Guest Cast:** Ralph Meeker, Henry Silva, Janet Blair.

Tycoon John Dexter goes on a fishing cruise to South America, where he captures an enormous and supposedly extinct "lizard-fish."

THE ZANTI MISFITS
Writer: Joseph Stefano. **Director:** Leonard Horn. **Guest Cast:** Michael Tolan, Robert F. Simon, Bruce Dern, Olive Deering.

The rulers of Planet Zanti are incapable of executing their criminals and send them to exile on Earth instead.

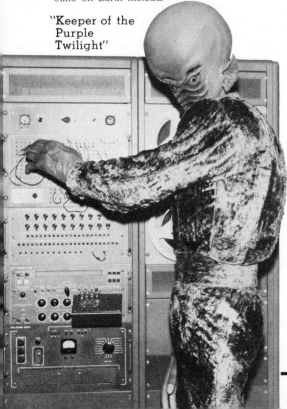

"Keeper of the Purple Twilight"

THE MICE
Writers: Joseph Stefano, Bill S. Ballinger. **Director:** Gerd Oswald. **Guest Cast:** Henry Silva, Diana Sands, Michael Higgins.

As an alternative to life imprisonment, a man volunteers for an inhabitant-exchange program being conducted with the planet Chromo.

CONTROLLED EXPERIMENT
Writer: Leslie Stevens. **Director:** Leslie Stevens. **Guest Cast:** Barry Morse, Carroll O'-Connor, Grace Lee Whitney.

Two Martians investigate Earth's "quaint" custom of homicide by using a machine that can replay a murder in fast and slow motion.

DON'T OPEN TILL DOOMSDAY
Writer: Joseph Stefano. **Director:** Gerd Oswald. **Guest Cast:** Miriam Hopkins, Melinda Plowman, Buck Taylor, Russell Collins, David Frankham, John Hoyt.

Eloping teenagers spend their wedding night in a bridal suite that hasn't been occupied since 1929. In it is a box containing a creature from another planet.

Z-Z-Z-Z-Z
Writer: Meyer Dolinsky. **Director:** John Brahm. **Guest Cast:** Phillip Abbott, Joanna Frank, Marsha Hunt, Booth Coleman.

A queen bee assumes human form to lure an entomologist into her world and make him a human drone.

THE INVISIBLES
Writer: Joseph Stefano. **Director:** Gerd Oswald. **Guest Cast:** Don Gordon, George Macready, Tony Mordente.

A government intelligence agent infiltrates a strange society known as "The Invisibles" which hopes to conquer mankind by attaching parasitic creatures to the spinal cords of human beings.

THE BELLERO SHIELD
Writer: Joseph Stefano. **Director:** John Brahm. **Guest Cast:** Martin Landau, Sally Kellerman, Chita Rivera, John Hoyt.

A scientist accidentally captures a space creature that protects itself with an impenetrable shield.

THE CHILDREN OF SPIDER COUNTY
Writer: Anthony Lawrence. **Director:** Leonard Horn. **Guest Cast:** Lee Kinsolving, Kent Smith, Burt Douglas, Dabbs Greer.

Five geniuses vanish and their father—an alien from a distant world—comes to Earth to claim them.

SPECIMEN: UNKNOWN
Writer: Stephen Lord. **Director:** Gerd Oswald. **Guest Cast:** Stephen McNally, Russell Johnson, Art Batanides, Richard Jaeckel.

Space station crewmen encounter mush-room-like organisms that emit a lethal gas and multiply at an enormous rate.

SECOND CHANCE (also titled JOY RIDE)
Writers: Lou Morheim, Lin Dane. **Director:** Paul Stanley. **Guest Cast:** Simon Oakland, Don Gordon, Janet DeGore, John McLiam.

A group of people board an amusement-park space ship, only to find out it's the real thing.

MOONSTONE
Writer: William Bast. **Director:** Robert Florey. **Guest Cast:** Ruth Roman, Alex Nicol, Tim O'Connor.

The staff of military and scientific personnel on the moon discovers a strange object that is round, smooth—and alive.

THE MUTANT
Writers: Allan Balter, Robert Mintz. **Director:** Alan Crosland, Jr. **Guest Cast:** Warren Oates, Betsy Jones Moreland, Walter Burke.

Caught in a strange silver downpour on another planet, a scientist turns into a telepathic killer.

THE GUESTS
Writer: Donald S. Sanford. **Director:** Paul Stanley. **Guest Cast:** Gloria Grahame, Geoffrey Horne, Luana Anders, Nellie Burt.

A drifter stumbles upon a house where time stands still and whose occupants are the captive guests of an alien.

FUN AND GAMES
Writers: Robert Specht, Joseph Stefano. **Director:** Gerd Oswald. **Guest Cast:** Nick Adams, Nancy Malone, Ray Kellogg, Bill Hart.

The "fun and games" on the satellite Arena involve pitting creatures from other worlds against each other with the losers forfeiting the lives of all the inhabitants of their own planet.

THE SPECIAL ONE
Writer: Joseph Stefano. **Director:** Gerd Oswald. **Guest Cast:** Richard Ney, Flip Mark, MacDonald Carey, Marion Ross.

An agent from the planet Xenon is tutoring brilliant Earth children for a special project—the conquest of Earth.

A FEASIBILITY STUDY
Writer: Joseph Stefano. **Director:** Byron Haskin. **Guest Cast:** Sam Wanamaker, Phyllis Love, Frank Puglia, David Opatoshu, Joyce Van Patton.

Six city blocks are transported to another galaxy.

PRODUCTION AND DECAY OF STRANGE PARTICLES
Writer: Leslie Stevens. **Director:** Leslie Stevens. **Guest Cast:** George Macready, Signe Hasso, Allyson Ames, Joseph Ruskin, John Duke, Leonard Nimoy.

"Soldier"

"Cold Hands, Warm Heart"

"I, Robot"

After a nuclear reactor goes out of control, a flood of radiation is released in the form of near-human creatures.

THE CHAMELEON
Writers: Robert Towne, Joseph Stefano. **Director:** Gerd Oswald. **Guest Cast:** Robert Duvall, Howard Caine, Henry Brandon.

An intelligence agent disguises himself to infiltrate a party of creatures from another planet.

THE FORMS OF THINGS UNKNOWN
Writer: Joseph Stefano. **Director:** Gerd Oswald. **Guest Cast:** Vera Miles, Barbara Rush, Sir Cedric Hardwicke, David McCallum.

An elusive and enigmatic madman devises a machine that can tilt time and bring the dead back to life. (This served as the pilot show for an unsold series titled *The Unknown*.)

Second Season: 1964-1965

SOLDIER
Writer: Harlan Ellison. **Director:** Gerd Oswald. **Guest Cast:** Lloyd Nolan, Michael Ansara, Tim O'Connor, Catherine McLeod, Jill Hill, Alan Jaffe.

An imaginative time-travel story by Harlan Ellison opens second season OUTER LIMITS, now produced by Ben Brady. Caught in a "laser light," a soldier of the future is catapulted backward into our present. Winner of a science fiction "Hugo" award.

COLD HANDS, WARM HEART
Writers: Dan Ullman, Milton Krims. **Director:** Charles Haas. **Guest Cast:** William Shatner, Geraldine Brooks, Lloyd Gough, Malachi Throne.

An astronaut returns from a successful orbit around Venus and finds that he can't keep himself warm.

BEHOLD, ECK!
Writer: John Mantley. **Director:** Byron Haskin. **Guest Cast:** Peter Lind Hayes, Joan Freeman, Parley Baer, Jack Wilson.

In this comedy, an eye-specialist fashions several pairs of glasses which enable the wearers to see a friendly but dangerous creature.

EXPANDING HUMAN
Writer: Francis Cockrell. **Director:** Gerd Oswald. **Guest Cast:** Skip Homeier, Keith Andes, James Doohan, Vaughn Taylor.

A university professor experiments with a drug that expands human consciousness.

DEMON WITH A GLASS HAND
Writer: Harlan Ellison. **Director:** Byron Haskin. **Guest Cast:** Robert Culp, Arline Martel, Abraham Sofaer, Rex Holman.

A suspenseful chase melodrama set in an eerie, abandoned office building. The last man on Earth returns to the twentieth century to find out why he was the only survivor of an attack by invaders from space. Winner of a science fiction "Hugo" award.

CRY OF SILENCE
Writer: Robert C. Dennis. **Director:** Charles Haas. **Guest Cast:** Eddie Albert, June Havoc, Arthur Hunnicut.

In a remote canyon, a couple is stalked by animated tumbleweeds possessed by an alien intelligence.

THE INVISIBLE ENEMY
Writer: Jerry Sohl. **Director:** Byron Haskin. **Guest Cast:** Adam West, Rudy Solari, Joe Maross, Chris Alcaide.

An expedition to Mars is menaced by a horde of monsters who dwell in a sea of sand.

WOLF 359
Writers: Seeleg Lester, Richard Landau. **Director:** Laslo Benedek. **Guest Cast:** Patrick O'Neal, Sara Shane, Peter Haskell, Ben Wright.

A professor reproduces a distant planet in miniature and watches evolution take place in a speeded-up fashion.

I, ROBOT
Writer: Robert C. Dennis. **Director:** Leon Benson. **Guest Cast:** Howard DaSilva, Marianna Hill, Red Morgan, Hugh Sanders, John Hoyt, Peter Brocco, Leonard Nimoy.

An almost-human robot is put on trial for murdering its creator.

THE INHERITORS
Writers: Sam Newman, Seeleg Lester, Ed Adamson. **Director:** James Goldstone. **Guest Cast:** Robert Duvall, Steve Ihnat, Ivan Dixon, Dee Pollock, James Frawley, Ted DeCorsia, Donald Harron, Dabbs Greer.

OUTER LIMITS' only two-part story is a meticulous, brilliantly conceived drama. In Part One, a meteor crashes in the Hui Tan Province and handsome bullets molded from its ore strike down four soldiers, creating a powerful alien intelligence, a "second brain" in each man that elevates his IQ to genius level. In Part Two the soldiers become engaged in a mysterious project involving a number of children.

KEEPER OF THE PURPLE TWILIGHT
Writer: Milton Krims. **Director:** Charles Haas. **Guest Cast:** Warren Stevens, Robert Webber, Gail Kobe, Curt Conway, Edward Platt.

An inquisitive alien trades his intellect for human emotions.

THE DUPLICATE MAN
Writer: Robert Dennis. **Director:** Gerd Oswald. **Guest Cast:** Ron Randell, Constance Towers.

To recapture the murderous space creature "Megasoid," a 21st century space anthropologist creates a duplicate of himself.

COUNTERWEIGHT
Writer: Milton Krims. **Director:** Paul Stanley. **Guest Cast:** Michael Constantine, Jacqueline Scott, Graham Denton.

Six ordinary people—and an extraordinary blob of light—board a rocketship for a simulated space flight.

THE BRAIN OF COLONEL BARHAM
Writer: Robert C. Dennis. **Director:** Charles Haas. **Guest Cast:** Grant Williams, Anthony Eisley, Elizabeth Perry.

Scientists decide that the ideal instrument for space exploration is a computer activated by a human brain.

THE PREMONITION
Writers: Sam Rocca, Ib Melchoir. **Director:** Gerd Oswald. **Guest Cast:** Dewey Martin, Mary Murphy, Emma Tyson, William Bramley.

A test pilot and his wife are saved from death by a sudden suspension of time.

THE PROBE
Writer: Seeleg Lester. **Director:** Felix Feist. **Guest Cast:** Mark Richman, Peggy Ann Garner, Ron Hayes, Janos Prohaska.

The survivors of a Pacific plane crash find themselves sitting motionless on a seemingly solid sea.

"Keeper of the Purple Twilight"

...If I can't blow up the world within the first ten minutes, then the show is a flop.

—Irwin Allen
Creator and Executive Producer

Before Irwin Allen discovered that moviegoers experience pure staring bliss in the face of the carnage and destruction he presented in *The Poseidon Adventure* and *The Towering Inferno,* he wowed the kiddies with his TV offerings: *Voyage to the Bottom of the Sea, Lost in Space, The Time Tunnel* and *Land of the Giants.* These shows, all debuting between 1964 and 1968, earned Allen the title of the dean of TV science fiction, as well as a pretty penny (all except *The Time Tunnel* were commercial hits).

Allen's career has combined two great gifts: the inventor's, for devising imaginative special effects, and the farmer's, for using everything twice.

VOYAGE TO THE BOTTOM OF THE SEA

Jules Verne's *Twenty Thousand Leagues under the Sea* spawned two generations of Irwin Allen productions. The first, a successful movie entitled *Voyage to the Bottom of the Sea,* fathered the 1964 TV series of the same name. The true star of this show was the research submarine *Seaview* with its two human sidekicks Richard Basehart as Admiral Harriman Nelson (ret.), who commanded the ship, and David Hedison as Captain Lee Crane. (Movie fans will remember Hedison for the title role in the 1959 movie *The Fly.*) The mission of the *Seaview,* though ostensibly research, was to defend the human race against sabotage, criminal organizations and goodness-knows-what from the depths of the sea.

As with most Allen productions, the plot and characterizations of *Voyage* were weak, but the special effects were strong. In the show's first season, which was shot in black and white, the majority of the dangers were of the enemy agent/saboteur/natural disaster genres. When the show began to be shot in color, the *Seaview* was menaced

Richard Basehart as Admiral Nelson in Allen's *Voyage to the Bottom of the Sea.*

by more colorful dangers: outer-spacemen, humanoid amphibians, ice creatures, dinosaurs (to re-use some stock footage from Allen's *Lost World*), werewolves, mummies, abominable snowmen, mad scientists, jellyfishlike monsters and even an army of marionettes. The show emphasized action and special effects but hardly wet its toes in science. Basehart, a former Shakespearean actor, played his role straight and with a sense of command, but silly plots and dialogue undermined his dignity. Hedison's role was bland, and he played it that way.

The *Seaview* was a spectacular hand-me-down from the feature film. Its initial cost for the movie was $400,000 (more than the entire cost of most TV pilots), a price which included the control room, viewing room and the missile and torpedo rooms. Sets, props, costumes and reels of underwater footage were also handed down from the film version. When Allen received the green light from ABC to start production, all the material was already on hand. Waste not, you-know-what not.

To convey the supposed four hundred-foot length of the submarine, three models, four-, eight- and eighteen-foot were built for filming the various sequences. The eight-footer was a fully automated working model with engines, lights and even working torpedoes. The eighteen-footer was used only for surface shots. There were also one- and two-foot models of the mini-subs housed in the mother ship and used on those indispensable exploratory missions—they would be the pride of any bathtub fleet. The price of all of these models: $200,000! L.B. "Bill" Abbott, the special effects chief at Twentieth Century Fox, won two Emmys for the subs and for the other special effects he created for the show. Howard Lydecker directed the filming of all the miniature scenes.

One of the best effects was the inside of a whale in the episode entitled "Jonah and the Whale." It was Allen's idea, but William Creber, the art director, executed it. He carried it off with such panache that Gia Scala, who literally starred *in* it, found it was "a horrible, frightening experience. It gave me goose pimples." To achieve the effect, a long tubular set (thirty by twenty by fifteen feet) was built and lined with enormous vinyl bags which were gradually inflated to simulate breathing. Membranes and the like

6023-967

6023965

One never knows
what lurks at the
bottom of Irwin
Allen's seas—
here, "The
Lobster Man."

were created using vinyl and foam rubber. For finishing
touches, red paint was sprayed over the lining, and the
entire structure was illuminated with red and yellow lights.

LOST IN SPACE

In 1965, after his success with *Voyage*, Allen looked
heavenward and tripped. *Lost in Space* was the tale of the
American Family Robinson (the pilot, never aired, was
called *Space Family Robinson*) who in 1997 sought to
leave an overcrowded earth for a quiet little spot in another
solar system. (Allen recently serialized the *Swiss Family
Robinson*, but it flopped.) A foreign agent, played by
Jonathan Harris, had planned to blow up the ship while the
Robinsons lay frozen for their long journey, but instead
catapulted it irreparably off course and got trapped on
board himself. It would be amusing to report that the family
thawed to the consistency of thawed strawberries—but no
such luck. Guy Williams and June Lockhart, as Dr. and Mrs.
Robinson, Marta Kristen, Billy Mumy and Angela Cartwright, as their children, and Mark Goddard, as their friend
and co-pilot, all came back to life in the proper consistency.
The plot, however, did not fare so well, nor did the acting. A
robot, whose lines were read by Bob May, was the most
interesting and popular member of the cast—if fan mail
can be taken as any indication. The show rarely rose above
the level of a Saturday morning cartoon and was laid to rest
in 1968.

LEFT: Irwin Allen on the set of *Lost in Space*.
OPPOSITE: The cast of *Lost in Space*.

THE TIME TUNNEL

After one series set below the sea and one set beyond the solar system, Allen adapted the idea of H.G. Wells' *The Time Machine* for his series *The Time Tunnel*, which debuted in 1967. Here, a group of scientists tries to demonstrate its invention—a machine that can transport people back and forth in time—to a U.S. senator who controls their research funds. Impetuous scientist Tony Newman (James Darren), desperate to prove that the still untested machine works, jumps into it and is hurled backward in time. Once inside, he learns that the machine has one particular flaw: it can't bring people back. But, if the government would just foot the bill...who knows? Anyway, as luck would have it, Tony lands on the Titanic a few days before the band strikes up "Nearer My God to Thee." Undaunted, he tries to convince the captain to change the course of the ship—and of history—but he gets put in the brig for his trouble. Stock footage from Twentieth Century Fox's *Titanic* was used in a special tinted, and very effective, form.

Meanwhile, back at the lab, the boys are watching on their viewing screen and getting perturbed. Concerned scientists all, they dispatch Doug Phillips (Robert Colbert) to help Newman and to deliver proof to the captain in the form of *The New York Sentinel,* its banner headline screaming of the Titanic catastrophe. Alas, the captain turns a deaf ear and is rewarded by having his ship ripped open by an iceberg. And what of our heroes? Just in the nick of you-know-what they are rescued by their dedicated friends in the lab and transported to another time slot. And so the series went; each week Newman and Phillips landed in the midst of another momentous and perilous event in history—it became a kind of hot-blooded *You are There.* Occasionally, they were thrown into the future, so that the thrifty Mr. Allen could have his makeup artist Ben Nye re-use some *Lost in Space* monster get-ups.

The Time Tunnel was magnificently photographed by Winton Hoch, and its elaborate illusions won Bill Abbott his

Series star Robert Colbert at the end of the time tunnel.

third Emmy for special photographic effects. The tunnel itself was the most extraordinary effect. It was a drum nine feet in diameter with a band five feet wide. The whole thing was covered with bits of cellophane and Christmas tinsel. When shot through an ultra-wide angle lens, the result was a dazzling kaleidoscope of "time fragments" flying through the shaft. The actors, suspended by wires in front of a blue screen, were matted into the scene. In the final episode, our two scientist heroes materialize once again on the deck of the Titanic, never to be heard from again. Viewers are left with the impression that the whole cycle will be repeated.

LAND OF THE GIANTS

Land of the Giants, Allen's fourth series, starts with people never heard from again. In the year 1983, the *Spindrift* is on a suborbital flight to London when it passes through an electrical storm and enters a strange white cloud. Its seven passengers never reach London, emerging instead, like Lemuel Gulliver in Brobdingnag, in a world identical to the one they left except for one thing: its scale is twelve times larger. The passengers and crew, played by Gary Conway, Don Marshall, Don Matheson, Heather Young, Deanna Lund, Kurt Kasznar and Stefan Arngrim, find themselves menaced by cats, terrorized by insects, imprisoned in a doll's house, strapped down and rendered helpless by cellophane tape and practically skewered by a paper clip.

The biggest thing about the show may have been its budget. At a cost of over $250,000 per episode, it was the most expensive series in TV history at the time. Producer Allen could have boasted that his ship was called the *Spendthrift*. The many technical problems involved in creating props like a slice of bread made from a four-foot slab of sponge rubber, a six-foot pencil and a nine-foot revolver were brilliantly, but expensively, solved. Also, many optical and photographic tricks enlivened an otherwise dull show.

ABOVE: Gary Conway and Deanna Lund find themselves held captive by Scotch tape in *Land of the Giants*. BELOW: Kurt Kaznar disembarks from the *Spindrift* into the *Land of the Giants*.

Allen's characters may have lost themselves above and below the sea or somewhere in time, but the financial returns have been phenomenal, and no doubt these TV shows paved the way for Allen's colossal success in his more recent feature films.

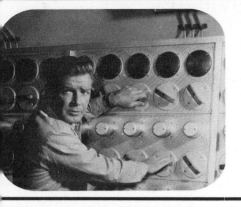

INDEXES OF EPISODES

VOYAGE TO THE BOTTOM OF THE SEA

1964-1968/110 Episodes
ABC/an Irwin Allen Production for 20th Century Fox Television
60 minutes/black & white (first season); color (second season on)

Regular Cast: Richard Basehart (Admiral Harrington Nelson); David Hedison (Captain Lee Crane); Bob Dowdell (Chip Morton); Terry Becker (Chief Sharkey); Del Monroe (Kowalski).

Executive Producer: Irwin Allen. **Creator:** Irwin Allen. **Story Consultant:** Sidney Marshall. **Director of Photography:** Carl Guthrie. **Special Effects:** L.B. Abbott. **Makeup:** Ben Nye.

First Season: 1964-1965

ELEVEN DAYS TO ZERO
Writer: Irwin Allen. **Director:** Irwin Allen. **Guest Cast:** Mark Slade, Hal Torey, Gordon Gilbert, Barney Biro, Eddie Albert, Theodore Marcuse, John Zaremba, Bill Hudson.

The *Seaview's* polar mission, which would save the world from huge tidal waves, is imperiled.

THE CITY BENEATH THE SEA
Writer: Richard Landau. **Director:** James Braham. **Guest Cast:** Hurd Hatfield, Linda Cristal, John Anderson.

While investigating the disappearance of two research ships, Crane and a lady diver are abducted to an underwater city.

THE FEAR MAKERS
Writer: Anthony Wilson. **Director:** Leonard Horn. **Guest Cast:** Edgar Bergen, Lloyd Bochner, Mark Slade.

Enemy agents are infecting our submarines with a strange "fear gas" to slow up our marine investigations.

THE MIST OF SILENCE
Writer: John McGreevey. **Director:** Leonard Horn. **Guest Cast:** Rita Gam, Alejandro Rey, Mike Kellin, Henry Del Gado, Edward Colmans, Doug Lambert, Booth Colman.

Unknown to the *Seaview* personnel, the Latin American President they're about to rescue is a reluctant member of a group of subversives.

THE PRICE OF DOOM
Writer: Harlan Ellison. **Director:** James Goldstone. **Guest Cast:** Jill Ireland, David Opatoshu, John Milford, Steve Ihnat, Pat Priest, Dan Seymour, Ivan Triesault.

While tackling an odd, expanding plankton specimen that threatens to destroy the vessel,

Seaview personnel must figure out who among them is a foreign agent.

THE SKY IS FALLING
Writer: Don Brinkley. **Director:** Leonard Horn. **Guest Cast:** Charles McGraw, Joseph di Reda, Frank Ferguson.

The rays of a spaceship knock out all *Seaview* power systems.

TURN BACK THE CLOCK
Writer: Sheldon Stark. **Director:** Alan Crosland. **Guest Cast:** Nick Adams, Yvonne Craig, Les Tremayne, Vitina Marcus, Robert Cornthwaite, Mark Slade.

Seaview investigations of the suspicious story of a man supposedly lost in Antarctica for several months lead the vessel to a prehistoric world.

THE VILLAGE OF GUILT
Writer: Berne Giler. **Director:** Irwin Allen. **Guest Cast:** Richard Carlson, Anna-Lisa, Steven Geray, Frank Richards, G. Stanley Jones.

The *Seaview* tackles a mad scientist's creation, a giant octopus-like creature that's holding a small village in the grip of terror.

HOT LINE
Writer: Berne Giler. **Director:** John Braham. **Guest Cast:** Everett Sloan, Michael Ansara.

A satellite is about to destroy San Francisco and one of the two Russian scientists who are going to disarm it is a fake.

SUBMARINE SUNK HERE
Writer: William Tunberg. **Director:** Leonard Horn. **Guest Cast:** Carl Reindel, Eddie Ryder, Robert Doyle.

A mine explosion temporarily cripples the *Seaview*.

THE MAGNUS BEAM
Writer: Alan Caillou. **Director:** Leonard Horn. **Guest Cast:** Monique Lemaire, Malachi Throne, Jacques Aubuchon, Mario Alcaide.

A night club singer says she has information about an aircraft-destroying weapon being used by enemy agents.

NO WAY OUT
Writer: Robert Hammer. **Director:** Felix Feist. **Guest Cast:** Than Wyenn, Danielle de Metz, Oscar Beregi, Jan Merlin, Don Wilbanks, Richard Webb.

A Soviet agent infiltrates the *Seaview* to kill a fellow who has defected and is hiding there.

THE BLIZZARD MAKERS
Writer: William Welch. **Director:** Joseph Leytes. **Guest Cast:** Werner Klemperer, Milton Selzer.

The scientist helping to check out strange changes in the Gulf Stream is turned into an enemy robot.

THE GHOST OF MOBY DICK
Writer: Robert Hamner. **Director:** Sobey Martin. **Guest Cast:** Edward Binns, June Lockhart, Bob Beekman.

The *Seaview* crew helps a deranged seaman to revenge himself on the whale that crippled him.

LONG LIVE THE KING
Writer: Raphael Hayes. **Director:** Laslo Benedek. **Guest Cast:** Carroll O'Connor, Michael Petit, Michael Pate, Sara Shane, Jan Arvan.

The *Seaview* crew tries to restore a young prince to his throne to avert a Communist overthrow of his country.

HAIL TO THE CHIEF
Writer: Don Brinkley. **Director:** Gerd Oswald. **Guest Cast:** Viveca Lindfors, Tom Palmer, Nancy Kovack, Lorence Kerr, James Doohan.

Enemy agents attempt to kill the President when he boards the *Seaview* for emergency treatment following an accident.

THE LAST BATTLE
Writer: Robert Hamner. **Director:** Felix Feist. **Guest Cast:** John Van Dreelen, Dayton Lummis, Joe De Santis, Ben Wright, Rudy Solari, Eric Feldary, Sandra Williams.

Nelson is captured by Nazis who still plan to take over the world.

MUTINY
Writer: William Reed Woodfield. **Director:** James Goldstone. **Guest Cast:** Harold J. Stone, Richard Bull, Jay Lanin.

While investigating a sub's disappearance, Nelson seems to be on the verge of a breakdown.

DOOMSDAY
Writer: William Reed Woodfield. **Director:** James Goldstone. **Guest Cast:** Donald Harron, Sy Prescott, Paul Genge, Ford Rainey, Richard Bull.

A missile attack by a foreign power puts the *Seaview* on fail-safe alert.

THE INVADERS
Writer: William Reed Woodfield. **Director:** Sobey Martin. **Guest Cast:** Robert Duvall, Michael McDonald.

The *Seaview* discovers—and releases—a manlike creature that has been in suspended animation for twenty million years.

THE INDESTRUCTIBLE MAN
Writer: Richard Landau. **Director:** Felix Feist. **Guest Cast:** None.

The *Seaview*ers discover that a robot used as part of a U.S. space probe has been reprogrammed into a murderous fiend.

THE BUCCANEER
Writers: William Welch, Albert Gail. **Director:** Laslo Benedek. **Guest Cast:** Barry Atwater, George Keymas, Emile Genest.

The *Seaview* is taken over by an insane art collector who has a plan to steal the Mona Lisa.

THE HUMAN COMPUTER

Writer: Robert Hamner. **Director:** James Goldstone. **Guest Cast:** Harry Millard, Simon Scott, Herbert Lytton, Walter Sande, Ted De Corsia.

Crane's belief that he is the only human aboard the *Seaview* during an atomic brain test is quickly proved wrong.

THE SABOTEUR

Writer: William Reed Woodfield. **Director:** Felix Feist. **Guest Cast:** Warren Stevens, Bert Freed.

Enemy agents brainwash Crane to sabotage the *Seaview* during an important mission.

CRADLE OF THE DEEP

Writer: Robert Hamner. **Director:** Sobey Martin. **Guest Cast:** John Anders, Howard Wendell, Derrick Lew, Robert Pane.

Experiments on a microscopic bit of matter yield an expanding creation that threatens to destroy everyone.

THE AMPHIBIANS

Writer: Rik Vollaerts. **Director:** Felix Feist. **Guest Cast:** Richard Bull, Skip Homeier, Curt Conway, Zale Parry.

Scientists turn themselves into amphibious creatures.

THE EXILE

Writer: William Reed Woodfield. **Director:** James Goldstone. **Guest Cast:** Edward Asner, David Sheiner, Harry Davis, James Frawley, Jason Wingreen.

A rendezvous between Nelson and the former leader of an enemy power ends up with the two stranded on a raft.

THE CREATURE

Writer: Rik Vollaerts. **Director:** Sobey Martin. **Guest Cast:** Leslie Nielsen, Pat Culliton, William Stevens.

The *Seaview* probes the cause of a failed missile launching.

THE ENEMIES

Writer: William Reed Woodfield. **Director:** Felix Feist. **Guest Cast:** Henry Silva, Malachi Throne.

Enemy agents use a medicine to turn Crane and Nelson into bitter foes.

SECRET OF THE LOCH

Writer: Charles Bennett. **Director:** Sobey Martin. **Guest Cast:** Torin Thatcher, Hedley Mattingly, George Mitchell, John McLiam.

The *Seaview* follows an underground conduit to Loch Ness, where they investigate a scientist's claim of having seen the famed monster.

THE CONDEMNED

Writer: William Reed Woodfield. **Director:** Leonard Horn. **Guest Cast:** J.D. Cannon, Arthur Franz, Alvy Moore.

A Presidential order turns control of the *Seaview* over to a glory-seeking scientist who plans to prove the vessel can break the "crush" barrier.

THE TRAITOR

Writers: William Welch, Albert Gail. **Director:** Sobey Martin. **Guest Cast:** George Sanders, Michael Pate, Susan Flannery.

A powerful government agent is actually the spy who masterminds a plot to obtain information from Nelson by abducting his young sister.

Second Season: 1965-1966

JONAH AND THE WHALE

Writer: Shimon Wincelberg. **Director:** Sobey Martin. **Guest Cast:** Gia Scala, Paul Trinka, Robert Pane, Pat Cullitan.

Admiral Nelson and a female Russian scientist are swallowed by a gigantic whale.

TIME BOMB

Writers: William Read Woodfield, Allen Balter. **Director:** Sobey Martin. **Guest Cast:** Susan Flannery, Ina Balin, John Zaremba, Richard Loo.

A war between Russian and the United States is nearly sparked when an Oriental secret agent attempts to turn Admiral Nelson into a human time bomb.

AND FIVE OF US ARE LEFT

Writer: Robert Vincent Wright. **Director:** Harry Harris. **Guest Cast:** James Anderson, Robert Doyle, Ed McCready, Phillip Pine, Francoise Ruggieri, Kent Taylor.

When Admiral Nelson investigates a sunken submarine, he is threatened by Japanese soldiers still fighting W.W. II.

THE CYBORG

Writers: William Reed Woodfield, Allan Balter. **Director:** Leo Penn. **Guest Cast:** Victor Buono, Brooke Bundy, Nancy Hsueh, Fred Crane.

In a plot to destroy a third of the world, an evil scientist creates an electronic duplicate of Nelson and orders it to fire *Seaview*'s warheads at various strategic points.

ESCAPE FROM VENICE

Writer: Charles Bennett. **Director:** Alex March. **Guest Cast:** Renzo Cesana, Danica D'Hondt, Vincent Gardenia, Delphi Lawrence.

Captain Crane is hunted by enemy agents in Venice.

THE LEFT-HANDED MAN

Writer: William Welch. **Director:** Jerry Hopper. **Guest Cast:** Regis Toomey, Cyril Delavanti, Charles Dierkop, Barbara Bouchet.

Admiral Nelson is nearly killed several times when he tries to foil a plot to infiltrate the Defense Department.

THE DEADLIEST GAME

Writer: Rik Vollaerts. **Director:** Sobey Martin. **Guest Cast:** Lloyd Bochner, Robert F. Simon, Audrey Dalton, Robert Cornthwaite.

An American general tries to kill the President and trigger a nuclear war.

LEVIATHAN

Writer: William Welch. **Director:** Harry Harris. **Guest Cast:** Karen Steele, Liam Sullivan.

A former colleague of Admiral Nelson grows into a gigantic menace after discovering an underwater fissure in the Earth's crust.

THE PEACEMAKER

Writers: William Read Woodfield, Allan Balter. **Director:** Sobey Martin. **Guest Cast:** John Cassavetes, Irene Tsu, Lloyd Kino, Whit Bissell.

A mad scientist tries to blow up the world with a super-bomb.

THE SILENT SABOTEURS

Writers: Sidney Marshall, Max Erlich. **Director:** Sobey Martin. **Guest Cast:** Pilar Seurat, George Takei, Bert Freed, Alex D'Arcy, Phil Posner.

Crane leaps into action on the Flying Sub when the enemy uses a secret computer to intercept manned Venus space probe capsules.

THE X FACTOR

Writer: William Welch. **Director:** Leonard Horn. **Guest Cast:** Jan Merlin, George Tyne, John McGiver, Bill Hudson, Anthony Brand.

Enemy agents kidnap a noted U.S. scientist, paralyze him and coat him with wax, then make plans to ship him to their country and pass him off as a mannequin.

THE MACHINES STRIKE BACK

Writers: John and Ward Hawkins. **Director:** Jerry Juran. **Guest Cast:** Roger C. Carmel, Francoise Ruggieri, Bert Remsen.

Receiving command signals from some unknown source, unmanned submarines turn their deadly missiles toward the United States.

THE MONSTER FROM OUTER SPACE

Writers: William Read Woodfield, Allan Balter. **Director:** James Clark. **Guest Cast:** Wayne Heffley, Lee Delano, Preston Hanson, Hal Torey.

A Saturn probe reenters the Earth's atmosphere with a tentacled monster attached to its surface.

TERROR ON DINOSAUR ISLAND

Writer: William Welch. **Director:** Leonard Horn. **Guest Cast:** Paul Carr.

Stock footage from Irwin Allen's "The Lost World" feature is used liberally in this story about a volcanic island inhabited by prehistoric beasts.

KILLERS OF THE DEEP

Writers: William Read Woodfield, Allan Balter. **Director:** Harry Harris. **Guest Cast:** Patrick

 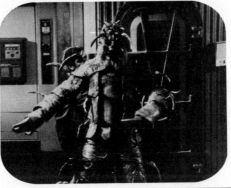 

Wayne, Michael Ansara, James Frawley, Bruce Mars.

Sabotage and stealing secrets from underwater hideouts provide the action for this tale.

DEADLY CREATURE BELOW

Writers: William Read Woodfield, Allan Balter. **Director:** Sobey Martin. **Guest Cast:** Nehemiah Persoff, Paul Comi, Wayne Heffley.

While a jellyfish-like sea monster menaces the *Seaview*, two escaped cons try to hijack the Flying Sub.

THE PHANTOM

Writer: William Welch. **Director:** Sutton Roley. **Guest Cast:** Alfred Ryder.

The ghostly captain of a phantom sub tries to reincarnate himself as Crane.

THE SKY'S ON FIRE

Writer: William Welch. **Director:** Sobey Martin. **Guest Cast:** David J. Stewart, Robert H. Harris, Frank Marth.

The Van Allen belt of radiation threatens the world.

GRAVEYARD OF FEAR

Writer: Robert Vincent Wright. **Director:** J. Addiss. **Guest Cast:** Robert Loggia, Marian Moses.

A scientist tries to force Nelson and Crane to retrieve a youth serum to keep his secretary-girl friend from reverting to old age.

THE SHAPE OF DOOM

Writer: William Welch. **Director:** Nathan Juran. **Guest Cast:** Kevin Hagen.

Another giant whale—this one's swallowed an atomic bomb.

DEAD MEN'S DOUBLOONS

Writer: Sidney Marshall. **Director:** Sutton Roley. **Guest Cast:** Albert Salmi, Allen Jaffe, Robert Brubaker.

An underwater pirate ship attacks the Flying Sub.

THE DEATH SHIP

Writers: William Read Woodfield, Allan Balter. **Director:** Abe Biberman. **Guest Cast:** Lew Gallo, Elizabeth Perry, June Vincent, David Sheiner.

A seven-nation peace conference is nearly blown up by a crackpot.

THE MONSTER'S WEB

Writers: Al Gail, Peter Packer. **Director:** J. Addiss. **Guest Cast:** Mark Richman, Barry Coe, Sea Morgan.

On a mission to retrieve highly explosive fuel cylinders, *Seaview* crewmen encounter a giant spider monster.

THE MENFISH

Writers: William Read Woodfield, Allan Balter. **Director:** Tom Giles. **Guest Cast:** Gary Merrill, Roy Jenson, Victor Lundin, John Dehner.

A mad scientist creates a horde of half-human, half-amphibian creatures.

THE MECHANICAL MAN

Writers: John and Ward Hawkins. **Director:** Sobey Martin. **Guest Cast:** James Darren, Arthur O'Connell, Seymour Cassel.

A lifelike robot seeks to control the world.

THE RETURN OF THE PHANTOM

Writer: William Welch. **Director:** Sutton Roley. **Guest Cast:** Alfred Ryder, Vitina Marcus, Richard Bull.

In this sequel to an earlier second season episode, the phantom sea captain returns from thee dead in a renewed attempt to possess Captain Crane's body.

Third Season: 1966-1967

MONSTER FROM THE INFERNO

Writer: Rik Vollaerts. **Director:** Harry Harris. **Guest Cast:** Arthur Hill.

A brain-shaped mass with notions of world conquest tries to take over the *Seaview*.

WEREWOLF

Writer: Donn Mullally. **Director:** J. Addiss. **Guest Cast:** Charles Aidman, Douglas Bank.

Nelson and his *Seaview* crewmen are transformed into werewolves.

THE DAY THE WORLD ENDED

Writer: William Welch. **Director:** Jerry Hopper. **Guest Cast:** Skip Homeier.

A fanatical senator, the greatest master of mass hypnosis who ever lived, convinces the crew of the *Seaview* that all the people in the world have suddenly disappeared.

NIGHT OF TERROR

Writer: Robert Bloomfield. **Director:** J. Addiss. **Guest Cast:** Henry Jones, Jerry Catron.

Nelson, Sharkey and a geologist are shipwrecked on a volcanic isle terrorized by a monster iguana, affording Allen the chance to use his "Lost World" lizard once again.

THE TERRIBLE TOYS

Writer: Robert Vincent Wright. **Director:** J. Addiss. **Guest Cast:** Paul Fix, Francis X. Bushman, Jim Mills.

Commanded by an alien intelligence, six windup toys wreak havoc aboard the *Seaview*.

DAY OF EVIL

Writer: William Welch. **Director:** Jerry Hopper. **Guest Cast:** None.

A stranger from outer space tries to force Nelson to blow up the Pacific Fleet with a nuclear missile.

DEADLY WATERS

Writer: Robert Vincent Wright. **Director:** G. Mayer. **Guest Cast:** Lew Gallo, Don Gordon, Harry Lauter.

Kowalski's injured and unreasonable brother manags to save the *Seaview* from a deep-sea death.

THING FROM INNER SPACE

Writer: William Welch. **Director:** A. March. **Guest Cast:** Hugh Marlowe, Dawson Palmer.

A well-known marine naturalist leads the *Seaview* in search of a terrible sea creature that killed his camera crew.

THE DEATH WATCH

Writer: William Welch. **Director:** Leonard Horn. **Guest Cast:** None.

Admiral Nelson and Captain Crane become subjects of an experiment in which they are ordered to murder each other.

DEADLY INVASION

Writers: John and Ward Hawkins. **Director:** Jerry Juran. **Guest Cast:** Warren Stevens, Michael Fox, Ashley Gilbert, Brent Davis.

Arriving in small metal cylinders, spaceships containing faceless aliens try to conquer Earth by taking over an underwater atomic base.

THE HAUNTED SUBMARINE

Writer: William Welch. **Director:** Harry Harris. **Guest Cast:** None.

Richard Basehart plays a dual role as Nelson plagued by his slave-trader ancestor.

THE PLANT MAN

Writer: Donn Mullally. **Director:** Harry Harris. **Guest Cast:** William Smithers.

An evil twin uses telepathy on his angelic brother in order to make him create an army of plant monsters.

THE LOST BOMB

Writer: Oliver Crawford. **Director:** J. Mayer. **Guest Cast:** John Lupton, Gerald Mohr, George Keymas.

The *Vulcan*, an enemy submarine, competes with *Seaview* for an underwater superbomb on the verge of exploding.

THE BRAND OF THE BEAST

Writer: William Welch. **Director:** J. Addiss. **Guest Cast:** None.

Exposure to radiation causes the Admiral to change into a hairy menace. (Richard Bull appears in the semiregular role of ship's doctor.)

THE CREATURE

Writers: John and Ward Hawkins. **Director:** J. Addiss. **Guest Cast:** Lyle Bettger.

An amoebalike sea creature, capable of shooting out lightning bolts, threatens to grow large enough to demolish entire cities. To make matters worse, exposure to the thing transforms *Seaview* officers into treacherous "creature-men."

DEATH FROM THE PAST
Writer: Sidney Marshall, Charles Bennett. **Director:** J. Addiss. **Guest Cast:** John Van Dreelen, Jan Merlin.

Two leftover Nazi soldiers awake from suspended animation and try to fire missiles at the Allied capital cities.

THE HEAT MONSTER
Writer: Charles Bennett. **Director:** J. Mayer. **Guest Cast:** Don Knight, Alfred Ryder.

Heat creatures found on an Arctic ice cap can make themselves invisible and plan to use the power to conquer our world.

THE FOSSIL MEN
Writer: James N. Whiton. **Director:** J. Addiss. **Guest Cast:** Brendan Dillon, Jerry Catron.

Fossil men, part human, part rock and all bad, want to take over Earth. They also want to turn Admiral Nelson into one of their stone-faced crew and use *Seaview* to fire deadly missiles at the United States.

THE MERMAID
Writer: William Welch. **Director:** Jerry Hopper. **Guest Cast:** Diane Webber.

Captain Crane finds himself enticed by a beautiful mermaid.

THE MUMMY
Writer: William Welch. **Director:** Harry Harris. **Guest Cast:** None.

A three-thousand-year-old monster puts a spell on Captain Crane and wreaks havoc aboard *Seaview*.

THE SHADOWMAN
Writer: Rik Vollaerts. **Director:** J. Addiss. **Guest Cast:** None.

When the *Seaview* sets out to launch the first interstellar space probe, it is enveloped by a mysterious alien mass and invaded by the equally unearthly "Shadowman."

NO ESCAPE FROM DEATH
Writer: William Welch. **Director:** Harry Harris. **Guest Cast:** None.

An outsized Portuguese man of war threatens the *Seaview* after the ship collides with an unidentified submarine.

DOOMSDAY ISLAND
Writer: Peter Germano. **Director:** Jerry Hopper. **Guest Cast:** Jock Gaynor.

Amphibian eggs, a mysterious uncharted atoll and marauding creatures spell danger for Nelson and his crewmen.

THE WAX MEN
Writer: William Welch. **Director:** H. Jones. **Guest Cast:** Michael Dunn.

This episode has become a minor classic among telefantasy enthusiasts. The *Seaview* picks up a shipment of wax dummies for a special exhibit to be held in Washington. Out of one of the crates pops a midget in clown costume who along with the dummies begins controlling the ship. Crane ultimately wins, the clown is electrocuted and the reign of terror ends.

DEADLY CLOUD
Writer: Rik Vollaerts. **Director:** Jerry Hopper. **Guest Cast:** Robert Carson.

A mysterious cloud containing invader aliens causes widespread destruction throughout the world. One of the monsters uses Captain Crane's body to further the invasion.

DESTROY SEAVIEW!
Writer: Donn Mullally. **Director:** J. Addiss. **Guest Cast:** Jerry Catron, Arthur Space.

A mysterious Voice brainwashes Admiral Nelson and orders him to blow up the *Seaview*.

Fourth Season 1967-1968

FIRES OF DEATH
Writer: Arthur Weiss. **Director:** Bruce Fowler. **Guest Cast:** Victor Jory.

Trying to obtain an elixir of youth from an erupting volcano, an aging alchemist endangers the entire southern hemisphere.

THE DEADLY DOLLS
Writer: Charles Bennett. **Director:** Harry Harris. **Guest Cast:** Vincent Price, Ronald P. Martin.

A deranged toymaster, the tool of a machine-ruled civilization, threatens *Seaview*.

CAVE OF THE DEAD
Writer: William Welch. **Director:** Harry Harris. **Guest Cast:** Warren Stevens.

A seaman from the past tries to transfer the curse of the Flying Dutchman on to Admiral Nelson.

JOURNEY WITH FEAR
Writer: Arthur Weiss. **Director:** Harry Harris. **Guest Cast:** Eric Matthews, Gene Dynarski, Jim Gosa.

Alien humanoids from Venus capture Nelson, Crane and Morton, then threaten to destroy the Earth.

SEALED ORDERS
Writer: William Welch. **Director:** Jerry Hopper. **Guest Cast:** None.

Strange fumes from a super-powered missile cause the men of the *Seaview* to experience mass hallucinations.

MAN OF MANY FACES
Writer: William Welch. **Director:** Harry Harris. **Guest Cast:** Jock Gaynor, Bradd Arnold, Howard Culver.

A mad scientist, capable of assuming the forms of others, imperils the Earth by drawing the Moon toward it.

FATAL CARGO
Writer: William Welch. **Director:** Jerry Hopper. **Guest Cast:** Woodrow Parfrey, John Lormer.

A gorilla-like creature wreaks havoc aboard *Seaview*.

TIME LOCK
Writer: William Welch. **Director:** J. Hoffer. **Guest Cast:** John Crawford, Paul Trinka.

A being from the future intends to add Admiral Nelson to his collection of zombie-like military officers.

RESCUE
Writer: William Welch. **Director:** J. Addiss. **Guest Cast:** Don Dubbins.

The *Seaview* plays cat-and-mouse with a deadly mystery sub.

TERROR
Writer: Sidney Ellis. **Director:** Jerry Hopper. **Guest Cast:** Damian O'Flynn, Pat Culliton, Brent Davis.

Admiral Nelson and crew members are possessed by alien plant monsters intent on conquering Earth.

A TIME TO DIE
Writer: William Welch. **Director:** R. Sparr. **Guest Cast:** Henry Jones.

Seaview is attacked by an odd little man capable of hurling people about in time.

BLOW UP
Writer: William Welch. **Director:** J. Addiss. **Guest Cast:** None.

When Admiral Nelson suddenly goes insane, he orders *Seaview* to fire upon Navy ships.

THE DEADLY AMPHIBIANS
Writer: Arthur Weiss. **Director:** Jerry Hopper. **Guest Cast:** Don Matheson, Joey Tata, Pat Culliton.

A race of amphibious aliens tries to take over *Seaview* and drain its nuclear power.

THE RETURN OF BLACKBEARD
Writer: Al Gail. **Director:** J. Addiss. **Guest Cast:** Malachi Throne.

During a critical diplomatic moment, Blackbeard the pirate appears and tries to take over *Seaview*.

THE TERRIBLE LEPRECHAUN
Writer: Charles Bennett. **Director:** Jerry Hopper. **Guest Cast:** Walter Burke, Ralph Garrett, Pat Culliton.

In order to prevent a nuclear explosion, the men of *Seaview* must thwart an evil leprechaun.

THE LOBSTER MAN
Writer: Al Gail. **Director:** J. Addiss. **Guest Cast:** Victor Lundin.

An evil crustacean from outer space threatens to destroy Earth.

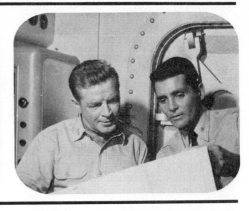

NIGHTMARE
Writer: Sidney Marshall. **Director:** C. Rondeau. **Guest Cast:** Paul Mantee.

Crane is alone and stalked by an alien testing Earth's defenses.

THE ABOMINABLE SNOWMAN
Writer: Robert Hamner. **Director:** R. Sparr. **Guest Cast:** Frank Babich, Bruce Mars, Dusty Cadis.

A scientific experiment with weather creates a terrifying creature capable of assuming human form.

SECRET OF THE DEEP
Writer: William Welch. **Director:** C. Rondeau. **Guest Cast:** Mark Richman.

A traitor aboard *Seaview* imperils Nelson's plan to stop world-threatening scientists.

MAN-BEAST
Writer: William Welch. **Director:** Jerry Hopper. **Guest Cast:** Lawrence Montaigne.

Following experimental descents in a diving bell, Captain Crane turns into a hate-crazed beast creature.

SAVAGE JUNGLE
Writer: Arthur Weiss. **Director:** B. Sparr. **Guest Cast:** Pat Culliton, Perry Lopez.

Aliens are planting a jungle growth that threatens to overrun the Earth.

FLAMING ICE
Writer: Arthur Browne, Jr. **Director:** B. Sparr. **Guest Cast:** Michael Pate, Frank Babich, George Robotham.

Frost Men create destructive world-wide floods.

ATTACK!
Writer: William Welch. **Director:** Jerry Hopper. **Guest Cast:** Skip Homeier, Kevin Hagen.

Nelson and Crane join forces with a peace-loving alien to stop a devastating attack on Earth.

THE EDGE OF DOOM
Writer: William Welch. **Director:** J. Addiss. **Guest Cast:** Scott McFadden.

Aboard *Seaview* is an enemy agent, impersonating one of the crew members.

THE DEATH CLOCK
Writer: Sidney Marshall. **Director:** Charles Rondeau. **Guest Cast:** Chris Robinson.

The *Seaview* crew encounters a fourth dimensional nightmare.

NO WAY BACK
Writer: William Welch. **Director:** B. Sparr. **Guest Cast:** Henry Jones, Barry Atwater, William Beckley.

In this sequel to "A Time to Die," Mr. Pem returns to confound the men of the *Seaview* with his time device.

LOST IN SPACE
1965-1968/83 episodes
CBS/an Irwin Allen Production in association with Van Bernard Productions for 20th Century Fox Television
60 minutes/black & white (first season); color (second season on)

Regular Cast: Guy Williams (Prof. John Robinson); June Lockhart (Maureen Robinson); Billy Mumy (Will Robinson); Mark Goddard (Don West); Marta Kristen (Judy Robinson); Angela Cartwright (Penny Robinson); Jonathan Harris (Dr. Zachary Smith).

Executive Producer: Irwin Allen. **Creator:** Irwin Allen. **Story Consultant:** Anthony Wilson. **Special Effects:** L.B. Abbott; Howard Lydecker. **Makeup:** Ben Nye. **Music:** Johnny Williams.

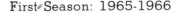

First Season: 1965-1966

THE RELUCTANT STOWAWAY
Writer: Shimon Wincelberg. **Director:** Tony Leader. **Guest Cast:** Don Forbes, Hal Torey, Brett Parker, Fred Crane, Tom Allen.

In the year 1997, the Robinson family blasts off in their spaceship, *Jupiter 2*, on a pioneer trip to settle another planet. The party becomes lost in space, however, through the villainous efforts of stowaway Dr. Zachary Smith. In this pilot episode, the family robot is a heavy and not the good guy it would eventually become.

THE DERELICT
Writer: Peter Packer. **Director:** Alex Singer. **Guest Cast:** Don Forbes, Dawson Palmer.

Drawn into a cavernous space craft, the Robinson family encounter a vastly advanced civilization composed of weird, bubblelike creatures.

ISLAND IN THE SKY
Writer: Norman Lessing. **Director:** Tony Leader. **Guest Cast:** None.

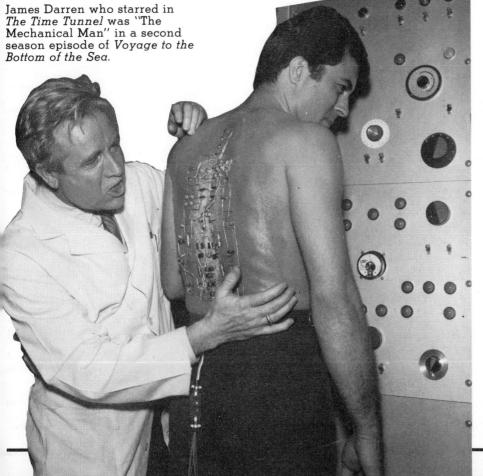

James Darren who starred in *The Time Tunnel* was "The Mechanical Man" in a second season episode of *Voyage to the Bottom of the Sea.*

After Smith tampers with its rockets, *Jupiter 2* crash-lands on a barren planet, where the recovered party launches an exhausting search of the missing Professor Robinson. This episode marked the first extensive use of the Robinsons' "space chariot," a combination tractor and bus.

THERE WERE GIANTS IN THE EARTH
Writer: Carey Wilber. **Director:** Leo Penn. **Guest Cast:** Dawson Palmer.

Trying to make their surroundings habitable, the Robinsons discover cyclopean giants in the vicinity.

THE HUNGRY SEA
Writer: William Welch. **Director:** Sobey Martin. **Guest Cast:** None.

Guiding the space chariot through storms and earthquakes, the Robinsons make their way across an island sea to the temporary safety of their spaceship.

WELCOME STRANGER
Writer: Peter Packer. **Director:** Alvin Ganzer. **Guest Cast:** Warren Oates.

Long lost astronaut Jimmy Hapgood, who has come to enjoy the life of a space rover, pays a visit.

MY FRIEND, MR. NOBODY
Writer: Jackson Gillis. **Director:** Paul Stanley. **Guest Cast:** None.

A delicate and charming fantasy about little Penny's "imaginary" companion, actually an invisible cosmic force with an uncontrollable attachment to its human friend.

INVADERS FROM THE FIFTH DIMENSION
Writer: Shimon Wincelberg. **Director:** Leonard Horn. **Guest Cast:** Ted Lehmann, Joe Ryan.

Searching for a humanoid brain to repair their computer, luminous alien creatures threaten the Robinsons.

THE OASIS
Writer: Peter Packer. **Director:** Sutton Roley. **Guest Cast:** None.

Dr. Smith grows into a giant after sampling some strange fruit.

THE SKY IS FALLING
Writers: Barney Slater, Herman Groves. **Guest Cast:** Don Matheson, Francoise Ruggieri, Eddie Rosson.

The Robinsons find themselves unable to understand the electronic language of a visiting space family.

WISH UPON A STAR
Writer: Barney Slater. **Director:** Sutton Roley. **Guest Cast:** None.

When Dr. Smith tampers with a magic cerebral machine that can materialize any wish, its original owner, a strange Rubberoid creature, arrives to reclaim it.

THE RAFT
Writer: Peter Packer. **Director:** Sobey Martin. **Guest Cast:** None.

After the Robinsons build a tiny space vehicle from parts of *Jupiter 2*, Dr. Smith steals the new exploratory craft and heads for Earth.

ONE OF OUR DOGS IS MISSING
Writer: William Welch. **Director:** Sutton Roley. **Guest Cast:** None.

The Robinsons befriend a twenty-year-old space dog, who later helps them save Judy from the clammy clutches of a great hairy mutant.

THE ATTACK OF THE MONSTER PLANTS
Writers: William Read Woodfield, Allan Balter. **Director:** J. Addiss. **Guest Cast:** None.

A sinister duplicate of Judy is manufactured by giant cyclamen plants.

RETURN FROM OUTER SPACE
Writer: Peter Packer. **Director:** Jerry Juran. **Guest Cast:** Reta Shaw, Walter Sande, Donald Losby, Sheila Mathews.

Young Will makes a Christmastime trip back to Earth through a matter-transfer machine.

THE KEEPER (two episodes)
Writer: Barney Slater. **Director:** Harry Harris. **Guest Cast:** Michael Rennie, Wilbur Evans.

In Part One of this two-part episode, an alien collector threatens to add Will and Penny to his incredible menagerie. In Part Two, Dr. Smith accidentally sets all the animals free, and the Keeper threatens to allow his monsters to overrun the planet unless Penny and Will are turned over to him as specimens.

THE SKY PIRATE
Writer: Carey Wilber. **Director:** Sobey Martin. **Guest Cast:** Albert Salmi.

Tucker, a space pirate, gives the Robinsons renewed hope of rescue while winning the friendship of young Will.

GHOST IN SPACE
Writer: Peter Packer. **Director:** Don Richardson. **Guest Cast:** None.

When a mysterious ghost threatens the Robinson party, Dr. Smith insists it's the troubled spirit of his Uncle Thaddeus.

THE WAR OF THE ROBOTS
Writer: Barney Slater. **Director:** Sobey Martin. **Guest Cast:** None.

An evil robotoid, created by an advanced civilization of aliens, is whipped into working shape by an unwitting Will. The mechanical monster differs from ordinary robots in that it has free choice, and it promptly chooses to enslave the Earth people and destroy their own robot. The robotoid is actually the world-famous Robby the Robot, who appeared in MGM science fiction thrillers.

THE MAGIC MIRROR
Writer: Jackson Gillis. **Director:** Jerry Juran. **Guest Cast:** Michael J. Pollard.

Penny and her pet Bloop Debbie enter into a magic mirror and find a mystical world inhabited by a lonely alien boy.

THE CHALLENGE
Writer: Barney Slater. **Director:** Don Richardson. **Guest Cast:** Michael Ansara, Kurt Russell.

To prove their superiority over Earth beings, an alien and his son challenge Prof. Robinson and Will to a test of strength and courage.

THE SPACE TRADER
Writer: Barney Slater. **Director:** Jerry Juran. **Guest Cast:** Torin Thatcher.

An alien space trader tries to trick the Robinson family into trading him a human being—Dr. Smith!

HIS MAJESTY SMITH
Writer: Carey Wilber. **Director:** Harry Harris. **Guest Cast:** Liam Sullivan, Kevin Hagen.

When Smith becomes king of a mysterious alien society, he little realizes the true purpose of this title. Actually, he has been chosen for his uselessness, and is intended as a sacrificial offering to primitive space gods.

THE SPACE CROPPERS
Writer: Peter Packer. **Director:** Sobey Martin. **Guest Cast:** Mercedes McCambridge, Sherry Jackson, Dawson Palmer.

A clan of galactic hillbillies grow a space crop that threatens to devour all life on the Robinson's planet.

ALL THAT GLITTERS
Writer: Barney Slater. **Director:** Harry Harris. **Guest Cast:** Werner Klemperer, Larry Ward.

The greedy Smith absconds with a magic key which holds the secret of great wealth, but which causes everyone whom its possessor touches to turn into platinum statues.

LOST CIVILIZATION
Writer: William Welch. **Director:** Don Richardson. **Guest Cast:** Kym Karath, Royal Dano.

Will stumbles into a strange underground world whose inhabitants are preparing to conquer the universe.

A CHANGE OF SPACE
Writer: Peter Parker. **Director:** Sobey Martin. **Guest Cast:** Frank Graham.

When Will is accidentally hurled into the sixth dimension, he returns to the Robinson party an intellectual giant. Smith, appreciating the possibilities for power, takes the trip also—and emerges a decrepit old man.

FOLLOW THE LEADER
Writer: Barney Slater. **Director:** Don Richardson. **Guest Cast:** Gregory Morton.

Dr. Zachary Smith (Jonathan Harris) and the robot were the most popular characters on *Lost in Space*.

An invisible alien spirit possesses the body and mind of Prof. Robinson. Will exorcises the diabolical force from his father's body through the power of his love.

Second Season: 1966-1967

BLAST OFF INTO SPACE
Writer: Peter Packer. **Director:** Jerry Juran. **Guest Cast:** Strother Martin.

John Robinson manages to pilot *Jupiter 2* into space before the planet his family had been living on disintegrates.

WILD ADVENTURE
Writers: William Read Woodfield, Allan Balter. **Director:** Don Richardson. **Guest Cast:** Vitina Marcus.

The first of a few appearances of Athena, the Green Girl. This seductive Lorelei lures an enchanted Dr. Smith out into space, and the efforts of the Robinson party to retrieve him forestall their return to Earth.

THE GHOST PLANET
Writer: Peter Packer. **Director:** Jerry Juran. **Guest Cast:** Sue England, Michael Fox.

Thinking he is landing on Earth, Smith adjusts *Jupiter 2's* controls and sets down on an alien world run by Cyborgs.

THE FORBIDDEN WORLD
Writer: Barney Slater. **Director:** Don Richardson. **Guest Cast:** Wally Cox, Janos Prohaska.

After drinking some alien nectar, Dr. Smith realizes that it is highly explosive and that he has become a human bomb!

SPACE CIRCUS
Writer: Bob and Wanda Duncan. **Director:** Harry Harris. **Guest Cast:** James Westerfield, Melinda Fee, Harry Varteresian.

Will nearly runs away with an intergalactic circus.

THE PRISONERS OF SPACE
Writer: Barney Slater. **Director:** Jerry Juran. **Guest Cast:** Dawson Palmer.

After an energized fence imprisons everyone in the Robinson campsite, the space party is tried by a mysterious tribunal for crimes committed in space.

THE ANDROID MACHINE
Writer: Bob and Wanda Duncan. **Director:** D. Richardson. **Guest Cast:** Dee Hartford, Fritz Feld.

The Robinsons cause an emotionless android to develop into a higher grade model by teaching her the meaning of love.

THE DEADLY GAMES OF GAMMA 6
Writer: Barney Slater. **Director:** Harry Harris. **Guest Cast:** Mike Kellin.

Smith must enter the ring to save the Earth from destruction on a planet of intergalactic fighting matches.

THE THIEF OF OUTER SPACE
Writer: Jackson Gillis. **Director:** Don Richardson. **Guest Cast:** Malachi Throne, Ted Cassidy, Maxine Gates.

A futuristic Arab chieftain enlists the aid of Will and Dr. Smith to find his long lost love.

THE CURSE OF COUSIN SMITH
Writer: Barney Slater. **Director:** J. Addiss. **Guest Cast:** Henry Jones.

Dr. Smith's rascally cousin Jeremiah tries to do him out of an inheritance.

THE DREAM MONSTER
Writer: Peter Packer. **Director:** Don Richardson. **Guest Cast:** John Abbott, Dawson Palmer, Harry Monty, Frank Delfino.

A space scientist tries to drain the Robinsons' emotions, to make his android more human.

THE GOLDEN MAN
Writer: Barney Slater. **Director:** Don Richardson. **Guest Cast:** Dennis Patrick, Ronald Gans, Bill Troy.

A lesson about prejudice, *Lost in Space*-style. The Robinsons must take sides in a confrontation between two alien civilizations. The representative of one is a handsome, courteous Golden Man, the other an inhospitable Frog. Guess who's the bad guy?

THE GIRL FROM THE GREEN DIMENSION
Writer: Peter Packer. **Director:** Jerry Juran. **Guest Cast:** Vitina Marcus, Harry Raybould.

The Green Girl Athena, whom we met several episodes back, returns to befuddle Dr. Smith.

THE QUESTING BEAST
Writer: Carey Wilbur. **Director:** Don Richardson. **Guest Cast:** Hans Conried, Sue England, Jeff County.

A sort of Don Quixote of space enlists the aid of Penny and Will in his life-long quest for a fire-breathing female beast.

THE TOYMAKER
Writers: Bob and Wanda Duncan. **Director:** Robert Douglas. **Guest Cast:** Fritz Feld, Walter Burke, Dawson Palmer.

Will and Dr. Smith are held prisoner in a fourth dimensional toyland.

MUTINY IN SPACE
Writer: Peter Packer. **Director:** Don Richardson. **Guest Cast:** Ronald Long.

Zahrk, a renegade space ship admiral, shanghais Will, Dr. Smith and the robot.

THE SPACE VIKINGS
Writer: Margaret Brookman Hill. **Director:** E. Stone. **Guest Cast:** Sheila Mathews, Bern Hoffman.

Smith is pitted against a space-age answer to the might God of Thunder, Thor.

ROCKET TO EARTH
Writer: Barney Slater. **Director:** Don Richardson. **Guest Cast:** Al Lewis.

Because of the bungling of a clumsy space magician named Zalto, Dr. Smith misses a chance to return to Earth.

CAVE OF THE WIZARDS
Writer: Peter Packer. **Director:** Don Richardson. **Guest Cast:** None.

Rock monsters, mummies and an evil computer threaten the Robinsons.

TREASURE OF THE LOST PLANET
Writer: Carey Wilbur. **Director:** Harry Harris. **Guest Cast:** Albert Salmi, Craig Duncan, Jim Boles.

A captain joins the robot, Will, Dr. Smith and Penny on a treasure hunt that yields disappointing booty.

REVOLT OF THE ANDROIDS
Writers: Bob and Wanda Duncan. **Director:** Don Richardson. **Guest Cast:** Dee Hartford, Don Matheson.

Smith thinks he can transform an android into the most powerful creature in the Universe.

THE COLONISTS
Writer: Peter Packer. **Director:** E. Stone. **Guest Cast:** Francine York.

It's up to Will to find a way to free his enslaved parents when a statuesque Amazon takes over their planet.

TRIP THROUGH THE ROBOT
Writer: Barney Slater. **Director:** Don Richardson. **Guest Cast:** None.

Will and Dr. Smith crawl into their suddenly outsized robot to fix the malfunction that caused his tremendous growth.

THE PHANTOM FAMILY
Writer: Peter Packer. **Director:** E. Stone. **Guest Cast:** Alan Hewitt.

A scientist from outer space makes android copies of Smith, Don and the girls, then forces Will to instruct them in the behavior of their human counterparts.

THE MECHANICAL MEN
Writer: Barney Slater. **Director:** S. Robbie. **Guest Cast:** None.

A horde of tiny mechanical men exchange the personalities of Dr. Smith and the robot.

THE ASTRAL TRAVELER
Writer: Carey Wilbur. **Director:** Don Richardson. **Guest Cast:** Sean McClory, Dawson Palmer.

After tumbling through a space warp, Will finds himself within a haunted Scottish Castle, guarded by a Loch Ness-like lagoon monster.

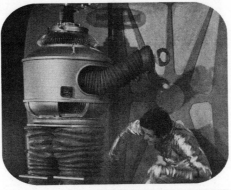

THE GALAXY GIFT
Writer: Barney Slater. Director: E. Stone. Guest Cast: John Carradine, Jim Mills.

Three aliens persuade Dr. Smith to trick Penny into giving up a magic amulet.

THE WRECK OF THE ROBOT
Writer: Barney Slater. Director: Jerry Juran. Guest Cast: Jim Mills.

The Robinsons' robot becomes the blueprint for a terrible machine with which a group of evil aliens hope to conquer the Earth.

A VISIT TO HADES
Writer: Carey Wilbur. Director: Don Richardson. Guest Cast: Gerald Mohr.

Smith literally goes to Hades, where a devilish character named Morbus is imprisoned.

WEST OF MARS
Writer: Michael Fessier. Director: Nathan Juran. Guest Cast: Allan Melvin, Charles Arthur, Mickey Manners, Lane Bradford.

Dr. Smith is mistaken for his lookalike, an interstellar gunslinger.

Third Season: 1967-1968

THE CONDEMNED OF SPACE
Writer: Peter Packer. Director: Jerry Juran. Guest Cast: Marcel Hillaire.

The Jupiter 2 stops to refuel and the Robinsons find themselves in the middle of a computerized space prison.

VISIT TO A HOSTILE PLANET
Writer: Peter Packer. Director: Sobey Martin. Guest Cast: Pitt Herbert, Robert Foulk, Robert Pine, Norman Leavitt.

The Robinson party finally succeeds in landing on Earth...but it is an Earth fifty years earlier than the one they left.

KIDNAPPED IN SPACE
Writer: Robert Hamner. Director: Don Richardson. Guest Cast: Grant Sullivan, Carol Williams, Joey Russo.

After kidnapping the Robinson party, mechanical men force the robot to turn surgeon so that he can operate on the defective cogs of their leader.

HUNTER'S MOON
Writer: Jack Turley. Director: J. Richardson. Guest Cast: Vincent Beck.

Professor Robinson, considered a prized quarry, is hunted by a humanoid creature named Megazor on a strange planet.

THE SPACE PRIMEVALS
Writer: Peter Packer. Director: Jerry Juran. Guest Cast: Arthur Batanides.

A race of primitive creatures, controlled by a gigantib computer, imperil the Robinsons.

THE SPACE DESTRUCTORS
Writer: Robert Hamner. Director: Don Richardson. Guest Cast: Tommy Farrell.

When Dr. Smith discovers a machine that manufactures Cyborgs, he dreams of conquering the galaxy with an army of such creatures.

THE HAUNTED LIGHTHOUSE
Writer: Jackson Gillis. Director: Sobey Martin. Guest Cast: Lou Wagner, Woodrow Parfrey, Kenya Coburn.

A little boy named J-5, the only surviving member of an alien colony from another planet, joins the Robinsons on their journey to a strange lighthouse.

FLIGHT INTO THE FUTURE
Writer: Peter Packer. Director: Sobey Martin. Guest Cast: Don Eitner, Lew Gallo.

Will, Dr. Smith and the robot find themselves on a planet that manufactures illusions by the dozens.

COLLISION OF THE PLANETS
Writer: Peter Packer. Director: Don Richardson. Guest Cast: Dan Travanty, Linda Gaye Scott, Joey Tata.

When four impulsive aliens threaten to destroy a planet that is on a collision course with their own, they consider the Robinsons expendable losses.

THE SPACE CREATURE
Writer: William Welch. Director: Sobey Martin. Guest Cast: None.

Will finds his innermost fears and anxieties turned into tangible dangers.

DEADLIEST OF THE SPECIES
Writer: Robert Hamner. Director: Sobey Martin. Guest Cast: Ronald Gans, Lyle Waggoner.

The robot flips his cogs over a female super-robot who is programmed for evil.

A DAY AT THE ZOO
Writer: Jackson Gillis. Director: I. Moore. Guest Cast: Leonard Stone, Gary Tigerman, Ronald Weber.

Penny is captured by an intergalactic showman named Farnum B., who puts her on display in his space zoo.

TWO WEEKS IN SPACE
Writer: Robert Hamner. Director: Don Richardson. Guest Cast: Fritz Feld, Richard Krisher, Eric Mathews, Edy Williams.

On the lam from Galactic law, a disguised quartet of space monsters convince Smith to turn the Jupiter 2 into a resort hotel for aliens.

CASTLES IN SPACE
Writer: Peter Parker. Director: Sobey Martin. Guest Cast: Alberto Monte, Corinna Tsopei.

When an impulsive bandito tries to abduct an ice princess protected by the Robinsons, the robot fights like "el Toro" to save her.

THE ANTI-MATTER MAN
Writers: Barney Slater and Robert Hamner. Director: Sutton Roley. Guest Cast: None.

An evil duplicate of Professor Robinson tries to substitute for the real Robinson.

TARGET: EARTH
Writer: Peter Packer. Director: Jerry Juran. Guest Cast: James Gosa, Brent Davis.

Will saves the day when shapeless aliens turn themselves into duplicates of the Robinson party and corrupt the robot as part of a scheme to conquer Earth.

PRINCESS OF SPACE
Writer: Jackson Gillis. Director: Don Richardson. Guest Cast: Robert Foulk, Arte Johnson.

Penny is mistaken for the princess of a far-away planet.

THE TIME MERCHANT
Writers: Bob and Wanda Duncan. Director: E. Stone. Guest Cast: John Crawford.

When Dr. Smith convinces a time merchant to return him to Earth sometime before the Jupiter's flight, he unwittingly endangers the others of the Robinson party.

THE PROMISED PLANET
Writer: Peter Packer. Director: E. Stone. Guest Cast: Gil Rodgers, Keith Taylor.

Smith's a hippie and Penny's a go-go dancer when the Robinsons land on a planet populated by mod youngsters.

FUGITIVES IN SPACE
Writer: Robert Hamner. Director: Ezra Stone. Guest Cast: Michael Conrad, Tol Avery.

Will and the robot try to rescue Don and Dr. Smith, who have been framed and jailed on a prison planet.

SPACE BEAUTY
Writer: Jackson Gillis. Director: I. Moore. Guest Cast: Leonard Stone, Dee Hartford.

Farnum B., who tried to turn Penny into a zoo attraction a few episodes ago, is now bribing Judy to enter his intergalactic beauty contest.

THE FLAMING PLANET
Writer: Barney Slater. Director: Don Richardson. Guest Cast: Abraham Sofaer.

A weird plant creature first tries to engulf the Jupiter 2, then develops a crush on Dr. Smith.

THE GREAT VEGETABLE REBELLION
Writer: Peter Packer. Director: Don Richardson. Guest Cast: Stanley Adams.

Members of the Robinson party are turned into human plants by an angry carrot monster.

JUNKYARD OF SPACE
Writer: Barney Slater. Director: Ezra Stone. Guest Cast: Marcel Hillaire.

With Dr. Smith's treacherous help, a mechanical junkman absconds with the robot's memory banks.

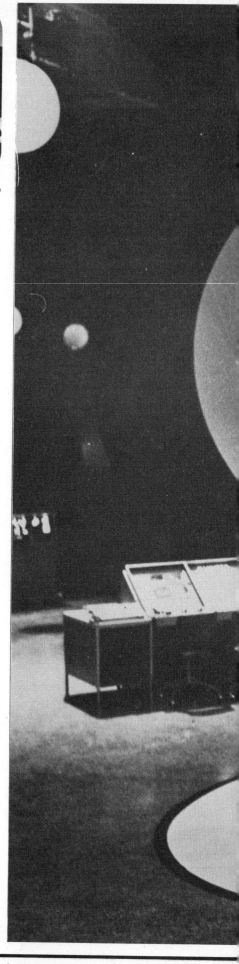

THE TIME TUNNEL

1966/30 episodes
ABC/an Irwin Allen Production for 20th
  Century Fox Television
60 minutes/color

Regular Cast: James Darren (Dr. Tony
Newman); Robert Colbert (Dr. Doug Phillips); Whit Bissell (Lt. Gen. Heywood Kirk);
John Zaremba (Dr. Raymond Swain); Wesley Lau (Army Master Sgt. Jiggs).

Executive Producer: Irwin Allen. **Creator:**
Irwin Allen. **Director of Photography:**
Winton Hoch. **Special Effects:** L.B. Abbott.
Makeup: Ben Nye. **Music:** Johnny Williams.

RENDEZVOUS WITH YESTERDAY
Writer: Harold Jack Bloom. **Director:** Irwin
Allen. **Guest Cast:** Michael Rennie, Susan
Hampshire, Gary Merrill, Don Knight.

Dr. Tony Newman hurls himself into the time
machine in order to prove it works, and lands
on the Titanic just before it sinks.

ONE WAY TO THE MOON
Writer: William Welch. **Director:** Harry
Harris. **Guest Cast:** James T. Callahan, Warren
Stevens, Larry Ward, Barry Kelley.

The time travelers materialize in a spaceship
bound for Mars.

END OF THE WORLD
Writers: William Welch, Peter Germano. **Director:** Sobey Martin. **Guest Cast:** Paul
Fix, Paul Carr, Gregory Morton, Nelson Leigh.

Landing in a small mining town at the time of
the appearance of Halley's Comet, the time
travelers try to convince townspeople that it is
not the end of the world.

THE DAY THE SKY FELL DOWN
Writer: Ellis St. Joseph. **Director:** William
Hale. **Guest Cast:** Sam Groom, Linden Chiles,
Lew Gallo, Bob Okazaki, Susan Flannery.

Tony and Doug at Pearl Harbor. Interesting
twist: Tony was born there and has the task of
warning his own father of the impending attack;
he also gets to confront himself as a child.

THE LAST PATROL
Writers: Wanda and Bob Duncan. **Director:**
Sobey Martin. **Guest Cast:** Carroll O'Connor,
Michael Pate, David Watson.

The time travelers are nearly executed as
spies in the War of 1812.

THE CRACK OF DOOM
Writer: William Welch. **Director:** William
Hale. **Guest Cast:** Torin Thatcher, Vic Lundin,
Ellen McRae, George Matsui.

The travelers encounter nerve-snapping adventure on the volcanic island of Krakatoa.

REVENGE OF THE GODS
Writers: William R. Woodfield, Allan Balter.
Director: Sobey Martin. **Guest Cast:** John
Douchette, Dee Hartford, Abraham Sofaer.

Tony and Doug meet Ulysses and Helen of
Troy in 500 B.C.

MASSACRE
Writer: Carey Wilber. **Director:** Murray
Golden. **Guest Cast:** Christopher Dark, Lawrence Montaigne, Joe Maross.

Tony and Doug are helpless to prevent the
massacre at Custer's Last Stand.

DEVIL'S ISLAND
Writers: Wanda and Bob Duncan. **Director:**
Jerry Hopper. **Guest Cast:** Marcel Hillaire,
Oscar Beregi, Theo Marcuse, Steven Geray.

The time travelers are taken prisoner on
Devil's Island.

REIGN OF TERROR
Writer: William Welch. **Director:** Sobey Martin. **Guest Cast:** David Opatoshu, Louis Mercier, Monique Lemaire, Joey Tata.

Materializing in Paris during the French Revolution, Tony and Doug encounter Marie
Antoinette and a young Napoleon Bonaparte.

SECRET WEAPON
Writer: Theodore Apstein. **Director:** Sobey
Martin. **Guest Cast:** Nehemiah Persoff, Sam
Groom, Michael Ansara, Gregory Gay.

Tony and Doug go back in time to dig up information on a scientist who they suspect is a
spy.

THE DEATH TRAP
Writer: Leonard Stodd. **Director:** William
Hale. **Guest Cast:** Scott Marlowe, R.G. Armstrong, Tom Skerritt.

It's the Civil War, and Tony and Doug get
mixed up in plot to assassinate Lincoln.

THE ALAMO
Writers: Wanda and Bob Duncan. **Director:**
Sobey Martin. **Guest Cast:** Edward Colmans,
John Lupton, Elizabeth Rogers.

March 16, 1836, the day the Alamo fell to
Santa Ana, and our intrepid travelers are there.

THE NIGHT OF THE LONG KNIVES
Writer: William Welch. **Director:** Paul Stanley. **Guest Cast:** David Watson, George Leymas, Dayton Lummis, Ben Wright.

An encounter with Rudyard Kipling teaches
Tony and Doug a few things.

INVASION
Writers: Wanda and Bob Duncan. **Director:**
Jerry Briskin. **Guest Cast:** Lyle Bettger, Robert
Carricart, Michael St. Clair.

It's Cherbourg this time—two days before
D-Day.

The time tunnel.

ROBIN HOOD
Writer: Leonard Stadd. **Director:** William Hale. **Guest Cast:** John Alderson, Erin O'Brien Moore, Ronald Long, Lames Lanphier.

Stock footage from *Prince Valiant* was used in this adventuresome episode.

KILL TWO BY TWO
Writers: Wanda and Bob Duncan. **Director:** Herschel Daugherty. **Guest Cast:** Mako Iwamtsu, Kam Tong, Phillip Ahn, Vince Howard.

A Pacific Island in 1945 holds our travelers, as well as a Japanese soldier determined to kill them.

VISITORS FROM BEYOND THE STARS
Writers: Wanda and Bob Duncan. **Director:** Sobey Martin. **Guest Cast:** Byron Foulger, Tris Coffin, Jan Merlin, John Hoyt.

Mullins, Arizona, in 1885, and aliens with silver skin have landed.

THE GHOST OF NERO
Writer: Leonard Stadd. **Director:** Sobey Martin. **Guest Cast:** Eduardo Ciannelli, Gunnar Hellstrom, John Hoyt.

Sci-fi and the supernatural blend as the ghost of emperor Nero is brought to the time of World War I.

THE WALLS OF JERICHO
Writer: Ellis St. Joseph. **Director:** J. Juran. **Guest Cast:** Michael Pate, Abraham Sofaer, Myrna Fahey, Rhodes Reason.

Tony and Doug are the spies who, according to the Bible, entered the walled city.

IDOL OF DEATH
Writers: Wanda and Bob Duncan. **Director:** Sobey Martin. **Guest Cast:** Rodolfo Hoyos, Lawrence Montaigne, Anthony Caruso, Peter Brocco.

Tony and Doug are nearly killed as spies when they materialize in Mexico at the time of Cortez.

BILLY THE KID
Writer: William Welch. **Director:** J. Juran. **Guest Cast:** Robert Walker, Jr., Allen Case, Pitt Herbert.

Tony is mistaken for the famous gunfighter.

PIRATES OF DEAD MAN'S ISLAND
Writer: Barney Slater. **Director:** Sobey Martin. **Guest Cast:** Regis Toomey, Victor Jory, James Anderson, Charles Bateman.

Tony and Doug are captured by pirates on the Barbary Coast.

CHASE THROUGH TIME
Writer: Carey Wilber. **Director:** Sobey Martin. **Guest Cast:** Robert Duvall, Lew Gallo, Vatina Marcus, Wesley Lau. Joe Ryan.

Tony and Doug travel from 1,000,000 A.D. to 1,000,000 B.C. during the course of this adventure.

THE DEATH MERCHANT
Writers: Wanda and Bob Duncan. **Director:** William Hale. **Guest Cast:** John Crawford, Kevin Hagen, Malachi Throne, Kevin O'Neal.

Tony and Doug find themselves on opposite sides at the Battle of Gettysburg.

ATTACK OF THE BARBARIANS
Writer: Robert Hammer. **Director:** Sobey Martin. **Guest Cast:** John Saxon, Arthur Batanides, Paul Mantee, Vatina Marcus.

The travelers are in a real dilemma—caught between the Mongol hordes and the forces of Kublai Khan.

MERLIN THE MAGICIAN
Writer: William Welch. **Director:** Harry Harris. **Guest Cast:** Christopher Cary, Lias Jak, Jim McMullan, Vincent Beck.

The magician of legend enlists Tony and Doug to help King Arthur rid his country of Vikings.

THE KIDNAPPERS
Writer: William Welch. **Director:** Sobey Martin. **Guest Cast:** Del Monroe, Michael Ansara, Bob May.

A woman colleague is whisked away to 8433 A.D. by a creature named Ott, and Tony and Doug are sent to the rescue.

RAIDERS FROM OUTER SPACE
Writers: Wanda and Bob Duncan. **Director:** J. Juran. **Guest Cast:** John Crawford, Kevin Hagen.

This time it's the battle of Khartoum; in addition, there is a monster from outer space—not to mention Tony and Doug.

TOWN OF TERROR
Writer: Carey Wilber. **Director:** Herschel Daugherty. **Guest Cast:** Mabel Albertson, Kelly Thordsen, Heather Young, Gary Haynes.

Aliens land in New England in 1978 and try to drain the Earth of oxygen.

LAND OF THE GIANTS
1968-1970/51 episodes
ABC/an Irwin Allen Production for 20th Century Fox Television
60 minutes/color

Regular Cast: Gary Conway (Steve Burton); Kurt Kasznar (Alexander Fitzhugh); Don Marshall (Dan Erickson); Heather Young (Betty Hamilton); Don Matheson (Mark Wilson); Deanna Lund (Valerie Scott); Stefan Arngrim (Barry Lockridge).

Executive Producer: Irwin Allen. **Creator:** Irwin Allen. **Director of Photography:** Howard Schwartz. **Special Effects:** L.B. Abbott; Art Cruickshank; Emil Kosa, Jr. **Makeup:** Ben Nye. **Music:** Johnny Williams.

First Season 1968-1969

THE CRASH
Writer: Anthony Wilson. **Director:** Irwin Allen. **Guest Cast:** Anne Dore, Don Watters, Pat Michenaud.

Pilots Steve Burton and Dan Erickson struggle to control their London-bound spaceship after it passes through a mysterious cloud. The passengers and crew discover that they have landed in a world of fantastic proportions: a giant cat, automobile and child provide dangerous encounters.

GHOST TOWN
Writers: Gil Ralston, William Welch, Anthony Wilson. **Director:** Nathan Juran. **Guest Cast:** Percey Helton, Amber Flower, Raymond Guth.

In a miniature "toy" town, a sadistic giant child dumps a bucket of sand on the little people, pours gasoline in their direction and tosses lighted matches at them, then tries to knock them out cold with a special force field.

FRAMED
Writer: Mann Rubin. **Director:** Harry Harris. **Guest Cast:** Paul Carr, Doodles Weaver, Linda Peck, Dennis Cross.

A giant hobo is framed for the murder of a photographer's model, and it's up to the little people to clear him.

UNDERGROUND
Writer: Ellis St. Joseph. **Director:** Sobey Martin. **Guest Cast:** John Abbott, Lance Le Gault, Jerry Catron, Paul Trinka.

A giant underground leader named Gorak enlists the aid of the little people to destroy a dangerous letter.

TERROR-GO-ROUND
Writer: Charles Bennett. **Director:** Sobey Martin. **Guest Cast:** Joseph Ruskin, Arthur Batanides, Gerald Michenaud, Arch Whiting.

A giant gypsy captures the Earthlings and plans to sell them to a circus.

THE FLIGHT PLAN
Writer: Peter Packer. **Director:** Harry Harris. **Guest Cast:** Linden Chiles, William Bramley, Myron Healey, John Pickard.

A giant, shrunk to miniature size, tries to use the space travelers in order to obtain valuable information from Earth.

MANHUNT
Writers: J.E. Selby, Stanley H. Silverman. **Director:** Sobey Martin. **Guest Cast:** John Napier.

The little people risk everything to save a giant convict who's trapped in quicksand... along with their spaceship.

THE TRAP
Writer: Jack Turley. **Director:** Sobey Martin. **Guest Cast:** Morgan Jones, Stewart Bradley.

When Betty and Valerie are captured by giants, the space travelers must sacrifice some of their precious fuel to rescue them.

THE CREED
Writers: Bob and Esther Mitchell. **Director:** Sobey Martin. **Guest Cast:** Paul Fix, Henry Corden, Harry Lauter, Grant Sullivan.

A giant doctor makes a spaceship-call when Barry has appendicitis and, using a magnifying glass, advises Steve on the boy's delicate operation.

DOUBLE-CROSS
Writers: Bob and Esther Mitchell. **Director:** Harry Harris. **Guest Cast:** Willard Sage, Lane Bradford, Howard Culver, Ted Jordan.

Fitzhugh, stricken with amnesia, helps two giants steal a ruby.

THE WEIRD WORLD
Writer: Ellis St. Joseph. **Director:** Harry Harris. **Guest Cast:** Glenn Corbett, Don Gazzaniga.

The space travelers encounter the nearly-mad survivor of an earlier space flight, who has been living in a giant gopher hole for several years.

THE GOLDEN CAGE
Writer: Jack Turley. **Director:** Sobey Martin. **Guest Cast:** Celeste Yarnall, Douglas Bank, Dawson Palmer, Page Slattery.

A Lorelei-like girl, brainwashed by the giants and sent out as bait to capture the Earthlings, nearly tricks Mark into betraying his friends.

THE LOST ONES
Writers: Bob and Esther Mitchell. **Director:** Harry Harris. **Guest Cast:** Tommy Webb, Jack Chaplain, Lee Jay Lambert, Zalman King.

More space-shipwreck victims, this time a group of mistrusting delinquents.

BRAINWASH
Writer: William Welch. **Director:** Harry Harris. **Guest Cast:** Warren Stevens, Leonard Stone, Len Lesser, Robert Dowdell.

A brainwashed Steve interferes with the little people's efforts to destroy a newly-found means of contacting Earth.

THE BOUNTY HUNTER
Writer: Dan Ullman. **Director:** Harry Harris. **Guest Cast:** Kimberly Beck, Paul Sorenson.

A reward is out for the capture of the little people! Before the giant bounty hunters arrive, the Earthlings step up efforts to repair their spaceship and leave.

ON A CLEAR NIGHT YOU CAN SEE EARTH
Writers: Sheldon Stark, Anthony Wilson. **Director:** Sobey Martin. **Guest Cast:** Michael Ansara.

A weird pair of binoculars and a flaky scientist figure prominently in this adventure.

DEADLY LODESTONE
Writer: William L. Stuart. **Director:** Harry Harris. **Guest Cast:** Kevin Hagen, Paul Fix, Bill Fletcher, Robert Emhardt.

The kindly doctor whom we met a few episodes back, is once again called on for help by the little people when a new method of detection is developed by the giants.

THE NIGHT OF THROMBELDINBAR
Writers: Bob and Esther Mitchell. **Director:** Sobey Martin. **Guest Cast:** Teddy Quinn, Michael A. Freeman, Jay Novello, Alfred Ryder.

Two giant orphans mistake Fitzhugh for a magic elf!

SEVEN LITTLE INDIANS
Writers: Bob and Wanda Duncan. **Director:** Harry Harris. **Guest Cast:** Kevin Hagen, Cliff Osmond.

Chipper, Barry's dog, is captured by giants and put on exhibition in a zoo.

TARGET: EARTH
Writer: Arthur Weiss. **Director:** Sobey Martin. **Guest Cast:** Kevin Hagen, Dee Hartford, Arthur Franz, Peter Mamakos.

If Mark can fix their nuclear guidance system, the giants agree to use it to send the little people back to Earth.

GENIUS AT WORK
Writers: Bob and Esther Mitchell. **Director:** Sobey Martin. **Guest Cast:** Ronny Howard, Jacques Aubuchon, Kevin Hagen, Vic Perrin.

Fitzhugh becomes giant-sized after drinking a scientific formula developed by a giant genius.

RETURN OF INIDU
Writers: Bob and Esther Mitchell. **Director:** Sobey Martin. **Guest Cast:** Jack Albertson, Tony Benson, Peter Haskell.

It's up to the Earthlings to prove that a friendly giant magician named Inidu is innocent of murder.

RESCUE
Writers: Bob and Esther Mitchell. **Director:** Harry Harris. **Guest Cast:** Kevin Hagen, Lee Meriwether, Don Collier, Buddy Foster.

The little people help rescue two giant children trapped in an abandoned shaft.

SABOTAGE
Writers: Bob and Esther Mitchell. **Director:** Harry Harris. **Guest Cast:** Robert Colbert, John Marley, Elizabeth Rogers.

The little people become involved in a struggle between a sympathetic giant and one hoping to gain power from their knowledge.

SHELL GAME
Writers: William Welch, Bob and Esther Mitchell. **Director:** Harry Harris. **Guest Cast:** Gary Dubin, Larry Ward, Jan Shepard, Tol Avery.

In exchange for their freedom, the little people must build a hearing aid for a giant deaf boy.

THE CHASE
Writers: Arthur Weiss, William Welch. **Director:** Sobey Martin. **Guest Cast:** Kevin Hagen, Erik Nelson, Timothy Scott.

The little people agree to help Inspector Kobick trap underground freedom workers. After discovering that Kobick planned to capture them, they turn the tables on him and help the rebels escape.

Second Season 1969-1970

THE MECHANICAL MAN
Writer: William L. Stuart. **Director:** Harry Harris. **Guest Cast:** Broderick Crawford, Stuart Margolin, James Daris.

A giant scientist seeks Mark's scientific

knowledge to figure out what's wrong with his super-robot.

SIX HOURS TO LIVE
Writer: Dan Ullman. **Director:** Sobey Martin. **Guest Cast:** George Mitchell, Anne Seymour, Richard Anderson.

The Earthlings endanger themselves to prove a giant innocent of murder.

THE INSIDE RAIL
Writer: Richard Shapiro. **Director:** Harry Harris. **Guest Cast:** Arch Johnson, Ben Blue, Joe Turkel.

Fitzhugh, a race-track fanatic, becomes partners with a giant and tells him which horse to bet on. Fitzhugh wins, but his winnings are too large to carry home.

DEADLY PAWN
Writer: Arthur Weiss. **Director:** Nathan Juran. **Guest Cast:** Alex Dreier, John Zaremba, Charlie Briggs.

Frozen by a polarizer, Fitzhugh, Valerie and Barry become human pawns on a giant's chessboard.

THE UNSUSPECTED
Writers: Bob and Esther Mitchell. **Director:** Harry Harris. **Guest Cast:** Kevin Hagen, Leonard Stone.

After sampling toxic toadstool spores, Steve is turned into a dangerous paranoid. One by one, he captures the rest of the party and tries to turn them over to Inspector Kobick.

GIANTS, AND ALL THAT JAZZ
Writer: Richard Shapiro. **Director:** Harry Harris. **Guest Cast:** Sugar Ray Robinson, William Bramley, Mike Mazurki.

When a down-and-out jazz trumpeter captures Valerie and Barry, Dan makes a deal with him. If he lets his friends go, Dan will instruct him in jazz playing.

COLLECTOR'S ITEM
Writers: Sidney Marshall, Bob and Wanda Duncan. **Director:** Sobey Martin. **Guest Cast:** Guy Stockwell, Robert H. Harris, Susan Howard.

The item in question is Valerie. She is captured by a penniless giant who dresses her in a fancy costume and places her in a music box— all part of an attempt to murder his wealthy uncle.

EVERY BOY NEEDS A DOG
Writer: Jerry Thomas. **Director:** Harry Harris. **Guest Cast:** Michael Anderson, Jr., Oliver McGowan, Bob Shayne.

When Chipper is injured by a giant German shepherd, Barry exposes the entire Earth party to danger by taking his pet to a veterinarian.

CHAMBER OF FEAR
Writer: Arthur Weiss. **Director:** Sobey Martin.

Guest Cast: Cliff Osmond, Christopher Cary, Joan Freeman.

While trying to rescue Fitzhugh, the little people become involved with jewel thieves who operate a wax museum.

THE CLONES
Writers: Oliver Crawford, Bob and Esther Mitchell. **Director:** Nathan Juran. **Guest Cast:** William Schallert, Sandra Giles.

A brilliant scientist experimenting with cloning makes exact duplicates of Valerie and Barry and returns them to the spaceship.

COMEBACK
Writer: Richard Shapiro. **Director:** Harry Harris. **Guest Cast:** John Carradine, Janos Prohaska, Jesse White, Fritz Feld.

The Earthlings meet a kindly but ugly giant who was once a famous star of monster movies, and they try to help him make a comeback.

A PLACE CALLED EARTH
Writer: William Welch. **Director:** Harmon Jones. **Guest Cast:** Warren Stevens, Jerry Douglas, Rex Holman, Jerry Quarry.

Silver-clad Earthlings from the future prove more of a danger than the giants.

LAND OF THE LOST
Writer: William Welch. **Director:** Sobey Martin. **Guest Cast:** Nehemiah Persoff, Clint Ritchie, Peter Canon, Brian Nash.

After four of the little people are accidentally carried away in a giant's balloon, they set down in a new land ruled by a foreign giant despot.

HOME SWEET HOME
Writer: William Welch. **Director:** Harry Harris. **Guest Cast:** William H. Bassett, William Benedict, Robert Alder.

After discovering a space capsule, Steve and Fitzhugh return briefly to Earth but are then forced to return to the giant's planet.

OUR MAN O'REILLY
Writer: Jackson Gillis. **Director:** Sobey Martin. **Guest Cast:** Alan Hale, Alan Bergman, Billy Halop.

The little people receive unexpected help from a superstitious giant who believes they are leprechauns.

NIGHTMARE
Writer: William Welch. **Director:** Nathan Juran. **Guest Cast:** Torin Thatcher, Yale Summers, Kevin Hagen.

Exposed to a dose of radiation from a new power device, the Earthlings suddenly become invisible to the giants.

PAY THE PIPER
Writer: Richard Shapiro. **Director:** Harry Harris. **Guest Cast:** Jonathan Harris, Peter Leeds, Michael James Wixted.

In one of the wackiest episodes of the series,

Dr. Smith from *Lost In Space* appears as a piper who plans to rid the Land of the Giants of its plague of Earthlings.

THE SECRET CITY OF LIMBO
Writers: Bob and Esther Mitchell. **Director:** Sobey Martin. **Guest Cast:** Malachi Throne, Joseph Ruskin, Peter Jason, Whit Bissell.

The shaken space travelers are caught in the middle of a war between giants both beneath and above the ground.

PANIC
Writers: Bob and Wanda Duncan. **Director:** Sobey Martin. **Guest Cast:** Mark Richman, Jack Albertson, Diane McBain, Edward G. Robinson, Jr.

Another chance to return home goes up in smoke as a scientist's marvelous invention—a "teleporter"—explodes after some preliminary testing.

THE DEADLY DART
Writer: William L. Stuart. **Director:** Harry Harris. **Guest Cast:** Christopher Dark, Kent Taylor, Madlyn Rhue, Willard Sage.

Mark is accused of murdering S.I.D. Inspector Swann.

DOOMSDAY
Writer: Dan Ullman. **Director:** Harry Harris. **Guest Cast:** Francine York, Ed Peck, Tom Drake, Kevin Hagen.

Bombs, saboteurs and Inspector Kobick spell danger for the little people.

A SMALL WAR
Writer: Shirl Hendryx. **Director:** Harry Harris. **Guest Cast:** Sean Kelly, Charles Drake, Miriam Schiller.

A giant boy and his army of toy soldiers endanger the space travelers.

THE MARIONETTES
Writer: William Welch. **Director:** Sobey Martin. **Guest Cast:** Frank Ferguson, Bob Hogan, Victoria Vetri, Sandra Giles.

The Earthlings help improve the act of a friendly puppeteer.

WILD JOURNEY
Writer: William Welch. **Director:** Harry Harris. **Guest Cast:** Bruce Dern, Yvonne Craig, Martin Liverman, Erik Nelson.

Using a space-time manipulator, Steve and Dan are given a chance to relive the hours before their ill-fated space flight.

GRAVEYARD OF FOOLS
Writer: Sidney Marshall. **Director:** Sobey Martin. **Guest Cast:** Albert Salmi, John Crawford, Michael Stewart.

Nasty giants send the little people off in toy airplanes that land in the "Graveyard of Fools," a terrifying place filled with giant insects and dinosaur-like creatures.

The regular cast of *Land of the Giants*. TOP TO BOTTOM: Barry Lockridge (Stefan Arngrim); Alexander Fitzhugh (Kurt Kaznar); Valerie Scott (Deanna Lund); Mark Wilson (Don Matheson) and Steve Burton (Gary Conway).

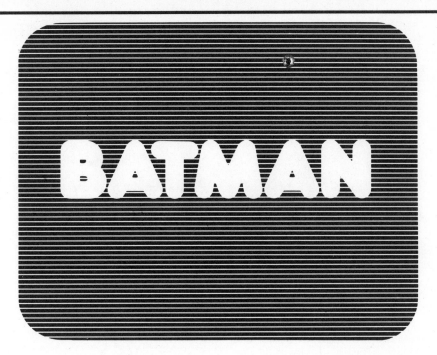

BATMAN

Certainly the show was unique; it was designed to be.
Batman was the only situation comedy on the air without a
laugh track!

—William Dozier
Executive Producer

ABC bought the *Batman* concept without the slightest idea what to do with it," recalls executive producer William Dozier. "Frankly, I had never heard of the Caped Crusader and was taken aback when they asked me to produce a biweekly series. I bought a dozen comic books, read them, and asked myself what do I do with this? Then I hit on the idea of 'camping' it."

"Camp," by popular definition, means something "so extreme as to amuse or have a perversely sophisticated appeal." Both Dozier and Lorenzo Semple, Jr., his story editor, considered the approach a long shot, but after considering the improbability of adapting *Batman* seriously, camp didn't seem like a bad alternative. Ironically, National Periodical Publications (the comic book firm that handles *Batman*) had been planning a straight video version of the character for some time, and *Tarzan* actor

Mike Henry had already donned the familiar blue and gray suit to elicit prepiloting interest. Dozier, however, convinced that camp was the only way to treat *Batman* successfully, persuaded National to abandon its plans and join in the fun.

"It came down to a fundamental reality," Dozier recalls. "We couldn't do a 7:30 show just for kids and justify it to the advertisers. Camp solved that problem. What we had on *Batman* was an exaggerated seriousness that became amusing to adults, and provided high adventure for the youngsters." Underlining this approach, Dozier and Semple, Jr. set out to make *Batman* the squarest hero ever. Borrowing from the old radio serials, each of the shows was planned as a two-part serial, with the first episode ending in a cliff-hanger. Another carry-over from the radio serials was a menacing "voice of doom" which exhorted everyone to tune in for the conclusion "same bat-time, same bat-channel." The voice was Dozier's, who with a kind of campy vanity, did all of the *Batman* narrations. During the episode that completed the bat-adventure, the Caped Crusader and the Boy Wonder would escape from their foul

OPPOSITE: Adam West and Burt Ward as
superheroes Batman and Robin.
BELOW: Speeding to the scene of a crime
in the batmobile.

The *batusi* became the dance craze of the nation after being introduced by Batman and Molly (Jill St. John) in the premiere episode. The show's musical theme also soared to the top of the charts within weeks.

attempt to brainwash the kiddies into becoming good citizens: "It can't miss," chortled one ABC executive. But the network still had some doubts; after all, camp was still an untried gimmick on television.

Ready or not, *Batman* debuted in mid-season of 1966. The show had been hyped to the hilt, and ABC even went so far as to stage a lavish premier in a theater in Manhattan at the same hour that the series was bowing on the air. The screening was followed by a cocktail party at a discotheque where bat-cowled Batgirls served popcorn and champagne to such luminaries as Roddy McDowell, Tammy Grimes and Andy Warhol. Unlike the rest of the nation, those who had attended the premier were treated to both parts of the first bat-adventure. According to one observer, everyone "laughed it up at every well-oiled cliche." But how would middle America respond to Dozier's gamble? Network executives bit their nails and prayed.

"Hi Diddle Riddle" and its followup, "Smack in the Middle," introduced *Batman* to his public. Written by Lorenzo Semple, Jr., they were lively and well-scripted comedies. In the guest roles, actor-impressionist Frank Gorshin played a neurotic villain called the Riddler, and Jill St. John was appropriately inviting as his henchwoman, Molly. Like most pilots, the production values were higher than in later entries. A small fortune was spent on sets and props, including a giant papier-mache elephant large enough to hold the two crime fighters in the final sequence. Floors, walls and secret passageways were blown up magnificently by L.B. Abbott's special effects team. There were, of course, some utterly absurd moments. We are expected to accept that the very shapely Molly would pass

predicament, clobber their nemeses in a splendidly choreographed fight sequence and set the world right once again.

A last-minute brainstorm that earned Dozier a special commendation from the National Safety Council was a shot of the heroes buckling up for safety in the Batmobile. First low-brow comedy, then high adventure and finally an

Frank Gorshin's manic portrayal of The Riddler set the standard for a long line of kinky supervillains.

for the Boy Wonder simply by putting on his life mask. Even more outrageous, the Caped Crusader casually strolls through a swinging discotheque, tells the *maitre d'*, "I shouldn't want to attract attention," then stolidly orders a glass of orange juice at the bar. Before long, Batman and his treacherous companion, the seductive Molly, are tearing around the dance floor. "You swing a pretty mean cape," compliments Molly. "It's nothing," replies Batman. This observation hardly seemed prophetic, but a few weeks later, the *batusi* was sweeping the nation.

The series was an overnight smash, completely burying the competition and convincing the network that camp was far from the disaster word they had feared so. The second week's doubleheader starred Burgess Meredith as the pointy-nosed Penguin, "that pompous, waddling perpetrator of foul play." As with the premier offering, audience ratings went through the roof.

"Part of our early success was largely due to surprise," admits Dozier's assistant Charles FitzSimons. "We were different. Ours was the only series built around the villain, not the hero." Among the colorful nogoodniks were the nefarious "clown prince of crime," the Joker, played by Cesar Romero, and the cold-blooded Mr. Freeze, played first by George Sanders and later by Otto Preminger and Eli Wallach. Julie Newmar was the deadly Catwoman, an alluring yet ingenuous female felon. Later, Eartha Kitt would reinterpret the role.

As the show became a nationwide fad, it was rumored that James Mason, Raymond Massey, Gloria Swanson and Bette Davis, among others, wrote to Dozier asking for the chance to be mean to Batman. Stars who in fact did have

Tallulah Bankhead was a natural guest villain as "The Black Widow." A friend had urged her to make this rare TV appearance, saying it would be a camp. The irrepressible Tallulah retorted, "Don't tell *me* about camp, dahling. I *invented* it!"

The Dynamic Duo's numerous nemeses included (left to right, top row): Anne Baxter (Zelda); John Astin (Riddler); Eartha Kitt (Catwoman); David Wayne (Mad Hatter); Roddy McDowell (Bookworm); (left to right,

the opportunity to menace the Caped Crusader include: Anne Baxter, David Wayne, Victor Buono, Art Carney, Barbara Nichols, Shelley Winters, Walter Slezak, Vincent Price, Edward Everett Horton, Liberace, Michael Rennie, Carolyn Jones, Estelle Winwood, Cliff Robertson, Maurice Evans, Talullah Bankhead, George Raft, Ethel Merman, Milton Berle, Rudy Vallee, Glynis Johns, Pierre Salinger, Barbara Rush, Monique Van Vooren, Ida Lupino, Howard Duff, Dina Merrill, Henny Youngman and Zsa Zsa Gabor. Veteran makeup artist Ben Nye had his hands full applying all the bushy eyebrows, strange noses and fright wigs that transformed a handsome army of actors into the most outrageous band of bad guys ever tailored for TV.

Although Dozier insisted on stellar names for his villains, his choice of a little-known actor named Adam West to play the title role was baffling to many. While West's voice and manner were square enough, his physique was

Cesar Romero (Joker), Julie Newmar (Catwoman), Frank Gorshin (Riddler), and Burgess Meredith (Penguin).

Adam West declared he didn't have one ounce of flab...

(bottom row) Cliff Robertson and Dina Merrill (Shame and Calamity Jan); Van Johnson (Minstrel); Art Carney (Archer); Vincent Price (Egghead); and Ethel Merman (Lola Lasagne).

...far from that of the well-muscled hero of the comics. As a result, West became the butt of many editorial jokes. Newsweek called him a "flabby travesty of muscle beach," to which West replied:

Please accept my thanks for your kind words about *Batman* and my pained look of personal injury for your less-than-kind words about my physical condition. After reading your story I raced instantly to my friendly neighborhood physician who assured me that I have not an ounce of "flab" and offered to provide a notarized statement to that effect. Granted, I am not Superman. But neither is Batman. Other than that, regards and thanks.

Dozier was much closer to the mark in his casting of Burt Ward as Robin. Ward stood five feet eight and held a brown belt in karate, making him something of a real-life Boy Wonder.

...Burt Ward was more suited to his role.

Whenever there was trouble in Gotham, Commissioner Gordon and Chief O'Hara contacted Bruce Wayne and Dick Grayson via the batphone. Within moments the heroes were in the batcave, caped, cowled and ready to go.

Unlike the leads, the remaining regulars were all seasoned pros whom Dozier considered "naturals" for the project: grim, deadpan Neil Hamilton as Batman's boss, Commissioner Gordon; Stafford Repp, with his excitable Irish brogue, played Chief O'Hara; Madge Blake was a perfect doting Aunt Harriet; and gaunt, gentlemanly Alan Napier was Wayne's loyal butler, Alfred.

As the bat craze grew, it spread out beyond the homescreen and entered the homes of America via every form of product merchandising imaginable. Special live appearances were arranged. In New York City, seven thousand children poured into Central Park to meet Batman, while another three thousand tots made it to Shea Stadium. That first year, the president of the FCC arrived at the annual convention in a bat suit! Possibly the most outrageous incident was the Soviet attack on America's caped hero in the Russian newspaper *Pravda*; that paper said of Batman:

He is nothing more than a glorified FBI agent, a capitalist murderer who kills his enemies beautifully, effectively and with taste, so that shoulder blades crack loudly and scalps break like cantaloupes.

To this Dozier replied:

Pravda, as usual, is a little mixed up. Batman doesn't kill anyone. He socks them—BIFF! POW! BAM!—but they always come back. The underlying theme of *Batman* is good triumphing over evil. Pravda seems to have trouble understanding this or the humor of *Batman*.

Despite the positive reactions and the cults, there were those, though few in number at first, who found Dozier's Bat series appalling. "Every ZONK is calculated," cried one dissenter. "They are making fun of Batman instead of making him come off in his own terms." Fans of the comic book hero were especially horrified. But, even the most conservative *aficionado* was forced to admire the elaborate bat paraphernalia created by the Twentieth Century Fox prop masters and designers. Recreating the proper comic book atmosphere was of prime importance to Dozier. Comments cameraman Howard Schwartz:

To us who worked on it the approach was highly specialized "comic strip." We tried to use color in an exciting way...and for that reason we used a great deal of colored light on the sets. For example, we did one episode with the Catwoman and, since we felt that

amber was a "cat color," we played everything in her office and lair in ambers. We went to greens for the Riddler, because he wore a green outfit, and on the Penguin we used purple.

Color wasn't the only visual trick employed by Schwartz and his fellow cinematographers Ralph Woolsey and Jack Marta. Tilted angles were used exclusively for an evil warped effect in the lairs of the villains. Most clever of all were the animated comic-book titles—ZAP! POW! BAM!—which were synched with the appropriate fisticuffs and superimposed on the fight scenes.

Part of Dozier's plan was to construct a simple formula for the show that would rarely veer from expectations. Lorenzo Semple, Jr. was the man responsible for setting the bat-style of the plots, and all writers employed by the show were encouraged to follow it. Whenever some oddly attired scoundrel begins to cause trouble in Gotham City, Police Commissioner Gordon and Chief O'Hara race to their red phone and call Batman. "I don't know who he is behind that mask of his," Gordon would invariably intone, "but, I know we need him, and we need him now!" Meanwhile, at Wayne Manor, the beeping Batphone alerts the millionaire playboy's loyal butler Alfred, who picks up the phone and takes a message. After coyly delivering the message in front of Wayne's unsuspecting Aunt Harriet, Wayne and his ward Dick Grayson disappear down the hidden

batpoles to emerge seconds later as the famed crime fighters Batman and Robin. They jump into their Batmobile and blast through the camouflaged Batcave exit and speed to Gotham City.

Though the antics of the villains vary, the Caped Crusader's *modus operandi* is always the same. Improbable clues lead the dynamic duo into the clutches of their dastardly adversaries, thus ending the first episode. Content with simple perils at first, Dozier and Semple later began to develop more absurd variations of fates worse than death. Force-feeding Bruce Wayne into a furnace wasn't inventive enough, but having the caped crusaders frozen into human frosty freezies was. One particularly bizarre cliff-hanger was dreamed up for a show where Van Johnson played a singing villain called The Minstrel. We leave our intrepid heroes frying, like a pair of plucked chickens, on an outsized radiant grill.

"Holy Inferno, Batman!" cries Robin. "Is this...the end?"

"If it is," Batman replies through the steam, "let us not lose...our dignity."

The first season and a half came and went quickly. By 1967, with a feature film and a fad behind it, Batmania was showing signs of age. The honeymoon was over for Dozier and company. As suddenly as interest had flared, it faded. Searching for a new angle to reactivate interest in the now-foundering series, Dozier and producer Howie Horwitz thought of adding a female crime fighter to the Bat-family. ABC, dissatisfied with the declining ratings, agreed to give the idea a chance.

Former Miss America Mary Ann Mobley was originally signed to play Batgirl—Commissioner Gordon's daughter. Last-minute studio decisions placed Mobley in the *Custer* series and Horwitz recruited Yvonne Craig, a ballerina turned actress who had appeared in his earlier *77 Sunset Strip* series, to play the part. In her form-fitting purple outfit with cowl and gold-lined cape, Craig was a knockout. A short sequence of Batgirl in action was quickly filmed and the network signed the series for another season on the strength of Craig's performance.

Horwitz, determined to maintain Batgirl's femininity during the fight sequences, avoided Emma Peel-like strongarming. Batgirl never punched out a male opponent, nor did she use judo or karate. "The Batgirl costume gave me a powerful feeling, like I ruled the world," remarked Craig, "but I was strictly feminine. In place of karate chops I used ballet techniques like high kicks and spins." Just as Batgirl is never unladylike in her assaults, any attacks on her are equally dainty. Subjected to fear, laughing and crying gasses, transformed into a slab of cardboard, or tied into a knot by a succession of fiends, the worst punishment Batgirl ever receives is a few bumps on the head. She emerges from all dangers unscathed, sound in wind and limb, and as delectable as ever.

But Batgirl proved to be only a temporary reprieve. At renewal time, the show again faced cancellation, and for lack of any new tricks up his or his producer's sleeve, Dozier threw in the cowl. Though he had fooled the Riddler, outfoxed Catwoman, penned the Penguin and turned the heat on Mr. Freeze, there was one fiend the Caped Crusader could not measure up to—the Rater, played by A.C. Nielsen. The cancellation notice came in February, 1968. SPLAT!

Yvonne Craig as Batgirl added higher excitement but not higher ratings.

INDEX OF EPISODES

BATMAN

1966-1968/120 episodes
ABC/a Greenway Production for 20th Century-Fox Television
30 minutes/color

Regular Cast: Adam West (Batman/Bruce Wayne); Burt Ward (Robin/Dick Grayson); Neil Hamilton (Police Commissioner Gordon); Stafford Repp (Chief O'Hara); Alan Napier (Alfred); Madge Blake (Aunt Harriet Cooper); Yvonne Craig (Batgirl/Barbara Gordon—third season).

Executive Producer: William Dozier. **Producer:** Howie Horwitz. **Story Consultant:** Lorenzo Semple, Jr. **Director of Photography:** Howard Schwartz. **Makeup:** Ben Nye. **Music:** Neal Hefti (theme); Nelson Riddle.

First Season: 1966

HI DIDDLE RIDDLE
SMACK IN THE RIDDLE
Writer: Lorenzo Semple, Jr. **Director:** Robert Butler. **Guest Cast:** Frank Gorshin (Riddler), Jill St. John, Allen Jaffe, Michael Fox.

Batman and Robin head to Gotham City to renew their battle against the Riddler. The Dynamic Duo finally thwart their foe by hiding in a gigantic papier-mache mammoth and surprising him, trojan-horse-style.

FINE FEATHERED FINKS
PENGUIN'S A JINX
Writer: Lorenzo Semple, Jr. **Director:** Robert Butler. **Guest Cast:** Burgess Meredith (Penguin), Leslie Parrish, Walter Burke.

The Penguin captures Bruce Wayne and tries to force-feed him into a furnace.

THE JOKER IS WILD
BATMAN GETS RILED
Writer: Robert Dozier. **Director:** Don Weiss. **Guest Cast:** Cesar Romero (Joker), Nancy Kovack, Jonathan Hole.

After escaping from prison, the Joker starts the greatest crime wave in Gotham's history, captures the Dynamic Duo and threatens to reveal their secret identities.

INSTANT FREEZE
RATS LIKE CHEESE
Writer: Max Hodge. **Director:** Robert Butler. **Guest Cast:** George Sanders (Mr. Freeze), Shelby Grant, Troy Metton.

Mr. Freeze, a villain who can live in only the coldest temperatures, turns the Dynamic Duo into icy zombies.

ZELDA THE GREAT
A DEATH WORSE THAN FATE
Writer: Lorenzo Semple, Jr. **Director:** Robert Butler. **Guest Cast:** Anne Baxter (Zelda), Jack Kruschen, Barbara Heller.

A female magician kidnaps Aunt Harriet, then locks Batman and Robin in an "inescapable doom trap."

A RIDDLE A DAY
KEEPS THE RIDDLER AWAY
WHEN THE RAT'S AWAY,
THE MICE WILL PLAY
Writer: Fred De Gorter. **Director:** Tom Gries. **Guest Cast:** Frank Gorshin (Riddler), Susan Silo, Tim Herbert.

The Riddler presents a visiting king with an exploding bouquet of roses and threatens to destroy the Dynamic Duo by shackling them to huge, spinning wheels.

THE THIRTEENTH HAT
BATMAN STANDS PAT
Writer: Charles Hoffman. **Director:** Norman Foster. **Guest Cast:** David Wayne (Mad Hatter), Richard La Starza, Sandra Wells, Diane McBain.

The Mad Hatter kidnaps the twelve jurors who put him away and makes plans to steal Batman's cowl.

THE JOKER GOES TO SCHOOL
HE MEETS HIS MATCH,
THE GRISLY GHOUL
Writer: Lorenzo Semple, Jr. **Director:** Murray Golden. **Guest Cast:** Cesar Romero (Joker).

The Joker sabotages the vending machines in Gotham High School and tries to electrocute the Dynamic Duo.

TRUE OR FALSE FACE
SUPER RAT RACE
Writer: Stephen Kandel. **Director:** William A. Graham. **Guest Cast:** Malachi Throne (False Face), Myrna Fahey, Billy Curtis.

False Face, a master of disguise, ties Batman and Robin to the subway tracks.

THE PURR-FECT CRIME
BETTER LUCK NEXT TIME
Writers: Stanley Ralph Ross, Lee Orgel. **Director:** James Sheldon. **Guest Cast:** Julie Newmar (Catwoman), Jock Mahoney, Ralph Manza.

Catwoman plans to give Robin a severe case of "cat-nip" by throwing him into a lion's pit.

THE PENGUIN GOES STRAIGHT
NOT YET, HE AIN'T
Writers: Lorenzo Semple, Jr., John Cardwell. **Director:** Les Martison. **Guest Cast:** Burgess Meredith (Penguin), Kathleen Crowley, Harvey Lembeck.

The Penguin joins the fight against crime, but resorts to his old methods by stringing up the Dynamic Duo behind a shooting gallery.

RING OF WAX
GIVE 'EM THE AX
Writers: Jack Paritz, Bob Rodgers. **Director:** James B. Clark. **Guest Cast:** Frank Gorshin (Riddler), Linda Scott, Michael Green.

Tied above a vat of bubbling wax, Batman and Robin are at their wick's end as the Riddler and henchgirl Moth watch gleefully.

JOKER TRUMPS AN ACE
BATMAN SETS THE PACE
Writers: Francis and Marian Cockrell. **Director:** Richard C. Sarafian. **Guest Cast:** Cesar Romero (Joker), Jane Wald, Dan Seymour, To Avery.

Joker traps the Dynamic Duo in a huge chimney and fills it with poison gas.

THE CURSE OF TUT
THE PHARAOH'S IN A RUT
Writers: Robert C. Dennis, Earl Barret. **Director:** Charles R. Rondeau. **Guest Cast:** Victor Buono (King Tut), Ziva Rodann, Don Barry.

After being struck in the head, a college professor fancies himself the reincarnation of an ancient Egyptian king.

THE BOOKWORM TURNS
WHILE GOTHAM CITY BURNS
Writer: Rik Vollaerts. **Director:** Larry Peerce. **Guest Cast:** Roddy McDowall (Bookworm), Francine York, Byron Keith.

The Bookworm fastens Robin to a huge bell, then plans to ring his neck.

DEATH IN SLOW MOTION
THE RIDDLER'S FALSE NOTION
Writer: Dick Carr. **Director:** Charles R. Rondeau. **Guest Cast:** Frank Gorshin (Riddler), Sherry Jackson, Francis X. Bushman, Thec Marcuse.

The Riddler decides to remake old silent movies—with Batman and Robin as his unwitting stars.

FINE FINNY FIENDS
BATMAN MAKES THE SCENE
Writer: Sheldon Stewart. **Director:** Tom Gries. **Guest Cast:** Burgess Meredith (Penguin), Juli Gregg, Victor Lundin.

Penguin draws the air from a room where Batman and Robin are imprisoned.

Second Season: 1966-1967

SHOOT A CROOKED ARROW
WALK THE STRAIGHT AND NARROW
Writer: Stanley Ralph Ross. **Director:** Sherman Marks. **Guest Cast:** Art Carney (Archer), Barbara Nichols, Doodles Weaver.

A villain called the Archer draws a bead on Batman and Robin, tying them to targets and charging with a lance.

HOT OFF THE GRIDDLE
THE CAT AND THE FIDDLE
Writer: Stanley Ralph Ross. **Director:** Don Weiss. **Guest Cast:** Julie Newmar (Catwoman), Jack Kelly.

Intense heat threatens to destroy Batman, and Robin as Catwoman plans to make off with two priceless violins.

THE MINSTREL'S SHAKEDOWN
BARBECUED BATMAN
Writers: Francis and Marion Cockrell. **Director:** Murray Golden. **Guest Cast:** Van Johnson (Minstrel), Leslie Perkins.

A singing villain known as the Minstrel threatens to level the Gotham City Stock Exchange, then binds the Dynamic Duo to an outsized radiant grill.

THE SPELL OF TUT
TUT'S CASE IS SHUT
Writers: R.C. Dennis, Earl Bennet. **Director:** Larry Peerce. **Guest Cast:** Victor Buono (King Tut), Marianna Hill, Peter Mamakos.

Tut traps Robin in an alligator pit; Commissioner Gordon's new secretary is actually Tut's henchgirl.

THE GREATEST MOTHER OF THEM ALL:
MA PARKER
Writer: Henry Slesar. **Director:** Oscar Rudolph. **Guest Cast:** Shelley Winters (Ma Parker), Tisha Sterling.

Ma Parker and her criminal brood invade Gotham Prison and strap the Dynamic Duo into electric chairs.

THE CLOCK KING'S CRAZY CRIMES
THE CLOCK KING GETS CROWNED
Writers: Bill Finger, Charles Sinclair. **Director:** James Neilson. **Guest Cast:** Walter Slezak (Clock King), Linda Lorimer, Roger Bacon.

The Clock King, a villain specializing in prime-time crimes, traps the Dynamic Duo in a huge hourglass where the sands of time threaten to bury them.

AN EGG GROWS IN GOTHAM
THE YEGG FOES IN GOTHAM
Writer: Stanley Ralph Ross. **Director:** George Waggner. **Guest Cast:** Vincent Price (Egghead), Edward Everett Horton, Ben Weldon.

Criminal genius Egghead kidnaps Gotham's millionaires and subjects them to a brain-drain to determine which one is actually Batman.

THE DEVIL'S FINGERS
DEAD RINGERS
Writer: Lorenzo Semple, Jr. **Director:** Larry Peerce. **Guest Cast:** Liberace (Chandell/Harry), Edy Williams, Marilyn Hanold.

The evil pianist Chandell woos Aunt Harriet while his twin brother Harry attempts to perforate the Dynamic Duo into rolls of music for a player piano.

HIZZONER THE PENGUIN
DIZZONER THE PENGUIN
Writer: Stanford Sherman. **Director:** Oscar Rudolph. **Guest Cast:** Burgess Meredith (Penguin), Byron Keith, George Furth, Judy Parker, Joe Besser, Don Wilson, Little Egypt, Paul Revere and the Raiders, Allen Ludden.

The Penguin conducts a foul campaign for the office of Mayor, with Batman as his opponent.

GREEN ICE
DEEP FREEZE
Writer: Max Hodge. **Director:** George Waggner. **Guest Cast:** Otto Preminger (Mr. Freeze), Dee Hartford, Nicky Blair.

Mr. Freeze tries to turn the caped crusaders into human frosty freezies.

THE IMPRACTICAL JOKERS
THE JOKER'S PROVOKERS
Writer: Jay Thompson. **Director:** James B. Clark. **Guest Cast:** Cesar Romero (Joker), Kathy Kersh, Luis Quinn.

A time device developed by the Joker enables him to commit crimes. During the course of this adventure, the Boy Wonder is nearly spray-waxed to death and Batman is imperiled by a giant key duplicator.

MARSHA, QUEEN OF DIAMONDS
MARSHA'S SCHEME
WITH DIAMONDS
Writer: Stanford Sherman. **Director:** James B. Clark. **Guest Cast:** Carolyn Jones (Marsha), Estelle Winwood, Woody Strode.

In order to get her criminal hands on the Batjewels, villainess Marsha decides to marry Batman.

COME BACK SHAME
IT'S THE WAY YOU PLAY THE GAME
Writer: Stanley Ralph Ross. **Director:** Oscar Rudolph. **Guest Cast:** Cliff Robertson (Shame).

A car-rustling villain named Shame imperils Batman and Robin with a cattle stampede.

THE PENGUIN'S NEST
THE BIRD'S LAST JEST
Writer: Lorenzo Semple, Jr. **Director:** Murray Golden. **Guest Cast:** Burgess Meredith (Penguin), Grace Gaynor, Vito Scotti.

The Penguin makes arrangements to be put into jail so that he and a master forger can join forces.

THE CAT'S MEOW
THE BAT'S KOW TOW
Writer: Stanley Ralph Ross. **Director:** James B. Clark. **Guest Cast:** Julie Newmar (Catwoman), Chad Stuart, Jeremy Clyde, Chuck Henderson, Sharyn Wynters, Judy Stragis.

Catwoman steals the singing voices of Chad & Jeremy and demands a ransom.

Commissioner Gordon, Chief O'Hara and the Dynamic Duo commiserate.

PUZZLES ARE COMING
THE DUO IS SLUMMING
Writer: Fred De Gorter. **Director:** Jeff Hayden.
Guest Cast: Maurice Evans (Puzzler), Barbara Stuart, Paul Smith.

The Puzzler traps Batman and Robin in an aerial balloon.

THE SANDMAN COMETH
THE CATWOMAN GOETH
Writers: Ellis St. Joseph, Charles Hoffman.
Director: George Waggner. **Guest Cast:** Julie Newmar (Catwoman), Michael Rennie (Sandman), Spring Byington, Don Ho, Gypsy Rose Lee.

The Sandman, a European criminal visiting Gotham City, places Robin in his power and orders the Boy Wonder to kill Batman. Later, Sandman joins forces with the Catwoman.

THE CONTAMINATED COWL
MAD HATTER RUNS AFOUL
Writer: Charles Hoffman. **Director:** Oscar Rudolph. **Guest Cast:** David Wayne (Mad Hatter), Jean Hale, Barbara Morrison.

Mad Hatter traps Batman and Robin in a fluoroscope cabinet where X-rays threaten to radiate them to death.

ZODIAC CRIMES
JOKER'S HARDTIMES
PENGUIN DECLINES
Writers: Stanford Sherman, Steve Kandal.
Director: Oscar Rudolph. **Guest Cast:** Cesar Romero (Joker), Burgess Meredith (Penguin).

The Joker joins forces with the Penguin in a marathon scheme to humiliate Batman. Among the perils are a falling meteorite and a man-eating clam.

BATMAN'S ANNIVERSARY
A RIDDLING CONTROVERSY
Writer: W.P. D'Angelo. **Director:** James Clark.
Guest Cast: John Astin (Riddler), Deanna Lund, Ken Scott.

On Batman's anniversary with the police force, the Riddler prepares a gigantic cake...with quicksand frosting!

PENGUIN IS A GIRL'S BEST FRIEND
THE PENGUIN SETS A TREND
THE PENGUIN'S DISASTROUS END
Writer: Stanford Sherman. **Director:** James Clark. **Guest Cast:** Burgess Meredith (Penguin), Carolyn Jones (Marsha), Bob Hastings, Alan Reed, Estelle Winwood.

The Penguin and Marsha, Queen of Diamonds, team up to make a movie in this three-part bat drama.

THAT DARN CATWOMAN
SCAT, CATWOMAN
Writer: Stanley Ralph Ross. **Director:** Oscar Rudolph. **Guest Cast:** Julie Newmar (Catwoman), Leslie Gore, J. Pat O'Mally.

With a hypnotic drug, Catwoman turns Robin into a criminal and orders him to murder Batman.

THE JOKER'S LAST LAUGH
THE JOKER'S EPITAPH
Writer: Lorenzo Semple, Jr. **Director:** Oscar Rudolph. **Guest Cast:** Cesar Romero (Joker), Phyllis Douglas.

In the wake of Joker's latest plunder, the Boy Wonder is nearly pressed into a comic book and Bruce Wayne becomes engaged to the Clown Prince of Crime's henchgirl.

CATWOMAN GOES TO COLLEGE
BATMAN DISPLAYS HIS KNOWLEDGE
Writer: Stanley Ralph Ross. **Director:** Robert Sparr. **Guest Cast:** Julie Newmar (Catwoman), Jacques Bergerac, Paul Mantee, Art Linkletter.

Catwoman enrolls at college and takes a course in criminology, then traps the Dynamic Duo in a huge coffee cup beneath an equally gigantic percolator filled with acid.

A PIECE OF THE ACTION
BATMAN'S SATISFACTION
Writer: Charles Hoffman. **Director:** Oscar Rudolph. **Guest Cast:** Van Williams (Green Hornet), Bruce Lee, Roger C. Carmel (Colonel Gumm), Diane McBain.

Crimefighters Green Hornet and Kato join Batman and Robin in their battle against a sticky adversary named Colonel Gumm, who nearly turns them all into human postage stamps.

KING TUT'S COUP
BATMAN'S WATERLOO
Writer: Stanley Ralph Ross. **Director:** James Clark. **Guest Cast:** Victor Buono (King Tut), Lee Meriwether, Grace Lee Whitney, Lloyd Haynes.

Trapped inside an Egyptian casket, Batman is

lowered into a pool of boiling oil by the villainous King Tut.

BLACK WIDOW STRIKES AGAIN
CAUGHT IN THE SPIDER'S DEN

Writer: Robert Mintz. **Director:** Oscar Rudolph. **Guest Cast:** Talullah Bankhead (Black Widow), George Raft, Donald Barry.

Batman joins the Black Widow's gang.

POP GOES THE JOKER
FLOP GOES THE JOKER

Writer: Stanford Sherman. **Director:** George Waggner. **Guest Cast:** Cesar Romero (Joker), Diana Ivarson, Reginald Gardiner.

In this parody on the world of pop art, the Joker's colorful assaults on famous paintings are hailed as artistic triumphs.

ICE SPY
THE DUO DEFY

Writer: Charles Hoffman. **Director:** Oscar Rudolph. **Guest Cast:** Eli Wallach (Mr. Freeze), Leslie Parrish, Elisha Cook.

The cold-blooded Mr. Freeze plans to vaporize the Dynamic Duo into oblivion.

Third Season: 1967–1968

ENTER BATGIRL, EXIT PENGUIN

Writer: Stanford Sherman. **Director:** Oscar Rudolph. **Guest Cast:** Burgess Meredith (Penguin), Elizabeth Harrower.

The Penguin kidnaps Batgirl and plans to make her his bride.

RING AROUND THE RIDDLER

Writer: Charles Hoffman. **Director:** Sam Strangis. **Guest Cast:** Frank Gorshin (Riddler), Joan Collins, Peggy Ann Garner, James Brolin.

The Riddler challenges Batman to a boxing match in Gotham Square Garden.

THE WAIL OF THE SIREN

Writer: Stanley Ralph Ross. **Director:** George Waggner. **Guest Cast:** Joan Collins (Siren), Mike Mazurki.

Lorelei Circe, alias the Siren, hypnotizes Police Commissioner Gordon with her seven-octave wail and orders him to find out Batman's true identity.

THE SPORT OF PENGUINS
HORSE OF ANOTHER COLOR

Writer: Charles Hoffman. **Director:** Sam Strangis. **Guest Cast:** Burgess Meredith (Penguin), Ethel Merman.

Penguin and Lola Lasagne switch horses and enter the Bruce Wayne handicap, but not before another entry makes the scene—Batgirl.

THE UNKINDEST TUT OF ALL

Writer: Stanley Ralph Ross. **Director:** Sam Strangis. **Guest Cast:** Victor Buono (King Tut), Patti Gilbert.

King Tut challenges Bruce Wayne and Batman to appear in public at the same time.

LOUIE THE LILAC

Writer: Dwight Taylor. **Director:** Sam Strangis. **Guest Cast:** Milton Berle (Louie), Lisa Seagram.

Gotham's flower children are under the power of Louie the Lilac, who tries to feed the Caped Crusaders to his carniverous plant.

THE OGG AND I
HOW TO HATCH A DINOSAUR

Writer: Stanford Sherman. **Director:** Oscar Rudolph. **Guest Cast:** Vincent Price (Egghead), Anne Baxter, Alfred Dennis.

After kidnapping Commissioner Gordon, Egghead and Olga assault the Terrific Trio with crying gas. Then they plan to hatch a million-year-old dinosaur egg and control Gotham City with their pet.

SURF'S UP! JOKER'S UNDER!

Writer: Charles Hoffman. **Director:** Oscar Rudolph. **Guest Cast:** Cesar Romero (Joker), Skip Ward, Sivi Aberg.

Batman hangs ten to keep the Joker from winning a surfing contest.

THE LONDINIUM LARCENIES
THE FOGGIEST NOTION
THE BLOODY TOWER

Writers: Elkan Allan, Charles Hoffman. **Director:** Oscar Rudolph. **Guest Cast:** Rudy Vallee (Lord Phogg), Glynis Johns (Lady Penelope Peasoup), Lyn Peters.

Batman, Robin and Batgirl travel to Londinium to prevent Lord Phogg and Lady Penelope Peasoup from making off with the crown jewels in this three-part show.

THE OGG COUPLE

Writer: Stanford Sherman. **Director:** Oscar Rudolph. **Guest Cast:** Vincent Price (Egghead), Anne Baxter, Violet Carlson.

Egghead and Olga, Queen of the Cossacks, try to drown Batgirl in a vat of caviar.

CATWOMAN'S DRESSED TO KILL

Writer: Stanley Ralph Ross. **Director:** Sam Strangis. **Guest Cast:** Eartha Kitt (Catwoman), James Griffith, Rudi Gernreich.

Catwoman captures Batgirl, straps her to a pattern cutting machine and threatens to bisect her if Batman interferes with her latest crime.

FUNNY FELINE FELONIES
THE JOKE'S ON CATWOMAN

Writer: Stanley Ralph Ross. **Director:** Oscar Rudolph. **Guest Cast:** Eartha Kitt (Catwoman), Cesar Romero (Joker), Pierre Salinger.

After serving a prison term, Joker teams with Catwoman for a series of thefts. Captured by the Terrific Trio, Catwoman hires famed criminal lawyer "Lucky Pierre" to defend her and her cowardly cohorts.

LOUIE'S LETHAL LILAC TIME

Writer: Charles Hoffman. **Director:** Sam Strangis. **Guest Cast:** Milton Berle (Louie), Ronald Knight.

After kidnapping Bruce Wayne and Dick Grayson, Louie the Lilac hypnotizes Batgirl.

NORA CLAVICLE AND HER LADIES' CRIME CLUB

Writer: Stanford Sherman. **Director:** Oscar Rudolph. **Guest Cast:** Barbara Rush (Nora), June Wilkinson, Inga Neilson.

A mini-skirted policewoman replaces Commissioner Gordon. Batman, Robin and Batgirl are tied into a human knot by Nora Clavicle and her female gang.

PENGUIN'S CLEAN SWEEP

Writer: Stanford Sherman. **Director:** Oscar Rudolph. **Guest Cast:** Burgess Meredith (Penguin), Monique Van Vooren.

Penguin breaks into the treasury and contaminates Gotham City's money.

I'LL BE A MUMMY'S UNCLE

Writer: Stanley Ralph Ross. **Director:** Sam Strangis. **Guest Cast:** Victor Buono (King Tut), Angela Dorian, Henny Youngman.

King Tut accidentally breaks into the Batcave and discovers Batman's true identity.

JOKER'S FLYING SAUCER

Writer: Charles Hoffman. **Director:** Sam Strangis. **Guest Cast:** Cesar Romero (Joker), Corinne Calvert.

A flying saucer and little green men, courtesy of the Joker, throw Gotham City into a panic.

THE ENTRANCING DR. CASSANDRA

Writer: Stanley Ralph Ross. **Director:** Sam Strangis. **Guest Cast:** Ida Lupino (Cassandra), Howard Duff, David Lewis.

An alchemist and her daffy mate transform the Terrific Trio into cardboard slabs, then free all of Gotham City's criminals and render them invisible.

THE GREAT ESCAPE
THE GREAT TRAIN ROBBERY

Writer: Stanley Ralph Ross. **Director:** Oscar Rudolph. **Guest Cast:** Cliff Robertson (Shame), Dina Merrill.

Cowboy criminal Shame uses fear gas on the Terrific Trio, turning Batman, Robin and Batgirl into sniveling cowards.

MINERVA, MAYHEM AND MILLIONAIRES

Writer: Charles Hoffman. **Director:** Sam Strangis. **Guest Cast:** Zsa Zsa Gabor (Minerva), Jacques Bergerac, William Smith.

At Minerva's mineral health spa, Batman and Robin are trapped in an oversized pressure cooker. Producer Howie Horwitz and executive producer William Dozier appear briefly in this final episode.

STAR TREK

Besides suggesting that there is a tomorrow, that there is challenge and romance in the world, besides suggesting that it's not all over, Star Trek *said something else. It goes rather like this: You human biped thing called Man, you strange creature, still in a sort of a violent childhood of your evolution, you're awkward and often illogical, you're weak, vain, but damn it, you're also gorgeous!*

—Gene Roddenberry
Creator and producer

Cancelled by NBC in 1969 after only three seasons, *Star Trek* reruns still flourish on local stations across the nation. Trekkies continue to gather at conventions, to circulate newsletters and to hold art exhibitions and masquerade parties, all in honor of their favorite show. Young and old, from all levels of society, Trekkies included Nelson Rockefeller, then Governor of New York, and writer Isaac Asimov, who said it was the only TV show he watched. In 1976, at the urging of Trekkies, President Gerald Ford named the United States' new space shuttle, our first re-usable orbiting vehicle, the *Enterprise*, in honor of the space ship on *Star Trek*. The fans' political clout was not so great with NBC, however.

After the show's cancellation, network offices were deluged with over one million letters, threatening, cajoling, imploring, clamoring for the return of Captain Kirk and his crew. One look at the marketplace eight years later shows that *Star Trek* is good business. Bookstores are still selling novelizations of episodes, as well as more serious tomes probing the series' development and significance, as well as maps of constellations and galaxies visited by the star fleet. You can purchase *Star Trek* model kits, lollipops, bubblegum cards, walkie-talkies, dolls, Spock ears, "phasers," stationery, pen and pencil sets, comic and coloring books, even tribbles, those furry pint-sized extra-terrestrials who purr when they're contented—if their batteries aren't drained.

Who would have guessed that this action-adventure series, which was sold to a skeptical network as a "*Wagon*

Train to the stars" and lambasted by Variety as a "crude... lower-case fantasia," would eventually become a major cultural phenomenon? To understand it, one must trace *Star Trek's* evolution.

Producer Gene Roddenberry tried to sell NBC an idea as old as Jules Verne's grandfather: a space ship exploring the galaxy to enhance man's knowledge and make contact with extraterrestrial life forms. This plot scheme had worn thin reel upon reel of celluloid (the show closely resembles "Forbidden Planet," a 1956 MGM space thriller). *Star Trek*, however, was television's first adult science fiction series with continuing characters.

Roddenberry's first pilot film was deemed too cerebral by the NBC brass, but he was encouraged to rewrite and resubmit it. That first pilot, which never was aired, starred Jeffrey Hunter as Captain Pike. It mutated into the *Star Trek* we know with William Shatner's Captain Kirk character heading the crew, supported by Leonard Nimoy as Science Officer Spock and DeForest Kelly as Chief Medical Officer Dr. Leonard McCoy.

Captain Kirk (William Shatner) headed up the Enterprise and its crew.

OPPOSITE: Pointy-eared Mr. Spock (Leonard Nimoy) is partly-human, partly-Vulcan.

Jeffrey Hunter, in the pilot episode, was Captain Pike.

Kirk, Spock and McCoy are the three main Trekkie heroes. Other regulars were James Doohan as Scotty the Engineering Officer, Majel Barrett as Nurse Christine Chapel, George Takei as Helmsman Sulu, Walter Koenig as Ensign Chekov and Nichelle Nichols as Communications Officer Uhura. Spock is the Science Officer by virtue of his logical turn of mind and vast scientific knowledge. His personality and unusual appearance—ba ears and eyebrows like windshield wipers 180 degrees out of phase—are characteristic of the natives of the plane Vulcan, where his father was born; his mother was an earthling. Mr. Spock, incidentally, was originally intended as a minor character whose dispassionate Vulcan nature would contrast with and comment on the Terran personality. However, he proved too interesting to remain in the background and soon developed into a major hero. Spock's cool logic inspires—like a mosquito bite does

The crew of the Starship Enterprise (left to right): Scotty (Jimmy Doohan); Ensign Chekov (Walter Koenig); Dr. McCoy (DeForest Kelley); Nurse Chapel (Majel Barret); Captain Kirk; Uhura (Nichelle Nichols); Lt. Sulu (George Takei); and Mr. Spock.

itching—the temper of "Bones" McCoy, and these two characters became the poles around which much of the show's conflict revolves. To settle these conflicts, we have Captain Kirk: handsome, athletic, always in command.

The basic premise of the show is that Kirk and his crew are emissaries of the United Federation of Planets—a loosely-knit organization of peaceloving planets. Their objective is to explore the cosmos, seeking new forms of life and civilizations. This peaceful mission is regularly thwarted by the vicious, dictatorial Klingons and their allies, the Romulans, who both seek to conquer the cosmos.

In concept, then, Star Trek could be almost any sci-fi action show, yet it has won a following unlike any other. Science fiction is prophecy. Special effects are used to fulfill that prophecy in advance of technology and are often the basis of the success of science fiction films. No effort was spared in bringing three major special effects studios

together to develop the spectacular out-of-this-galaxy illusions of Star Trek. Because of Roddenberry's insistence on scientific accuracy, every detail of the Enterprise was painstakingly planned, and opinions of experts in space, the military, the scientific community and medicine were sought. Their creations were so good that the Navy became interested in the plans for the Enterprise's landing deck, and hospital authorities were interested in the diagnostic beds in the sick bay.

Handling the bulk of the early assignments were technicians from Howard A. Anderson's company. Their association with Star Trek began a full year before the

original pilot was filmed, and the staff worked closely with series art director Matt Jeffries on the design and construction of the *Enterprise*. As conceived by Roddenberry, the *Enterprise* was much larger than a modern battleship. It had a crew of over four hundred on eight separate decks. After Roddenberry approved Jeffries' final design (the result of countless attempts), the next step was translating it into several models: one four inches long, a three-foot version and an elaborate fourteen-footer. Although some interesting changes were made in the cruiser between the two pilot films, it remained generally the same. For Roddenberry's second *Star Trek* adventure, "Where No Man Has Gone Before," a complex lighting system was installed, conveying a feeling of life and activity aboard ship. Also at his suggestion, a rear landing deck was added. Beyond changes in physical design, a "swooshing" sound was later developed and dubbed in, which—although sound does not occur in the vacuum of space—greatly enhanced the sensation of speed as the *Enterprise* zoomed dramatically across the heavens.

Perhaps the most curious effects used on the show were the "de-materialization" and "re-materialization" in the transporter room. Hoping to develop something a bit more distinctive than a simple photographic "matte" (optical outline) and "dissolve," Anderson's technicians livened up this process by scattering aluminum dust through a beam of high-intensity light: The transporting effect is achieved by first filming the crew or cargo to be "beamed down" in the transporter set. Next, the camera freezes and whatever is being transported is removed; the camera films the now-empty set. From a duplicate negative, a "matte" is made of the person or object at the freeze point. An identically shaped matte containing the falling particles is also made. Using the two mattes, the person or cargo is slowly dissolved out, leaving only the glittering aluminum, which, in turn, is dissolved to leave nothing but the empty transporter chamber.

In addition to creating breathtaking optical paintings of strange alien landscapes, Anderson also tackled the problem of having the *Enterprise* appear to speed through space. He knew that without a background, an object seems to move slowly despite its actual velocity, but provide a background and it appears to move faster. For instance, a horse galloping through the woods appears to be moving faster than one galloping across a meadow. Using this principle to simulate velocity involved complex matte work and the construction of several background "skies" (with stars, painted black on a white surface, later reversed in the optical printing). By superimposing tracking shots of the galaxy at different speeds, the illusion of a speed faster than light was created.

All three effects studios working on *Star Trek* were heavily involved in the *Enterprise's* functions, although it was Anderson's team that originated most of the major processes. Film Effects of Hollywood, Inc. had two starship models to work with: a twenty-four-inch and a twelve-foot version, the latter equipped with interior and exterior lights and twin motors. These models were used when certain complicated shots were required, such as combining the action of the *Enterprise* with that of other ships. Also rebuilt

LEFT (top to bottom): Step-by-step matte and dissolve process used to beam crew members from place to place. Here, crew members in position in the transporter room, next disappearing, then the empty transporter room and, finally, reappearing on alien soil.

for finer control was the flight deck with rear clam-shell doors opening to permit the take-off of the miniature shuttlecraft (which were maneuvered by invisible wires). Continuing the fine work started by the Anderson company, Film Effects contributed some mind-boggling psychedelic illusions. This type of effect has little to do with advanced distortion of contrasts and color values. As Film Effects President Linwood G. Dunn explains it:

> Churning, weaving forms and masses hanging in space, as seen through the *U.S.S. Enterprise's* viewing screen, were created by photographing the action of special dyes fed into a tank of clear liquid. With a certain measure of control over the action of the dyes, fascinating and often unexpected varieties of weird, shapeless forms and colors evolved.

Technicians for the third special effects studio, the Westheimer Company, did nothing less than create miniature planets and develop the "phaser" or special *Star Trek* weapon which could be set either to stun or to disintegrate its target. To depict a typical phaser zapping, the phaser ray beam was animated across the screen until it reached its unfortunate target who was then dissolved out, leaving a matte of the beam glow which, in turn, was dissolved out. Similar opticals were used for the *Enterprise's* viewing screen and for optically superimposing a figure on an extraterrestrial landscape.

Although Roddenberry's show was geared to the tube in its action-adventure format, science fiction was con-

ABOVE: The Enterprise speeding through the galaxies.
BELOW: An asteroid is zapped by the Enterprise.

sidered a risky vehicle for a weekly series. The reason is obvious: most science fiction shows attempt to dazzle the viewer with their ingenious gimmickry and gadgetry. This strategy is devised for a single show, though; in a series with the same setting, the novelty would soon lose its brilliance and the show its viewers. For *Star Trek,* gimmickry was to be played down; to emphasize it would have been similar to spotlighting the furniture in *All in the Family.* The "warp drives," "photon torpedoes" and "tricorders," accordingly, were accepted by the characters as the commonplaces they would soon become to the audience. The special effects, fascinating as they were, contribute to, but do not account for, the *Star Trek* phenomenon.

If the special effects, the mainstay of most science fiction, cannot explain the phenomenon, what can? Gene Roddenberry believes the show's success

> ...reveals a great deal more about the fan than it does about the series. The typical *Star Trek* enthusiast is invariably a remarkably gentle human being. It was this capacity for affection, of course, which led him to approve and appreciate our view that humankind is not best characterized by evil—as the visionless would have us believe—but, rather, that its past has been a lusty infant's.

Star Trek was first aired in a gloomy era, a time in which respectable scientists, not religious nuts, were predicting the world's doom. All signs pointed toward

The futuristic settings were carefully planned, leaving out no detail from the utensils they employed for eating, to the weapons they used and the games they played. **ABOVE:** Captain Kirk and Mr. Spock relax with a game of 3-dimensional chess. **BELOW:** Kirk aims his phaser rifle.

future disaster. One could, and still can, select one's preferred form of destruction: nuclear holocaust, pollution, overpopulation and starvation, floods resulting from the melting of the polar ice caps, a new ice age resulting from the expansion of the polar ice caps, race war, revolution. ...In the midst of this, *Star Trek's* message was hopeful, portraying man as frail and flawed but, most often, motivated by a vision of morality and nobility. The mission of the *Enterprise* was to learn from others, beings of different races and cultures, literally of different worlds. Our differences here on Earth paled by comparison. Captain Kirk and his colleagues sought to cooperate, not to coerce; they sought equality, not domination. This moral tone and the friendship among different beings made the future on Earth seem possible, even worth striving for, and captured both the idealism and enthusiasm of the audience. Trekkies call it the "optimism effect."

The inspiring message was also supported by the show's excellent scripts. All the shows began with Kirk's voice-over narration as the *Enterprise* appeared traveling across the starry heavens.

Space, the final frontier. These are the voyages of the *Starship Enterprise*. Its five-year mission: to explore new worlds, to seek out new life and new civilizations, to boldly go where no man has gone before.

Not surprisingly, the most interesting and novel installments were produced during the first season.

"The Corbomite Maneuver," written by Jerry Sohl and directed by Joseph Sargent, is a dramatization of an *Enterprise* mission. Kirk and the crew encounter a horrifying-looking alien named Balok but after an impressive display of the captain's ingenuity, the thing is revealed to be a sort of scarecrow designed by the real Balok in order to test the earthlings. The aliens discover that man is not a savage but

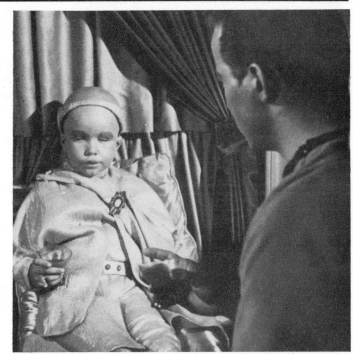

In The Corbomite Maneuver," an eerie childlike creature turned out to be the alien Balok.

an intelligent being that greets the unknown with an open mind and heart.

Another significant early episode is John D.F. Black's "The Naked Time." This tale is set almost completely aboard the starship. Investigating a frozen planet with Mr. Spock, a crewman (Stewart Moss) contracts a strange virus which disrupts his capacity for judgment and self-control. Black and director Marc Daniels use the effects of the disease to probe the contrasting psyches of Trek regulars.

Mr. Spock and his parents, Amanda (Jane Wyatt) and Sarak (Mark Lenard), in "Journey to Babel."

Spock, weeping his heart out in the deserted briefing room, confides to Captain Kirk that he can never accept love or friendship, a tragic consequence of his Vulcan heritage. Even more interesting is Kirk's revelation about his fanatical devotion to the *Enterprise*—he thinks of himself as married to *her*.

Fans of the series are quick to boast that *Star Trek*, unlike rival science fiction series, employed top science fiction writers. Actually, their teleplays were often extensively rewritten by *Trek* story editors, usually for the better. Probably the most successful *Trek* tale to originate from the pen of a noted writer was Richard Matheson's "The Enemy Within," which probed the roles of good and evil in a man. Captain Kirk, victim of a transporter malfunction, is divided into two separate and distinct people. Both look exactly like him, with one being a heroic composite of all his best points and the other, of his negative aspects. Much of Matheson's intelligent vision survives the rewrite, although his original portrait of McCoy as a resentful enemy of Kirk's was discarded. Veteran fantasist Jerome Bixby, who, like Matheson, was a regular contributor to *Twilight Zone*, wrote the excellent "Mirror, Mirror," then went on to write "By Any Other Name," one of the worst. Most mystifying of all, however, is Harlan Ellison's "City on the Edge of Forever," which won a science fiction Hugo award. To maintain character consistency and stay within the budget, Roddenberry and D.C. Fontana completely overhauled the brilliant but impossible-to-produce script, eliminating costly special effects and a bit on drug smuggling considered too daring for TV in 1967. Ellison created much ado about the changes but quietly accepted the Hugo.

By the third season the show had acquired a large following, but sponsor interest and Nielson ratings remained low. The staff's ingenuity grew stale, and as a result

This Star Trek alien from "The Menagerie" made its debut several years earlier on an episode of *Outer Limits* called "Fun and Games" (see page 63).

they began to depend on the appeal of their heroes and on special effects rather than well-written scripts. The plots became familiar parables, mediocre historical adventures based on time travel and even gangster stories. These were pitfalls they had wisely avoided at the beginning, but once they fell into them, *Star Trek* was buried. The show was cancelled as of June 3, 1969.

Star Trek paraphernalia:

The show's popularity has spawned an entire industry of related products including books, tee-shirts, dolls, maps, posters, walkie-talkies, the control center of the Enterprise, and even Tribbles that move.

INDEX
OF
EPISODES

STAR TREK

1966-1969/78 episodes
NBC/a Norway Production for Paramount Television.
60 minutes/color

Regular Cast: William Shatner (Capt. James T. Kirk), Leonard Nimoy (Mr. Spock), DeForest Kelley (Dr. Leonard "Bones" McCoy), Nichelle Nichols (Uhura), George Takei (Lt. Sulu), Jimmy Doohan (Scotty), Majel Barret (Nurse Christine Chapel), Walter Koenig (Ensign Chekov, from the second season), Grace Lee Whitney (Yeoman Janice Rand, first season only).

Executive Producer: Gene Roddenberry. **Producers:** Gene Roddenberry; Gene Coon; John Meredyth Lucas; Fred Freiberger (last season only). **Creator:** Gene Roddenberry. **Story Consultants:** Steven Carabatsos; D.C. Fontana. **Director of Photography:** Ernest Haller; Jerry Finnerman. **Special Effects:** Howard Anderson Company; Westheimer Company; Film Effects of Hollywood, Inc.; Jim Rugg. **Make-up:** Fred Phillips. **Music:** Alexander Courage, Gerald Fried.

First Season: 1966-1967

THE MAN TRAP
Writer: George C. Johnson. **Director:** Marc Daniels. **Guest Cast:** Jeanne Bal, Alfred Ryder, Bruce Watson.

Nancy Crater, a former flame of Dr. McCoy's, is actually a murderous creature capable of assuming human form.

CHARLIE X
Writers: D.C. Fontana, Gene Roddenberry. **Director:** Lawrence Dobkin. **Guest Cast:** Robert Walker, Jr., Abraham Sofaer.

Reared to an early manhood on an alien planet, a teenaged boy threatens the *Enterprise* with his unearthly powers when he finds himself unable to cope with human emotions.

WHERE NO MAN HAS GONE BEFORE
Writer: Sam Peeples. **Director:** James Goldstone. **Guest Cast:** Gary Lockwood, Sally Kellerman, Paul Carr, Paul Fix, Lloyd Haynes, Andrea Dromm. (The last three were original regulars.)

After journeying through a strange barrier at the edge of the galaxy, two crew members become superior beings with god-like powers.

THE NAKED TIME
Writer: John D.F. Black. **Director:** Marc Daniels. **Guest Cast:** Bruce Hyde, William Knight, Stewart Moss, John Bellah.

A virus strips the *Enterprise* crew of their mental and emotional controls as the vessel spirals downward to destruction on a frozen planet.

THE ENEMY WITHIN
Writer: Richard Matheson. **Director:** Leo Penn. **Guest Cast:** Jim Goodwin, Edward Madden, Garland Thompson.

A transporter malfunction transforms Kirk into two people—one meek and mild, the other violent and animalistic.

MUDD'S WOMEN
Writer: Robert Bloch. **Director:** Harvey Hart. **Guest Cast:** Roger C. Carmel, Karen Steele, Susan Denberg, Maggie Thrett.

After tracking an unidentified spaceship, Kirk beams aboard its captain—Harry Mudd—and his cargo of three lovely women.

WHAT ARE LITTLE GIRLS MADE OF?
Writer: Robert Bloch. **Director:** James Goldstone. **Guest Cast:** Michael Strong, Ted Cassidy, Sherry Jackson, Harry Basch.

Nurse Chapel's fiance, Dr. Corby, is readying a race of androids for conquest. Among those he intends to replace with a robot double is Kirk.

MIRI
Writer: Adrian Spies. **Director:** Vincent McEveety. **Guest Cast:** Kim Darby, Michael J. Pollard, Ed Macready.

The survivors of a planet-wide catastrophe look like children, but are over 300 years old. One of them falls in love with Kirk.

DAGGER OF THE MIND
Writer: Shimon Wincelberg. **Director:** Vincent McEveety. **Guest Cast:** Marianna Hill, James Gregory, Morgan Woodward, Susann Wasson.

Kirk investigates the "advanced" reformatory methods of a noted penal colony.

THE CORBOMITE MANEUVER
Writer: Jerry Sohl. **Director:** Joseph Sargent. **Guest Cast:** Anthony Call, Clint Howard.

Kirk uses a tactical bluff to save the *Enterprise* from Balok, commander of a gigantic space vehicle.

THE MENAGERIE
Writer: Gene Roddenberry. **Directors:** Marc Daniels (new footage), Robert Butler (old footage). **Guest Cast:** Jeffrey Hunter, Malachi Throne, Julie Parrish, Sean Kenny, John Hoyt, Susan Oliver, Meg Wyllie, Laurel Goodwin, M. Lee Hudec.

This two-part show used footage from "The Cage"—Star Trek's original pilot. In Part One, Spock mutinies and kidnaps his former commanding officer, Captain Pike. He then sets the *Enterprise* on a course for Talos IV, a forbidden planet shrouded in mystery. In Part Two, Spock, on trial for mutiny and abduction, tells Captain Kirk and Commander Mendez the story of Captain Pike's bizarre experience on Talos IV. Winner of a Hugo Award.

THE CONSCIENCE OF THE KING
Writer: Barry Trivers. **Director:** Gerd Oswald. **Guest Cast:** Arnold Moss, Barbara Anderson, William Sargent, Bruce Hyde.

Spock and Pike in the series pilot "The Cage." Footage from it was used in a two-part episode called "the Menagerie."

The star of a troupe of actors is suspected of being Kodos the Executioner, who had vanished mysteriously many years before.

BALANCE OF TERROR

Writer: Paul Schneider. **Director:** Vincent McEveety. **Guest Cast:** Mark Lenard, John Warburton, Paul Comi, Barbara Baldwin.

Kirk engages in a duel of wits and courage with the commander of a Romulan ship.

SHORE LEAVE

Writer: Theodore Sturgeon. **Director:** Robert Spear. **Guest Cast:** Emily Banks, Bruce Mars, Shirley Bonne, Oliver McGowan.

Shore leave on a beautiful planet turns into a frightening adventure as the *Enterprise* crew encounter people and images from their pasts.

THE GALILEO SEVEN

Writer: Oliver Crawford. **Director:** Robert Gist. **Guest Cast:** John Crawford, Don Marshall, Rees Vaughn, Peter Marko.

While commanding a shuttlecraft investigation of a mysterious solar system, Spock and his crew are marooned on a planet inhabited by murderous gorilla-like creatures.

THE SQUIRE OF GOTHOS

Writer: Paul Schneider. **Director:** Donald McDougall. **Guest Cast:** William Campbell, Venita Wolf, Michael Barrier, Richard Carlyle.

Kirk plays a game of death with the maniacal alien Trelane who plans to use the *Starship Enterprise* as a toy.

ARENA

Writers: Gene Coon, F. Brown. **Director:** Joseph Pevney. **Guest Cast:** Carole Shelyne, Vic Perrin.

Kirk is pitted against the commander of a rival space vehicle—a scaly, man-sized powerful creature called Gorn.

TOMORROW IS YESTERDAY

Writer: D.C. Fontana. **Director:** Michael O'Herlihy. **Guest Cast:** Roger Perry, Jim Spencer, Sherri Townsend, Ed Peck.

The *Enterprise* catapults back in time to the 1960s, where it is thought to be a UFO.

COURT MARTIAL

Writers: Don Mankiewicz, Steven Carabatsos. **Director:** Marc Daniels. **Guest Cast:** Elisha Cook, Alice Rawlings, Richard Webb.

Kirk goes on trial for his life after the *Enterprise*'s computer accuses him of murdering a fellow officer.

RETURN OF THE ARCHONS

Writer: Boris Sobelman. **Director:** Joseph Pevney. **Guest Cast:** Harry Townes, Jon Lormer, Torin Thatcher, Charles Macaulay.

Kirk must cause Landru—the computer ruler of an alien planet—to self-destruct if the planet's population is to survive.

SPACE SEED

Writers: C. Wilbur, Gene Coon. **Director:** Marc Daniels. **Guest Cast:** Ricardo Montalban, Madlyn Rhue, Mark Tobin, Kathy Ahart.

The *Enterprise* encounters a derelict spacecraft containing 72 bodies in suspended animation. Khan, the leader, is revived, and he and his companions turn out to be tyrannical supermen.

A TASTE OF ARMAGEDDON

Writers: R. Hamner, Gene Coon. **Director:** Joseph Pevney. **Guest Cast:** David Opatoshu, Barbara Babcock, Sean Kenny, David L. Ross.

Kirk and Spock become involved in a computer war on the planet Eminar 7.

THIS SIDE OF PARADISE

Writer: D.C. Fontana. **Director:** Ralph Senensky. **Guest Cast:** Jill Ireland, Frank Overton, Grant Woods, Michael Barrier.

Alien spores lull crew members into a peaceful tranquility, allowing Spock to experience true love for the first time.

THE DEVIL IN THE DARK

Writer: Gene Coon. **Director:** Joseph Pevney. **Guest Cast:** Ken Lynch, Barry Russo, Brad Weston, Janos Prohaska.

In a mining colony, Kirk and Spock battle a strange creature capable of tunneling through rock.

ERRAND OF MERCY

Writer: Gene Coon. **Director:** John Newland. **Guest Cast:** John Abbott, David Hilary Hughes, Peter Brocco, John Colicos.

Kirk and Spock try to persuade the inhabitants of the planet Organia to protect themselves against the Klingons.

THE ALTERNATIVE FACTOR

Writer: Don Ingalls. **Director:** Gerd Oswald. **Guest Cast:** Robert Brown, Richard Derr, Janet MacLachlan, Arch Whiting.

The *Enterprise* officers investigate an uncharted planet where they discover Lazarus, a raving time traveler who is battling some unseen force.

THE CITY ON THE EDGE OF FOREVER

Writer: Harlan Ellison. **Director:** Gene Roddenberry. **Guest Cast:** Joan Collins, David L. Ross, John Harmon.

Kirk and Spock follow a deranged McCoy through a time doorway to New York City in the Roaring Twenties.

OPERATION ANNIHILATE!

Writer: Steven Carabatsos. **Director:** Herschel Daugherty. **Guest Cast:** Joan Swift, Craig Hundley, Fred Carson, Jerry Catron, Maurishka.

Enterprise officers attempt to save the inhabitants of Deneva from parasites that invade their bodies and drive the hosts insane.

AMOK TIME

Writer: Theodore Sturgeon. **Director:** Joe Pevney. **Guest Cast:** Arlene Martel, Celia Lovsky, Lawrence Montaigne, Byron Morrow.

Spock is overwhelmed with the Vulcan mating drive that must end in marriage or death.

WHO MOURNS FOR ADONAIS?

Writers: Gene Coon, Gilbert Ralston. **Director:** Marc Daniels. **Guest Cast:** Michael Forest, Leslie Parrish, John Winston.

An alien named Apollo, who claims that he is the last of a race once hailed on Earth as gods, seizes the *Enterprise*.

THE CHANGELING

Writer: John M. Lucas. **Director:** Marc Daniels. **Guest Cast:** Vic Perrin, Barbara Gates, Arnold Lessing.

The *Enterprise* faces destruction by Nomad, an ancient robot probe programmed to eliminate all life forms deemed not perfect.

MIRROR, MIRROR

Writer: Jerome Bixby. **Director:** Marc Daniels. **Guest Cast:** Barbara Luna, Vic Perrin, Ben Andrews, John Winston.

An ion storm causes Kirk and three crew members to exchange places with their counterparts on another ship in another universe.

THE APPLE

Writers: Max Erlich, Gene Coon. **Director:** Joe Pevney. **Guest Cast:** Celeste Yarnall, David Soul, Keith Andes, Shari Nims.

Kirk and the crew encounter a primitive society ruled by a powerful "god" machine.

THE DOOMSDAY MACHINE

Writer: Norman Spinrad. **Director:** Marc Daniels. **Guest Cast:** William Windom, John Copage, Richard Compton, Elizabeth Rogers.

After rescuing Commodore Decker from a disabled starship, The *Enterprise* and its crew are nearly destroyed by a "doomsday machine" on a rampage through space.

CATSPAW

Writers: Robert Bloch, D.C. Fontana. **Director:** Joe Pevney. **Guest Cast:** Antoinette Bower, Theo Marcuse, Michael Barrier.

Kirk and his top aides are captured by two weird creatures who can assume various magical forms.

I, MUDD

Writer: Stephen Kandel. **Director:** Marc Daniels. **Guest Cast:** Roger C. Carmel, Kay Elliot, Richard Tatro.

A sophisticated android abducts the starship and its crew and delivers them to Harry Mudd, who controls 2000 beautiful androids programmed to grant his every wish.

METAMORPHOSIS

Writer: Gene L. Coon. **Director:** Ralph Senensky. **Guest Cast:** Glenn Corbett, Elinor Donahue.

A space pioneer is kept alive by a cloudlike alien life form in one of the strangest "love stories" ever filmed.

JOURNEY TO BABEL

Writer: D.C. Fontana. **Director:** Joe Pevney. **Guest Cast:** Jane Wyatt, Mark Lenard, William O'Connell, Reggie Nalder.

Transporting delegates, including Spock's parents, to a meeting on the planet Babel, Kirk is plagued with one crisis after another.

FRIDAY'S CHILD

Writer: D.C. Fontana. **Director:** Joe Pevney. **Guest Cast:** Julie Newmar, Tige Andrews, Michael Dante, Cal Bolder.

Kirk violates a tribal taboo on the planet Capella, and he and the crew are forced to take to the hills along with the chief's wife.

THE DEADLY YEARS

Writer: David P. Harmon. **Director:** Joe Pevney. **Guest Cast:** Charles Drake, Sarah Marshall, Felix Locher, Beverly Washburn.

Kirk, Spock, Scotty and Dr. McCoy begin to age at an astonishing rate after visiting the planet Gamma Hydra IV.

LEFT: The scarecrow alter ego of Balok in "The Corbomite Maneuver."

OBSESSION

Writer: Art Wallace. **Director:** Ralph Senensky. **Guest Cast:** Stephen Brooks, Jerry Ayres.

For the second time in his career, Kirk encounters a deadly gaseous creature and disregards orders to proceed to another planet in order to destroy it.

WOLF IN THE FOLD

Writer: Robert Bloch. **Director:** Joe Pevney. **Guest Cast:** John Fiedler, Charles Macaulay, Pilar Seurat, James Bernard.

Scotty is suspected of murdering three women until Kirk discovers that the spirit of historical villain Jack the Ripper is actually responsible.

THE TROUBLE WITH TRIBBLES

Writer: David Gerrold. **Director:** Joe Pevney. **Guest Cast:** William Schallert, William Campbell, Stanley Adams, Whit Bissell.

Kirk has his hands full—literally—with *tribbles*, tiny, purring creatures that multiply at an alarming rate.

THE GAMESTERS OF TRISKELION

Writer: Margaret Armen. **Director:** Gene Nelson. **Guest Cast:** Joseph Ruskin, Steven Sandor, Angelique Pettyjohn, Victoria George.

Kirk and the crew visit a planet where some of the residents perform in "games" for the amusement of their masters.

A PIECE OF THE ACTION

Writers: David Harmon, Gene Coon. **Director:** James Komack. **Guest Cast:** Anthony Caruso, Victor Tayback, Lee Delano, John Harmon.

Investigating the disappearance of a Starship which had been lost for a hundred years, the crew lands on a planet that is run like the mobs in old Chicago.

THE IMMUNITY SYNDROME

Writer: Robert Sabaroff. **Director:** Joe Pevney. **Guest Cast:** John Winston.

The *Enterprise* must destroy a giant amoeba-like creature which threatens to engulf the galaxy.

A PRIVATE LITTLE WAR

Writer: Gene Roddenberry. **Director:** Marc Daniels. **Guest Cast:** Nancy Kovak, Michael Whitney, Ned Romero, Janos Prohaska.

When the natives of a primitive planet receive weapons from the Klingons, Kirk finds that he must furnish the rival tribes with guns to maintain the balance of power.

RETURN TO TOMORROW

Writer: John Kingsbridge. **Director:** Ralph Senensky. **Guest Cast:** Diana Muldaur.

The bodies of Kirk, Spock and a woman doctor are inhabited by the "minds" of an advanced civilization that intends to build robot bodies for their brains to live in.

PATTERNS OF FORCE

Writer: John Meredyth Lucas. **Director:** Vincent McEveety. **Guest Cast:** Richard Evans, Valora Norand, Skip Homeier, David Brian, Gilbert Green.

The *Enterprise* officers alight on a planet run like the Nazi regime.

BY ANY OTHER NAME

Writers: Jerome Bixby, D.C. Fontana. **Director:** Marc Daniels. **Guest Cast:** Warren Stevens, Barbara Bouchet, Julie Cobb, Carl Byrd.

The *Enterprise* is hijacked by aliens intent on destroying all human existence.

THE OMEGA GLORY

Writer: Gene Roddenberry. **Director:** Vincent McEveety. **Guest Cast:** Morgan Woodward, Roy Jensen, Irene Kelly, David L. Ross.

A starship captain mistakenly believes that he has found the secret of immortality on the planet Omega.

THE ULTIMATE COMPUTER

Writer: D.C. Fontana. **Director:** John Meredyth Lucas. **Guest Cast:** William Marshall, Barry Russo.

The *Enterprise* is a guinea pig in an experiment to prove that a multitronic computer system can run a space vessel more efficiently than humans.

BREAD AND CIRCUSES

Writer: Gene Coon. **Director:** Ralph Senensky. **Guest Cast:** William Smithers, Logan Ramsey, Ian Wolfe, Rhodes Reason, Lois Jewell.

The *Enterprise* crew find themselves on a planet whose society is just like ancient Rome, complete with gladiators and arena games.

ASSIGNMENT: EARTH

Writers: Art Wallace, Gene Roddenberry. **Director:** Marc Daniels. **Guest Cast:** Robert Lansing, Terri Garr.

The *Enterprise* beams aboard Gary Seven—he's a human raised by aliens, and he hopes to save mankind from itself. (Originally a pilot for a new series that never made it.)

Third Season: 1968-1969

SPOCK'S BRAIN

Writer: Lee Cronin. **Director:** Marc Daniels. **Guest Cast:** Marj Dusay.

A beautiful and mysterious woman materializes aboard the *Enterprise* and kidnaps Mr. Spock's brain.

THE ENTERPRISE INCIDENT

Writer: D.C. Fontana. **Director:** John Meredyth Lucas. **Guest Cast:** Joanne Linville.

Kirk and Spock disguise themselves as Romulans in order to steal a cloaking device.

  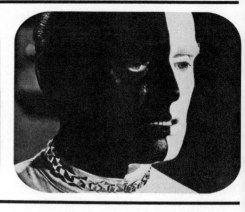

THE PARADISE SYNDROME
Writer: Margaret Armen. **Director:** Jud Taylor. **Guest Cast:** Sabrina Scharf, Rudy Solari.

Kirk, suffering from amnesia, marries a beautiful alien woman and is oblivious to the impending destruction of her planet.

AND THE SMALL CHILDREN SHALL LEAD
Writer: Edward J. Lasko. **Director:** Marvin Chomsky. **Guest Cast:** Melvin Belli, Craig Hundley, James Wellman.

Children under the spell of alien villain Gorgan play on the secret fears of crew members in an attempt to conquer the *Enterprise.*

IS THERE NO TRUTH IN BEAUTY?
Writer: Jean Lisette Aroeste. **Director:** Ralph Senensky. **Guest Cast:** Diana Muldaur, David Frankham.

Spock gazes on a Medusan and is doomed to death by madness unless Kirk can persuade a jealous woman to save him by performing a dangerous mind-link with the Vulcan hero.

SPECTRE OF THE GUN
Writer: Lee Cronin. **Director:** Vince McEveety. **Guest Cast:** Rex Holman, Bill Zuckert, Sam Gilman.

After violating Melkotian space, Kirk, Spock and McCoy are trapped in a bizarre reconstruction of the gunfight at the OK Corral.

DAY OF THE DOVE
Writer: Jerome Bixby. **Director:** Marvin Chomsky. **Guest Cast:** Michael Ansara, Susan Howard.

Klingons and *Enterprise* officers clash as a transparent monster feeds upon their hatred and grows to alarming proportions.

FOR THE WORLD IS HOLLOW AND I HAVE TOUCHED THE SKY
Writer: Rik Vollaerts. **Director:** Tony Leader. **Guest Cast:** Kate Woodville.

The queen of a hollow world camouflaged as an asteroid enslaves a dying Dr. McCoy.

THE THOLIAN WEB
Writers: Judy Burns, Chet Richards. **Director:** Ralph Senesky. **Guest Cast:** None.

With Captain Kirk trapped in hyperspace, the *Enterprise* is attacked by the Tholians and surrounded by their powerful web.

PLATO'S STEPCHILDREN
Writer: Meyer Dolinsky. **Director:** David Alexander. **Guest Cast:** Michael Dunn, Liam Sullivan, Barbara Babcock.

The *Enterprise* officers respond to a distress call on Platonius and become slaves to creatures possessing advanced telepathic powers.

WINK OF AN EYE
Writer: Arthur Heinemann. **Director:** Judd Taylor. **Guest Cast:** Kathie Brown, Eric Holland, Geoffrey Binney, Jason Evers.

For the Scalosians, one of our seconds is like an hour. Their queen, Deela, uses their speed to take over the *Enterprise,* and chooses Captain Kirk as a temporary mate.

THE EMPATH
Writer: Joyce Muscat. **Director:** John Erman. **Guest Cast:** Kathryn May Hays, Alan Bergman, Willard Sage, Jason Wingreen.

Under the observation of powerful alien creatures, a mute girl with the gift of sensing emotions and transferring pain learns compassion from the reactions of Kirk, Spock and Dr. McCoy.

ELAAN OF TROYIUS
Writer: John Meredyth Lucas. **Director:** John Meredyth Lucas. **Guest Cast:** France Nuyen, Jay Robinson, Tony Young, Lee Duncan, Victor Brandt.

Kirk falls prey to the tears of an alien woman.

WHOM GODS DESTROY
Writer: Lee Erwin. **Director:** Herb Wallerstein. **Guest Cast:** Steve Ihnat, Yvonne Craig, Richard Geary, Gary Downey.

Garth, a madman planning to conquer the galaxy, has two curious advantages: an explosive and the ability to alter his shape.

LET THAT BE YOUR LAST BATTLEFIELD
Writers: Lee Cronin, Oliver Crawford. **Director:** Judd Taylor. **Guest Cast:** Frank Gorshin, Lou Antonio.

Two aliens attempt to transform the *Enterprise* into a battlefield to end a 50,000-year struggle.

MARK OF GIDEON
Writers: George F. Slavin, Stanley Adams. **Director:** Judd Taylor. **Guest Cast:** Sharon Acker, David Hurst, Gene Kynarski, Richard Derr.

Lured onto a fake and deserted *Enterprise,* Kirk is approached by the inhabitants of the planet Gideon, to remain with them as a source of alien infection.

THAT WHICH SURVIVES
Writers: D.C. Fontana, John Meredyth Lucas. **Director:** Herb Wallerstein. **Guest Cast:** Lee Meriwether, Arthur Batanides, Naomi Pollack.

After the *Enterprise* is hurtled a thousand light years away, Kirk and McCoy face starvation and a deadly female enemy on a hostile and barren planet.

THE LIGHTS OF ZETAR
Writers: Jeremy Tarcher, Shari Lewis. **Director:** Herb Kenwith. **Guest Cast:** Jan Shutan, Libby Erwin, John Winston.

A living electrical storm endangers Lt. Mira and Chief Engineer Scott, who has fallen in love with her.

REQUIEM FOR METHUSELAH
Writer: Jerome Bixby. **Director:** Murray Golden. **Guest Cast:** James Daly, Louise Sorel.

Flint is a powerful alien who claims to possess eternal life and to have lived on Earth as Methuselah, Solomon, Da Vinci and other famous figures.

THE WAY TO EDEN
Writers: Michael Richards, Arthur Heinemann. **Director:** David Alexander. **Guest Cast:** Skip Homeier, Charles Napier, Mary Linda Rapelye, Deborah Downey.

Dr. Sevrin, an explorer disillusioned with modern technology, leads a group of space hippies in search of a planetary paradise.

THE CLOUD MINDERS
Writer: Margaret Armen. **Director:** Judd Taylor. **Guest Cast:** Jeff Corey, Diana Ewing, Charlene Polite.

The *Enterprise* officers are caught in a slave rebellion after responding to an emergency call to save a planet.

THE SAVAGE CURTAIN
Writers: Gene Roddenberry, Arthur Heinemann. **Director:** Herschel Daugherty. **Guest Cast:** Lee Bergere, Barry Atwater, Phil Pine, Robert Herron.

Historical figures Abraham Lincoln and Surak aid Captain Kirk and his men in a bizarre battle against the most evil characters in history.

ALL OUR YESTERDAYS
Writer: Jean Lisette Aroeste. **Director:** Marvin Chomsky. **Guest Cast:** Ian Wolfe, Mariette Hartley.

A strange machine on a doomed planet hurtles Kirk, Spock and Dr. McCoy into different eras of Earth's past.

TURNABOUT INTRUDER
Writer: Arthur M. Singer. **Director:** Herb Wallerstein. **Guest Cast:** Sandra Smith, Harry Landers.

A mind-body transfer imprisons the mind of Captain Kirk in the body of Dr. Janice Lester while she takes over the *Enterprise* as Kirk.

Years after cancellation, the show remains as popular as ever. Fans have accepted the fact that no new television shows will be produced, but one and all anxiously await the release of a feature film starring all of their heroes, who stand ready for the next adventure.

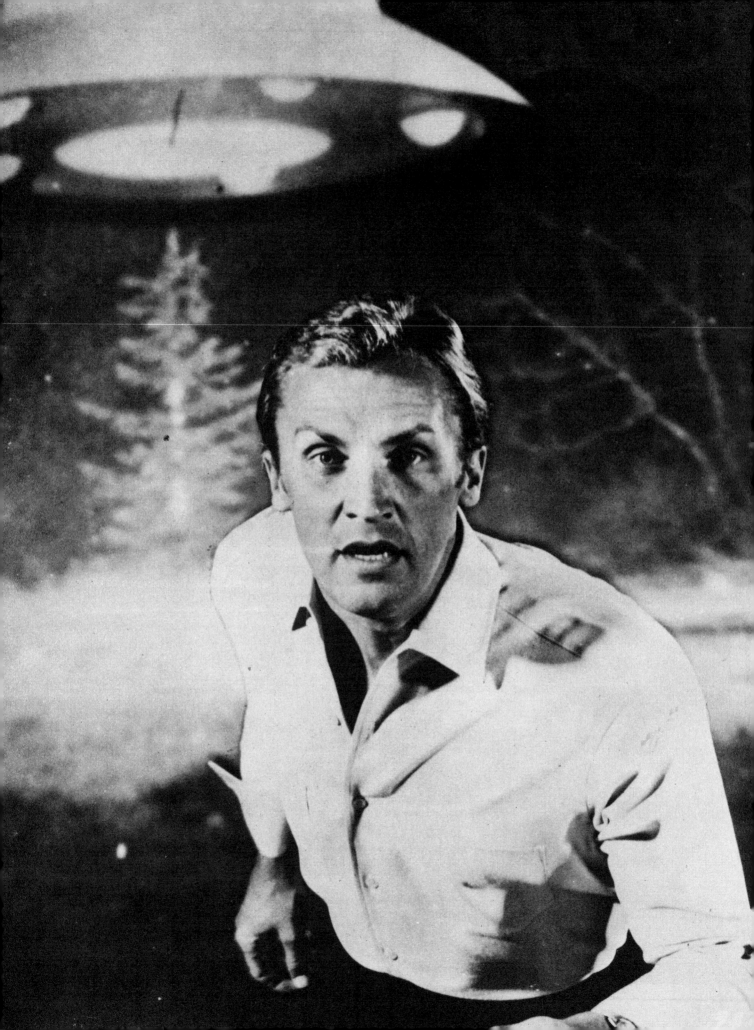

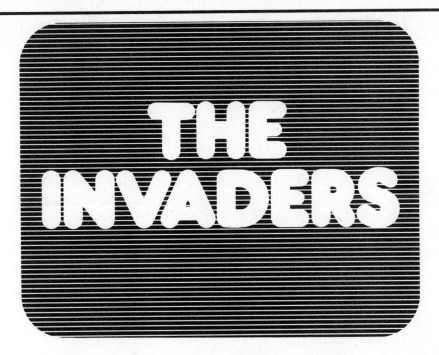

THE INVADERS

I think people like to be scared out of their wits, but they're no longer frightened by three-headed monsters, so we've made the Invaders look just like the folks next door, and the audience is going along with it. What we're after, quite simple, is fear.

—Alan A. Armer
Producer

The *Invaders* debuted in January, 1967, slowly increased its audience until it peaked in September and then limped to its demise at the end of the 1968 season. Executive producer Quinn Martin's (*The Fugitive, The F.B.I., Barnaby Jones, Cannon* and others) objective was to scare viewers out of their wits, which he may have succeeded in doing initially. Toward the end of the show's run, though, its inflexible plot just dulled their wits.

Producer Armer explained the premise this way:

They're here among us now...in your city...maybe on your block. They're invaders...alien beings from another planet...but they look *just like us!* Take a look around. Casually. No sense letting them know you're suspicious. The new neighbors across the street. The substitute teacher. That too-pretty secretary in your husband's office. Any one of them might be an invader from outer space. How can you tell? Sometimes their hands are mutated, the little finger jutting out awkwardly. Sometimes, rarely, they will begin to glow, when they are in need of regeneration in order to retain their human form. And always they are without a pulse or a heartbeat. For, of course, they possess no hearts.

The first episode sets the theme for all succeeding shows. In it we meet our hero David Vincent (Roy Thinnes) as he pulls his car over to the side of the road to catch a few winks. He is abruptly awakened by a loud whirring and is astounded to see a flying saucer landing. Later, he returns to the scene with the police and his business partner; they find nothing but a young couple on their honeymoon who claim they never saw a thing. The police think Vincent is

crazy; his business partner thinks he's overworked. Vincent notices that the pinkies of the honeymooners jut out at an odd angle.

Vincent, convinced that the fate of the human race rests in his hands, repeats his story to whoever will listen. Of course, no one believes him until he meets Kathy Adams (Diane Baker), a widow who runs the local hotel. She believes his tale and tries to help him. For the remainder of the episode, Vincent is, in turn, held in a psychiatric ward, nearly run over, beaten and almost burned to death in his hotel room before he begins to suspect that Kathy, too, is an alien. Vincent finally learns that Kathy and the others are from a doomed planet; they hope to take over one whose environment is hospitable and whose inhabitants won't resist too strenuously. They plan to use their ability to take on human form to infiltrate all the institutions of human society: the government, the police force, the news media, the PTA—until they control the planet. "Don't fight us," he is advised, "it's going to *happen.*" At the conclusion of the first show, this modern-day David has accepted the challenge of a multitude of Goliaths and the human race can only hope that he is invincible.

OPPOSITE: Roy Thinnes as David Vincent. RIGHT: Diane Baker in "Beachhead," the premiere episode.

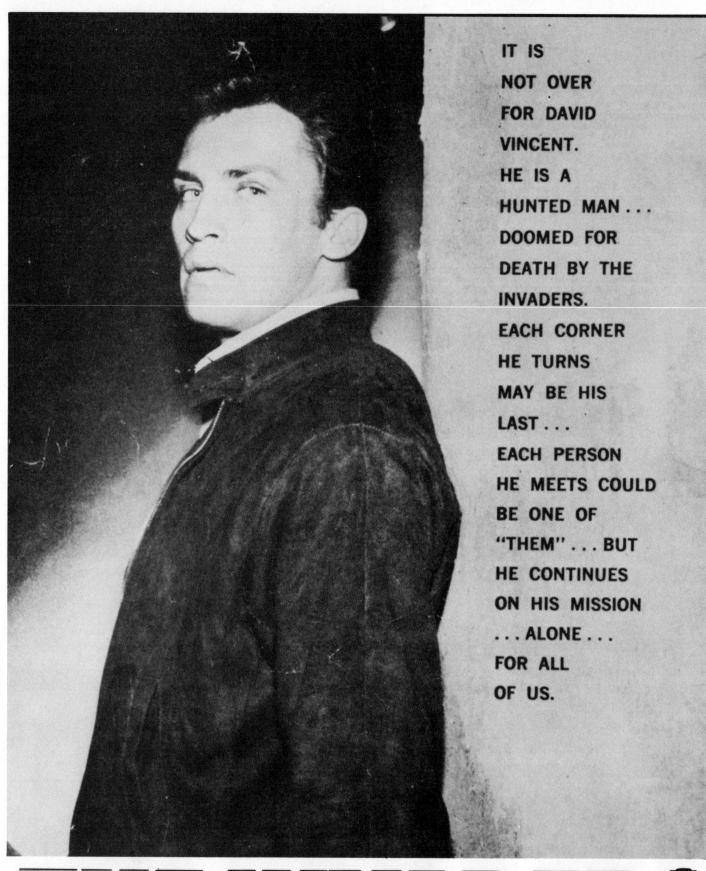

IT IS NOT OVER FOR DAVID VINCENT. HE IS A HUNTED MAN . . . DOOMED FOR DEATH BY THE INVADERS. EACH CORNER HE TURNS MAY BE HIS LAST . . . EACH PERSON HE MEETS COULD BE ONE OF "THEM" . . . BUT HE CONTINUES ON HIS MISSION . . . ALONE . . . FOR ALL OF US.

THE INVADERS

When one of the alien invaders is destroyed, it goes up in a cloud of red smoke, leaving nothing but ashes behind.

A later episode, "The Mutation," is remarkably similar in content and well directed by Paul Wendkos. Vincent hears that flying saucers have been sighted in the Mexican desert. He finds two men to take him there and, when they get to the spot, they beat the tar out of him. Vincent lives to tell his story yet again to a skeptical but sympathetic newspaperman, Mark Evans (Edward Andrews). He introduces Vincent to a nightclub stripper named Vikki (Suzanne Pleshette) who also claimed to have witnessed the saucers. Vikki suggests that they go to the landing site to conduct their own investigation. Unaware that she is truly an alien luring him into a trap, Vincent agrees to go. As they get close to their destination, Vikki begins to act confused, and says she can't identify the spot. She knows this is a trap for Vincent but because she is different from the other aliens—a mutation—she feels affection for Vincent and wants to spare his life. For her disloyality, the aliens kill her, and Vincent, armed with a rifle, kills many of them.

Roy Thinnes was an admirable choice for the lead—handsome and athletic enough to handle the action scenes believably. Yet he was ordinary enough for the viewer to identify with him in his extraordinary situation. Thinnes believed in the show and spent a great deal of time traveling around the country to promote it and stimulate thought about UFOs: "We are theorizing with reality, theorizing as to who flies flying saucers and why they are here." The premise of the show may have been thought-provoking but, even though the players changed, the game adhered to the same rigid formula in nearly every episode: the people Vincent trusts betray him because they are aliens; the others think he's crazy and don't listen. Realizing that this tactic could not carry the series, the producers tried to add more players to Vincent's side in an episode called "The Believers." In this and the following episodes, the "believers" offered Vincent money, assistance and business and political connections. One of the believers, Edgar Scoville, played by Kent Smith, began to appear on a regular basis until the end of the series.

However, changing the game from singles to a team sport did not enliven it and it wasn't long before the viewers had become as complacent as the townspeople. Maybe Vincent *was* crazy after all.

Suzanne Pleshette (Bob Newhart's TV wife) guest-starred as a mutant invader—her mutation gave her sympathy for an Earthling—joins Vincent in a chase in "The Mutation."

INDEX OF EPISODES

THE INVADERS

1967-1968/43 episodes
ABC/a Q-M (Quinn-Martin) Production
60 minutes/color

Regular Cast: Roy Thinnes (David Vincent), Kent Smith (Edgar Scoville—second season only).

Executive Producer: Quinn Martin. **Producer:** Alan Armer. **Creator:** Larry Cohen. **Music:** Dominic Frontiere.

First Season: 1967

BEACH HEAD
Writer: Anthony Wilson. **Director:** Joseph Sargent. **Guest Cast:** Diane Baker, J.D. Cannon, James Daly, John Milford, Ellen Corby, James Ward, Bonnie Beecher, Vaughn Taylor.

David Vincent desperately searches for someone who will believe he sighted the landing of a space ship.

THE EXPERIMENT
Writer: Anthony Spinner. **Director:** Joseph Sargent. **Guest Cast:** Roddy McDowall, Laurence Naismith, Harold Gould, Dabbs Greer, Willard Sage, Stuart Lancaster, Jackie Kendall.

Vincent forestalls an assassination attempt on a famous scientist who has evidence of the landing of a space ship.

THE MUTATION
Writers: David Chandler, George Eckstein. **Director:** Paul Wendkos. **Guest Cast:** Suzanne Pleshette, Edward Andrews, Lin McCarthy, Roy Jenson, Rudolfo Hoyos, Val Avery, Argentina Brunetti.

With the assistance of a nightclub stripper, Vincent continues his search for the alien space craft.

THE LEECHES
Writer: Dan Ullman. **Director:** Paul Wendkos. **Guest Cast:** Arthur Hill, Mark Richman, Diana van der Vlis, Robert H. Harris, Theo Marcuse, Peter Brocco, Noah Keen.

Vincent is called on by a renowned electronics expert who fears he is next in line to be abducted by the alien invaders.

GENESIS
Writer: John W. Bloch. **Director:** Richard Benedict. **Guest Cast:** Carol Rossen, Louise Latham, Tim McIntire, William Sargent, Phillip Pine, John Larch, Frank Overton.

Vincent's search for the invaders leads him to an underwater sea lab.

VIKOR
Writer: Don Brinkley. **Director:** Paul Wendkos. **Guest Cast:** Jack Lord, Alfred Ryder, Diana Hyland, Richard O'Brien, Sam Edwards, Joe DiReda, Larry Duran, Hal Baylor.

A dying telephone lineman's fantastic story leads Vincent to investigate a huge industrial plant owned by a famous war hero.

NIGHTMARE
Writer: John Kneubuhl. **Director:** Paul Wendkos. **Guest Cast:** Kathleen Widdoes, Robert Emhardt, Jeanette Nolan, James Callahan, William Bramley, Irene Tedrow, Nellie Burt.

Vincent travels to a small town to check out a possible link between the invaders and an attack of carnivorous insects.

DOOMSDAY MINUS ONE
Writer: Louis Vittes. **Director:** Paul Wendkos. **Guest Cast:** William Windom, Andrew Duggan, Wesley Addy, Robert Osterloh, Lee Farr, Tom Palmer, Rick Murray, Lew Brown.

Vincent is called upon to help avert possible alien infiltration into a nuclear test site.

QUANTITY UNKNOWN
Writer: Don Brinkley. **Director:** Sutton Roley. **Guest Cast:** James Whitmore, Milton Selzer, William Talman, Susan Strasberg, Barney Phillips, Douglas Henderson.

While investigating the theft of a mysterious cylinder from the site of a plane crash, Vincent is captured on suspicion of being an alien.

THE INNOCENTS
Writer: John W. Bloch. **Director:** Sutton Roley. **Guest Cast:** William Smithers, Michael Rennie, Robert Doyle, Patricia Smith, Paul Carr, Katherine Justice, Dabney Coleman.

Vincent is captured by aliens and told he's being taken to a paradise as proof of the invaders' benevolent intentions toward the human race.

THE IVY CURTAIN
Writer: Don Brinkley. **Director:** Joe Sargent. **Guest Cast:** Jack Warden, Susan Oliver, David Sheiner, Murray Matheson, Barry Russo, Clark Gordon, Byron Morrow, Paul Pepper.

Vincent discovers that a school is being used by the invaders as an indoctrination center.

THE BETRAYED
Writer: John W. Bloch. **Director:** John M. Lucas. **Guest Cast:** Ed Begley, Laura Devon, Nancy Wickwire, Normal Fell, Bill Fletcher, Victor Brandt, Ivan Bonar, Gil Stuart.

Vincent discovers a mysterious, complex computer tape that could stand as evidence of the alien invasion.

STORM
Writer: John Kneubuhl. **Director:** Paul Wendkos. **Guest Cast:** Joseph Campanella, Barbara Luna, Simon Scott, Carlos Romero, John McLiam, Paul Comi, John Mayo, Dean Harens.

A meteorologist calls on Vincent to help investigate the suspicious nature of a hurricane on the east coast.

PANIC
Writer: Robert Sherman. **Director:** Robert Butler. **Guest Cast:** Robert Walker, Lynn Loring, R.G. Armstrong, Len Wayland, Ross Hagen, Ford Rainey, Rayford Barnes.

It's a close race between the invaders and Vincent to capture a wounded alien whose touch brings on a freezing death.

MOONSHOT
Writer: Alan Armer. **Director:** Paul Wendkos. **Guest Cast:** Peter Graves, John Ericson, Joanne Linville, Kent Smith, Anthony Eisley, Richard X. Slattery, Paul Lukather, Strother Martin.

Vincent and a security officer investigate the deaths of two lunar astronauts in a strange red fog.

WALL OF CRYSTAL
Writer: Don Brinkley. **Director:** Joe Sargent. **Guest Cast:** Burgess Meredith, Linden Chiles, Julie Sommars, Edward Asner, Lloyd Gough, Russ Conway, Jerry Ayres, Peggy Lipton.

The aliens resort to kidnapping his brother and pregnant wife to keep Vincent from publicizing his discoveries about them.

THE CONDEMNED
Writer: Robert Sherman. **Director:** Richard Benedict. **Guest Cast:** Ralph Bellamy, Marilyn Mason, Murray Hamilton, Larry Ward, John Ragin, Wright King, Garry Walberg, Harlan Wade.

The aliens frame Vincent for the apparent death of a communications plant owner who had made some startling discoveries.

Second Season: 1967-1968

CONDITION: RED
Writer: Laurence Heath. **Director:** Don Medford. **Guest Cast:** Antoinette Bower, Jason Evers, Roy Engel, Mort Mills, Robert Brubaker, Burt Douglas, Forrest Compton, Jim Raymond.

Vincent must thwart the alien infiltration of an Air Defense Command unit.

THE SAUCER
Writer: Dan B. Ullman. **Director:** Jesse Hibbs. **Guest Cast:** Anne Francis, Charles Drake, Dabney Coleman, Robert Knapp, Kelly Thordsen, Sandy Kenyon, John Ward.

By battling and destroying an alien guard, Vincent captures one of the aliens' space craft.

THE WATCHERS
Writers: Jerry Sohl, Earl Hamner, Jr. **Director:** Jesse Hibbs. **Guest Cast:** Shirley Knight, Kevin

McCarthy, Leonard Stone, Walter Brooke, Robert Yuro, Harry Hickox, James Seay.

Vincent heeds a terrified hotel manager's hysterical warning that "they" are taking over his hotel.

VALLEY OF THE SHADOW
Writers: Howard Merrill, Robert Sabaroff. **Director:** Jesse Hibbs. **Guest Cast:** Ron Hayes, Nan Townes, Harry Townes, Joe Maross, Ted Knight, Hank Brandt, Jon Lormer, Wayne Heffley.

When an alien is unknowingly captured in a small town, Vincent tries to warn the inhabitants, who at first think he's mad.

THE ENEMY
Writer: John W. Bloch. **Director:** Robert Butler. **Guest Cast:** Barbara Barrie, Richard Anderson, Russell Thorson, Paul Mantee, Gene Lyons, George Keymas.

Despite Vincent's warnings, a nurse tries to help the injured alien survivor of a saucer crash.

THE TRIAL
Writers: George Eckstein, David W. Rintels. **Director:** Robert Butler. **Guest Cast:** Don Gordon, Lynda Day, Harold Gould, John Rayner, William Zuckert, James McCallion, Russell Johnson, Selette Cole.

A man goes on trial for murder in the incineration death of an alien.

THE SPORES
Writers: George Eckstein, David W. Rintels, Ellis Kadison, Joel Kane. **Director:** William Hale. **Guest Cast:** Gene Hackman, John Randolph, James Gammon, Judee Morton, Kevin Coughlin, Mark Miller, Patricia Smith, Brian Nash.

Vincent learns of a horrifying alien plot by which new, fully-grown aliens would be born instantly of strange seed spores.

DARK OUTPOST
Writer: Jerry Sohl. **Director:** George McCowan. **Guest Cast:** William Sargent, Tim McIntire, Andrew Prine, Dawn Wells, Tom Lowell, Kelly Jean Peters, Whit Bissell.

While checking out alien susceptibility to minor human ailments, Vincent is unknowingly taken aboard one of the space ships.

SUMMIT MEETING
Writer: George Eckstein. **Director:** Don Medford. **Guest Cast:** William Windom, Diana Hyland, Michael Rennie, Eduard Franz, Ford Rainey, Martin West, Peter Hobbs, Victoria Hale, Richard Eastham, Hank Simms, Troy Melton.

In the first episode of a two-part story, a diabolical alien plot to destroy all of the world's leaders is put forth. In the second show, Vincent

must defuse an experimental rocket that's being tested at a world summit meeting and which will destroy everyone present if released.

THE PROPHET
Writer: Warren Duff. **Director:** Robert Douglas. **Guest Cast:** Pat Hingle, Zina Bethune, Roger Perry, Richard O'Brien, Byron Keith, Dan Frazer, Ray Kellogg.

Vincent must stop an invader who is converting humans to an alien way of thinking by posing as an evangelist.

LABYRINTH
Writer: Art Wallace. **Director:** Murray Golden. **Guest Cast:** Ed Begley, Sally Kellerman, James Callahan, John Zaremba, Martin Blaine, Ed Peck, Virginia Christine.

Vincent takes an alien's chest X-ray to Washington as proof that the invaders have arrived.

THE CAPTIVE
Writer: Laurence Heath. **Director:** William Hale. **Guest Cast:** Dana Wynter, Fritz Weaver, Don Dubbins, Lawrence Dane, Peter Coe, K.L. Smith, Douglas Henderson, Robert Patten.

When an alien is caught in the building of the Communist delegation to the U.N., he threatens to start World War III.

THE BELIEVERS
Writer: Barry Oringer. **Director:** Paul Wendkos. **Guest Cast:** Carol Lynley, Kent Smith, Than Wyenn, Donald Davis, Kathleen Larkin, Rhys Williams, Anthony Eisley.

When Vincent joins forces with several people who believe his claims, the group is attacked by the aliens.

THE RANSOM
Writer: Robert Collins. **Director:** Lewis Allen. **Guest Cast:** Alfred Ryder, Anthony Eisley, Laurence Naismith, Karen Black, Lawrence Montaigne, John Ragin, Christopher Held.

While investigating an alien regeneration center, Vincent and his believers are attacked, but escape by taking a hostage who turns out to be a key alien figure.

TASK FORCE
Writer: Warren Duff. **Director:** Gerald Mayer. **Guest Cast:** Linden Chiles, Nancy Kovack, Martin Wolfson.

The alien plot for conquest leads them to try to undermine the nation's news media, beginning with a huge publishing empire.

THE POSSESSED
Writer: John W. Bloch. **Director:** William Hale. **Guest Cast:** Michael Tolan, Michael Constantine, Katherine Justice, William Smithers, Charles Bateman.

A letter from a colleague alerts Vincent to the notion that the aliens are using electronic programming devices to control humans.

COUNTERATTACK
Writer: Laurence Heath. **Director:** Robert Douglas. **Guest Cast:** Anna Capri, Lin McCarthy, John Milford, Ken Lynch, Donald Davis, Warren Vanders, Don Chastain, Pamela Curran.

When a jamming signal causes one of the saucers to crash, Vincent is accused of murder.

THE PIT
Writer: Jack Miller. **Director:** Louis Allen. **Guest Cast:** Charles Aidman, Joanne Linville, Donald Harron.

A professor who claims proof of an alien invasion is institutionalized as a lunatic.

THE ORGANIZATION
Writer: Franklin Barton. **Director:** William Hale. **Guest Cast:** J.D. Cannon, Chris Robinson.

An alien theft of a valuable shipment of illegal drugs brings a crime syndicate into the search for the invaders.

THE PEACEMAKER
Writer: David W. Rintels. **Director:** Robert Day. **Guest Cast:** James Daly, Phyllis Thaxter.

A top military commander suggests attempting peaceful settlement with the aliens.

THE VISE
Writers: Robert Sabaroff, William Blinn. **Director:** William Hale. **Guest Cast:** Raymond St. Jacques, Roscoe Lee Browne, Lanet MacLachlan.

The alien threat fires the passions of racial tension: a black man may lose a government appointment if Vincent can prove he's an invader.

THE MIRACLE
Writer: Robert Collins. **Director:** Robert Day. **Guest Cast:** Barbara Hershey.

A young woman who witnesses the incineration death of a wounded alien is sure she's had a miraculous vision.

THE LIFE SEEKERS
Writer: Laurence Heath. **Director:** Paul Wendkos. **Guest Cast:** Barry Morse, Diana Muldaur.

Vincent goes to meet two aliens who are willing to stop the invasion of Earth if he'll give them his help.

THE PURSUED
Writer: Don Brinkley. **Director:** William Hale. **Guest Cast:** Suzanne Pleshette.

When an alien woman is given human emotions she finds she cannot control them and turns to Vincent for help.

INQUISITION
Writer: Barry Oringer. **Director:** Robert Glatzer. **Guest Cast:** Mark Richman, Susan Oliver.

When an explosion kills a senator shortly after he meets with Vincent, a government official tries to pin the death on Vincent and his group of fanatical "believers."

I've always been obsessed with the idea of prisons in a liberal democratic society. I believe in democracy, but the inherent danger is that with an excess of freedom in all directions we will eventually destroy ourselves.
— Patrick McGoohan
Creator, producer and star

On June 1, 1968, *The Jackie Gleason Show* was replaced for the summer by a very mysterious series, *The Prisoner*. The openings of the first and of all succeeding episodes are identical. We see a car driving very fast down the center of a road. Then a man, played by Patrick McGoohan, taking long, triumphant strides into a plush office, slaps his resignation down on a desk, and strides out. He had held a highly confidential intelligence post, but has now declared himself through. Back in his apartment, he is packing for an undoubtedly much-deserved vacation but suddenly it looks as though his holiday will be postponed: gas is seeping under his door and he falls, unconscious. We next see him waking up in a lovely little cottage. Puzzled, he ventures out on the balcony to get his bearings. The cottage is situated in a beautiful village of very distinctive architecture surrounded by mountains, a forest and the sea. (Later he will receive a detailed map opaquely identifying the place as "The Village" and the geographical features as "The Mountains," "The Forest," and "The Sea.") While on the balcony he senses that he is being watched.

Other residents are aware that he is a newcomer and refer to him as "Number 6," after the number of his cottage. Number 6 soon discovers that the village phones make only local calls and taxis don't leave the place. But where *is* it? The village is a quirky place with a babble of architectural accents; it could be put anywhere, in the tropics, in the Orient, on the Mediterranean, in Scandinavia, but it belongs nowhere. It is a jumble with spires, turrets, domes, towers and a campanile. Bright red, yellow, blue and white cottages dot the shoreline. There are no post cards to identify the village; and anyway the mail doesn't go *out*. Why is he there? Who has abducted him—his own people or enemies?

He discovers that the whole village is bugged, monitored by television and other spying devices. But it *is* a lovely place. His cottage has maid service, even a butler, a semiregular character played by Angelo Muscat, and every other conceivable comfort. There is entertainment—chess, dancing, films, theater, even a Palace of Fun. The village has its own water supply and electricity generators, a local government run from Town Hall by an elected Town Council. There is a hospital, and a cemetery. All in all, it's an idyllic spot to stay—which is fortunate since there doesn't seem to be any way to leave. He is a prisoner.

Number 6 is summoned to meet Number 2 (Guy Doleman), who informs him that he has been abducted because, "The information in your head is priceless. I don't think you realize what a valuable property you have become. A man like you is in great demand on the open market." When Number 6 begins to ask questions, Number 2 will only say, "A lot of people are curious about what lies behind your resignation...they want to know why you suddenly left."

As soon as his audience with Number 2 is over, Number 6 tries to take a sudden leave again, but his escape is thwarted by very large, very insistent balloons, called "rovers," and he is returned to Number 2. But this time there is a different Number 2 (George Baker). Because Number 1, who calls the shots, doesn't seem to appreciate rivals, the various Number 2s are replaced with the frequency of tissues during a bout with the flu. The current Number 2 tells Number 6 that it is impossible to escape—although he was beginning to formulate ideas along those lines himself.

As Number 6 explores the village, he discovers that the other residents come from many countries and that all of them had once held jobs with intelligence agencies. There are two types of prisoners, those who were brought to the village and those who run it. But it's difficult to tell which is which. Some urge him to escape, others tell him escape is foolhardy, warning him that the rovers can kill. He finds out personally that a major portion of the hospital is devoted to brainwashing the prisoners. Some fight it, some submit to it—after all it's a pleasant, leisurely existence.

No. 6 campaigned to be elected No. 2 in "Free for All."

Number 6 is a fighter, he refuses to be molded like a lump of clay.

This series was perplexing, the issues it raised kept sliding into and out of focus, but it was basically entertainment. As such, it was intriguing, suspenseful, great fun and far more imaginative and intelligent than the common ruck of TV programs. Each of the seventeen episodes dealt with the constant thrust and parry between the village managers and the prisoner; they would attempt to coerce an explanation of his resignation but he would keep silent; he would attempt to escape but they would catch him. For instance, in "A, B, and C" Number 2 (Colin Gordon, this time) attempts to manipulate Number 6's dreams to determine why he quit. That bright Number 14 (Sheila Allen) had developed a process by which dreams are projected onto a television screen; outside elements also can be projected onto the screen, and once an external element is added to the projection, it becomes part of the dream. Number 2 believed that the prisoner was going to sell his secrets but didn't know to whom. His plan was to project each suspected "buyer" into the dream to determine not only that Number 6 had planned to sell his secrets, but to whom he'd planned to sell. When suspects A and B are projected, the dream makes it clear that Number 6 would never sell his secrets, at least not to them. Number 2 doesn't know the identity of suspect C, however, and tries to pry it out of Number 6's dream. But Number 6 is on to him and counters by projecting Number 2 himself into the dream.

The meaning of this Kafkaesque world is as intriguing to the viewer as it is to Number 6. On one level we ask the same questions Number 6 asks: Why was he abducted? By whom? Where is the village? On another level, we ponder the analogy of the village to society in general: Are we all

The Prisoner stands alone in The Village.

prisoners made content with the comforts of our prosperous liberal democracy so long as we don't press too hard for answers, push too much for absolute freedom?

At least one of these questions can be answered definitely. The village is actually a resort, Hotel Portmeirion, near Penrhyndeudraeth on Cardigan Bay in North Wales. It is the work of a single man, Sir Clough Williams-Ellis. Now in his 90's, Sir Clough is a Welsh architect, though he had no formal training, and is still at work on the village after some fifty years. Its idiosyncrasies have made it a favorite retreat for writers, such as Bertrand Russell, George Bernard Shaw and Noel Coward. McGoohan himself often stayed there and the isolated, self-contained village, more fantastic than any set could possibly be, partly inspired him to create the series.

McGoohan was born in New York City of Irish parents who returned to the old sod, to County Leitrim, when he was quite young. He quit school at sixteen and worked successively in a rope factory, a bank, a chicken farm and, after illness ended his farming career, the theater. He was the assistant stage manager of the Sheffield Repertory Company—which meant that he made coffee and performed other menial services. But he was soon seized with the desire to perform larger roles, and starting with bit parts, ended his four years with the company as one of its leading players. McGoohan had a successful, even illustrious, career on the British stage as well as on television and in films before he was selected to play the lead, John Drake, of the highly successful TV series *Secret Agent*, which led to international recognition. With the demise of this show, McGoohan started working on *The Prisoner*.

Not only was the original idea for *The Prisoner* McGoohan's but he was the executive producer, sometime writer and director and the only continuing character on the show, as well. It was his show. Nevertheless, no one can do everything on a television show, and McGoohan had capable help from David Tomblin, the producer, and George Markstein, the script editor; both also wrote some of the scripts. The director of photography was Brendan Stafford and the art direction was done by Jack Shampan. Don Chaffey was the director for most of the episodes.

McGoohan knows his own mind. Though his role as John Drake in *Secret Agent* stood in the shadow of James Bond, he refused to let Drake carry a gun or even to kiss the girl. There was no sex, though there are lots of beautiful women, in *The Prisoner*, since he thought such a sexual focus improper for a family show. Though he was urged to clarify the enigmas in *The Prisoner* in order to make it a popular success, McGoohan adamantly refused. He even refused to reveal the final outcome to the script writers and wrote the last two episodes himself.

All the questions which baffled Number 6 and the viewer are supposedly cleared up in these last two installments, "Once Upon a Time" and "Fall Out." In "Once Upon a Time," the prisoner is subjected to the most brutal form of brain-washing: his mind is electronically probed. This procedure forces him to relive his whole life. In this installment he is referred to once, very briefly, as "Drake." John Drake, of course, is the star of *Secret Agent*. He refuses, however, to reveal the reason for his resignation or to reveal any other secret he holds from his past as an espionage agent.

In "Fall Out," for having refused to cooperate, to be coerced, to be molded, fumigated or fondled, and for his incessant escape attempts, Number 6 wins the right not to be called by a number. He has "vindicated the right of the individual to be an individual," implying that if enough people assert their individuality, society won't become a conformist, dehumanized mass. When Number 6 asks who Number 1 is, the startling answer is that *he* is Number 1. He quit his intelligence post, therefore, for two reasons: first, to protest the repression fostered by the intelligence community as represented by the rovers and the omnipresent bugs; and second, to imprison himself, thereby demonstrating that each man is his own warden, conforming to society's design only by his own commands. His continual escape attempts demonstrated—even though they were continually thwarted—that society's (i.e., his own) repression must be matched by individual steadfastness if freedom and democracy will ever be safe from the conspiracy of Number 1 (i.e., himself) and his ilk. At the very end of this last episode, the prisoner finally does escape the village and drives to London. In the final scene we see his car speed down the road just as it had in the opening of each episode, implying that the cycle is continuing; though he is no longer imprisoned in the village, he remains imprisoned within himself. Got it?

In every episode attempts were made to pick the brain of No. 2 and find out his secrets.

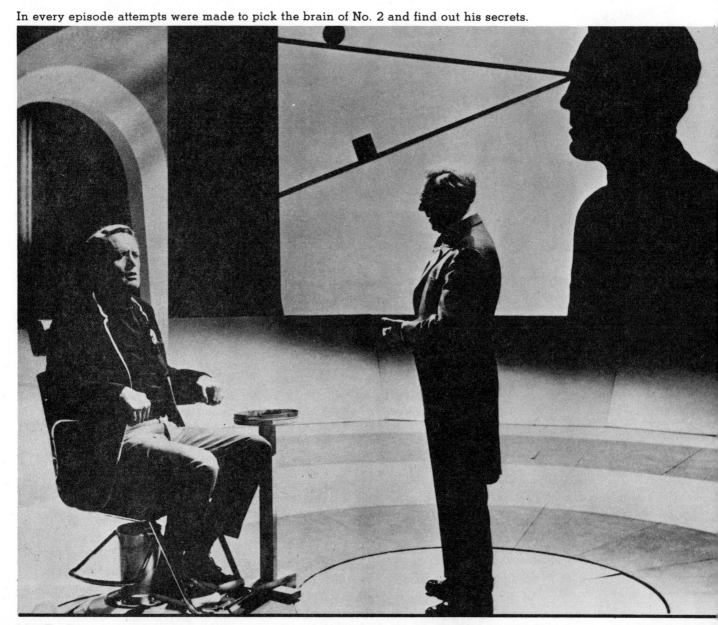

INDEX OF EPISODES

THE PRISONER
1968—one season/17 episodes
CBS/an I.T.C. Production
60 minutes/color

Regular Cast: Patrick McGoohan (Number Six), Angelo Muscat (the butler).

Producer: David Tomblin. **Creator:** Patrick McGoohan. **Director of Photography:** Brandon Stafford, B.S.C. **Music:** Ron Grainer.

ARRIVAL
Writers: George Markstein, David Tomblin. **Director:** Don Chaffey. **Guest Cast:** Virginia Maskell, Guy Doleman, Paul Eddington, George Baker, Angelo Muscat, Barbara Yu Ling, Stephanie Randall.

This opening episode sets the premise for the entire series. A man is abducted to a weird, lovely and dangerously isolated mini-world known as "The Village," where he is told that his capture was necessitated by his curious resignation from a high-level government intelligence post.

THE CHIMES OF BIG BEN
Writer: Vincent Tilsley. **Director:** Don Chaffey. **Guest Cast:** Leo McKern, Nadia Ginlay, Finlay Currie, Richard Wattis, Angelo Muscat, Kevin Stoney, Christopher Benjamin.

The huge London clock tips off the Prisoner that his seemingly successful escape attempt had been used as part of a complex scheme to get information from him.

A, B, & C
Writer: Anthony Skene. **Director:** Pat Jackson. **Guest Cast:** Katherine Kath, Sheila Allen, Colin Gordon, Peter Bowles, Angelo Muscat, Georgina Cookson, Annette Carel.

In the hope that his subconscious holds the key to Number 6's mysterious resignation, Number 2 attempts to manipulate his dreams, using a process developed by Number 14.

FREE FOR ALL
Writer: Paddy Fitz. **Director:** Patrick McGoohan. **Guest Cast:** Eric Portman, Rachel Herbert, George Benson, Harold Berens, John Cazabon, Angelo Muscat, Dene Cooper.

The Prisoner becomes a contender for the post of "Number 2," the physical leader of The Village, but finds that his rights and powers would be just as limited in the new position.

THE SCHIZOID MAN
Writer: Terence Feely. **Director:** Pat Jackson. **Guest Cast:** Jane Merrow, Anton Rodgers, Angelo Muscat, Earl Cameron, Gay Cameron, David Nettheim, Pat Keen, Gerry Crampton.

The leaders of The Village use a double of the Prisoner to convince him he's someone else.

THE GENERAL
Writer: Joshua Adam. **Director:** Peter Graham Scott. **Guest Cast:** Colin Gordon, John Castle, Peter Howell, Angelo Muscat, Al Mancini, Betty McDowall, Peter Swanwick.

The Prisoner tries to thwart an "instant knowledge" system that would give Village leaders the power to control men's minds.

MANY HAPPY RETURNS
Writer: Anthony Skene. **Director:** Joseph Serf. **Guest Cast:** Donald Sinden, Patrick Cargill, Georgina Cookson, Brian Worth, Richard Caldicot, Dennis Chinnery, Jon Laurimore.

When The Village appears abandoned one day, the Prisoner attempts to escape back to London.

DANCE OF THE DEAD
Writer: Anthony Skene. **Director:** Don Chaffey. **Guest Cast:** Mary Morris, Duncan MacRae, Norma West, Angelo Muscat, Aubrey Morris, Bee Duffell, Camilla Hasse, Alan White.

The Prisoner's attempt to smuggle out a plea for help with a corpse is foiled by Number 2, who then puts him on trial.

DO NOT FORSAKE ME OH MY DARLING
Writer: Vincent Tilsley. **Director:** Pat Jackson. **Guest Cast:** Zena Walker, Clifford Evans, Nigel Stock, Angelo Muscat, Hugo Schuster, John Wentworth, James Bree.

A strange procedure puts the Prisoner's personality and his mind into the body of another man.

IT'S YOUR FUNERAL
Writer: Michael Cramoy. **Director:** Robert Asher. **Guest Cast:** Derren Nesbitt, Annette Andre, Mark Eden, Andre Van Gyseghem, Martin Miller, Wanda Ventham, Angelo Muscat.

Village leaders feed the Prisoner misinformation about an assassination attempt in order to prevent him from foiling their own plans.

CHECKMATE
Writer: Gerald Kelsey. **Director:** Don Chaffey. **Guest Cast:** Ronald Radd, Patricia Jessel, Peter Wyngarde, Rosalie Crutchley, George Coulouris, Angelo Muscat, Bee Duffell.

The Prisoner becomes a pawn in a life-sized chess game, where the leaders of The Village try to use his attraction to the Queen to destroy him.

A CHANGE OF MIND
Writer: Roger Parkes. **Director:** Joseph Serf. **Guest Cast:** Angela Browne, John Sharpe, Angelo Muscat, George Pravda, Kathleen Breck, Peter Swanwick, Thomas Heathcote.

In another attempt to discover the Prisoner's secrets, Village leaders use an electronic method for transforming human mental processes.

HAMMER INTO ANVIL
Writer: Roger Woddis. **Director:** Pat Jackson. **Guest Cast:** Patrick Cargill, Victor Maddern, Basil Hoskins, Norman Scace, Derek Aylward, Angelo Muscat, Hilary Dwyer.

To avenge the murder of a young girl, the Prisoner tries to trick Number 2 into believing he is a decoy sent to spy on him.

THE GIRL WHO WAS DEATH
Writer: Terence Feely. **Director:** David Tomblin. **Guest Cast:** Kenneth Griffith, Justine Lord, Christopher Benjamin, Michael Brennan, Harold Berens, Sheena Marsh.

The Prisoner faces a lethal struggle with a young woman, who introduces herself as "Death." She believes them to be made for each other—he, a born survivor, she, a born killer.

ONCE UPON A TIME
Writer: Patrick McGoohan. **Director:** Patrick McGoohan. **Guest Cast:** Leo McKern, Angelo Muscat, Peter Swanwick, John Cazabon, John Maxim.

The Prisoner and Number 2 face a deadly conflict of wills when a dangerous electronic mind probe is used to establish why the Prisoner resigned.

FALL OUT
Writer: Patrick McGoohan. **Director:** Patrick McGoohan. **Guest Cast:** Leo McKern, Kenneth Griffith, Alexis Kanner, Angelo Muscat, Peter Swanwick, Michael Miller.

The prisoner finally wins the right not to be called by a number, to be an individual. He escapes The Village but not the prison of himself.

LIVING IN HARMONY
Writer: David Tomblin. **Director:** David Tomblin. **Guest Cast:** Alexis Kanner, David Bauer, Valerie French, Gordon Tanner, Gordon Sterne, Michael Balfour, Larry Taylor.

In this episode which was never aired on the network, but has been shown in syndication, the Prisoner suddenly finds himself in a western town where he has been appointed sheriff. He faces mental conflict when he must decide whether or not to carry a gun.

ROD SERLING'S NIGHT GALLERY

The way the studio wants to do it, a character won't be able to walk by a graveyard, he'll have to be chased. They're trying to turn it into a Mannix *in a shroud.*

—Rod Serling
Creator

Rod Serling was not idle after *Twilight Zone's* cancellation in 1964. He worked on a few other television shows and wrote the screenplays for the movie versions of *The Planet of the Apes,* based on a novel by Pierre Boulle, and *The Man,* adapted from a book by Irving Wallace. In the fall of 1970, his new series, *Rod Serling's Night Gallery,* appeared as one of four dramatic shows, which ran six episodes each, under the umbrella title *Four-In-One.* In 1971, it appeared on its own as NBC's entry opposite *Mannix.* In both the initial six segments and the 1971 series, it was an hour long and comprised of two or three different playlets. In the 1972-'73 season (its last) it was pared down to a half hour. The series was produced by Jack Laird, and Rod Serling had less to do with it than one might have guessed.

Whereas *Twilight Zone* dealt with science fiction and fantasy, *Night Gallery* was a venture into the occult. Each show opened with Serling in an art gallery after closing time. He would begin his narration strolling past the pictures, then pause at one that represented the evening's story. For example, there was "Pickman's Model," adapted by Alvin Sapinsley from a classic horror tale by H. P. Lovecraft. Serling stopped by a portrait of a terrifying creature prowling a graveyard. In the story, a young artist has rented a studio in New England where the famous, but mad, Richard Upton Pickman (Bradford Dillman), painter of ghouls and monsters, had lived and worked. As the young artist and a friend discuss Pickman's life, the scene flashes back to the turn of the century....

Pickman teaches painting to wealthy young women in order to support himself and be free to pursue his real passion, painting monsters and ghouls. He reveals the subject of his latest project to one of his students, Miss Goldsmith (Louise Sorel). The bizarre paintings are based on a local legend about a race of manlike creatures who dwell in tunnels beneath the city, surfacing only to capture

OPPOSITE: Host Rod Serling strolled through a gallery at the opening of each show. **ABOVE:** Veteran Hollywood actress Joan Crawford made one of her infrequent TV appearances on the series' pilot episode. She played an evil blind woman capable of robbing other people of their sight in a segment directed by Steven (Jaws) Spielberg.

human females to propagate the race. Miss Goldsmith expresses a desire to see Pickman's work, but, greatly disturbed at the prospect of a private showing, he flees, leaving one of his paintings behind. Miss Goldsmith goes to his home to return it. Upon arriving she finds the house empty and sneaks into Pickman's studio. There she finds horrifying portraits of monsters, including one of a monster carrying off a young girl. Suddenly, Pickman returns and is enraged to find her there. He shouts that she must leave immediately but that it may already be too late. In the midst of this raving, they both hear animal noises. He orders her to go upstairs, to lock the door and not to come down under

any circumstances. Locked upstairs, she hears the sound of a fight...then silence...then footsteps on the stairs. T her horror, the locked door protecting her is pulled off it hinges revealing a hideous scaly monster. As the creatur is about to claim her as his bride, Pickman recovers to figh the monster off and enables Miss Goldsmith to escape.

We return to the present as the young artist is finishin the narrative, saying that the paintings as well as Pickma had been missing ever since. The pair decide to search fc Pickman's missing paintings. They begin in the basemer and prepare to break into a concrete block above the floo thinking that the paintings might be there. Inside, howeve we glimpse the waiting monster....

"The Messiah of Mott Street" written by Serling was nominated for an Emmy. It starred Edward G. Robinson and Yaphet Kotto.

In sharp contrast to *Twilight Zone, Night Gallery* wa panned by critics. Among those not infatuated with th show was Rod Serling himself. No stranger to the inte ference of sponsors, networks and censors, Serling onc again found himself locked by contract into an untenabl situation. Imagine a clothing company started by a tailc whose name is sterling to his customers—Gluckman, let call him. Gluckman's success and popularity are based o his flawless reputation. His main competitor is Schwartz Ready-to-Wear, where everything is done by machine. Th day comes when Gluckman produces a few designs an finds that they can't be marketed because his compan too, has hired machines to imitate the stuff being cranke out by Schwartz. And there is nothing Gluckman can d about it.

That is the kind of situation Rod Serling found himse in. He owned *Night Gallery,* created it and it was sold t network and audience on his reputation. The competitio on CBS was *Mannix,* a formula private-eye shoot-anc rough-'em-up. Serling felt that NBC and Universal wer doing their best to imitate *Mannix,* with an emphasis c monsters, chases and fights. They turned down many of h; scripts as "too thoughtful." Serling lamented, "They don want to compete against *Mannix* in terms of contrast, bu similarity." Not only was Serling unable to sell them script he was also barred from casting sessions, and couldn make decisions about his show—he had signed awa creative control. As a result, he tried to have his nam removed from the title, but NBC had him contract-bound t play host and cordially to introduce the parasite to the T audience.

Oddly enough, despite executive hassling, two of th shows that Serling did write were nominated for Emmy "They're Tearing Down Tim Riley's Bar" starred Williar Windom and Diane Baker. In it, a lonely widower sees parallel between the tearing down of his beloved local ba and the shambles of his life. "The Messiah of Mott Street starred Edward G. Robinson as an old, ill Jew anxious stay alive to care for his young grandson. The old man als wants to live to see his faith in the coming of the Messia realized. His grandson decides to help and goes looking fc Him.

When Rod Serling's *Night Gallery* was canceled at th end of the 1973 season, Serling retired from TV to teach Ithaca College in Upstate New York, not far from where h grew up.

On June 28, 1975, Rod Serling died of complication following open-heart surgery. He was fifty years old. In hi twenty-five-year career, though the medium fought hir every inch of the way, he had given it many of its very be moments.

"The Dead Man"

INDEX OF EPISODES

"The Little Black Bag"

ROD SERLING'S NIGHT GALLERY
1971/90 plays
NBC/a Jack Laird Production for Universal TV
60 minutes (first two seasons); 30 minutes (third season)/color

Host: Rod Serling.

Producer: Jack Laird. **Creator:** Rod Serling. **Makeup:** Bud Westmore; John Chambers. **Music:** Gil Melle.

First Season: 1970
(part of Four-In-One)

THE DEAD MAN
Writer: Douglas Heyes. Director: Douglas Heyes. Guest Cast: Carl Betz, Jeff Corey, Louise Sorel, Michael Blodgett.
A doctor carries an experiment in hypnosis to terrifying conclusion.

THE HOUSEKEEPER
Writer: Matthew Howard. Director: John M. Lucas. Guest Cast: Jeanette Nolan, Larry Hagman, Suzy Parker, Cathleen Cordell.
After hiring an unwanted old woman with a heart of gold, a man plans to transfer her kindly soul into the body of his nagging wife.

ROOM WITH A VIEW
Writer: Hal Dresner. Director: Jerrold Freedman. Guest Cast: Joseph Wiseman.
With the unwitting aid of his nurse, an invalid schemes to revenge himself on his unfaithful wife.

THE LITTLE BLACK BAG
Writer: Rod Serling. Director: Jeannot Szwarc. Guest Cast: Burgess Meredith, Chill Wills.
A wino on skid row for twenty years, a discredited doctor discovers a medical bag filled with miraculous medicine which was accidentally hurled back through time from the twenty-first century.

THE NATURE OF THE ENEMY
Writer: Rod Serling. Director: Allen Reisner. Guest Cast: Joseph Campanella.
A scientist monitors the efforts of an astronaut investigating the weird disappearance of a team that landed on the moon.

THE HOUSE
Writer: Rod Serling. Director: John Astin. Guest Cast: Joanna Pettet, Paul Richards, Steve Franken.
A beautiful girl, who is a patient in a sanitarium, has persistent dreams about a house that seems to beckon her.

CERTAIN SHADOWS ON THE WALL
Writer: Rod Serling. Director: Jeff Corey. Guest Cast: Louis Hayward, Agnes Moorehead, Rachel Roberts, Grayson Hall.
Three sisters and a brother fight for their lives in a house haunted by ghosts, memories, jealousies and fear.

MAKE ME LAUGH
Writer: Rod Serling. Director: Steven Spielberg. Guest Cast: Godfrey Cambridge, Tom Bosley, Jackie Vernon.
An unsuccessful, depressed comedian is willing to pay any price to make people laugh and gets a chance when he encounters a genie anxious to prove his own powers.

CLEAN KILLS AND OTHER TROPHIES
Writer: Rod Serling. Director: Walter Doniger. Guest Cast: Raymond Massey, Barry Brown.
A hunter insists that his son prove his manliness before he can inherit the family fortune, by hunting and killing a deer.

PAMELA'S VOICE
Writer: Rod Serling. Director: Richard Benedict. Guest Cast: Phyllis Diller, John Astin.
A man has killed his wife because she never stopped nagging him about his many faults—but her death has not solved his problems.

THE ACADEMY
Writer: Rod Serling. Director: Jeff Corey. Guest Cast: Pat Boone, Leif Erickson.
A father checks out a military school reputed to employ slightly unorthodox methods for handling delinquent boys.

THE FUNERAL
Writer: Richard Matheson. Director: Jeannot Szwarc. Guest Cast: Werner Klemperer, Joe Flynn.
A man returns from the dead in order to stage a more lavish funeral than the one he had.

THE LATE MR. PEDDINGTON
Writer: Jack Laird. Director: Jeff Corey. Guest Cast: Kim Hunter, Harry Morgan.
A funeral director is curious when a woman starts making some strange arrangements for her still-alive husband.

LONE SURVIVOR
Writer: Rod Serling. Director: Gene Levitt. Guest Cast: John Colicos, Torin Thatcher.
A man who put on woman's clothing to save his life when the Titanic sank is doomed to be taken aboard other ships also destined to go down.

THE DOLL
Writer: Rod Serling. Director: Rudi Dorn. Guest Cast: Shani Wallis, John Williams, Henry Silva.

After returning to England from India, a man finds his niece in possession of a doll that seems strangely alive.

THEY'RE TEARING DOWN TIM RILEY'S BAR
Writer: Rod Serling. Director: Don Taylor. Guest Cast: William Windom, Diane Baker, Bert Convy, John Randolph.
When a lonely widower sees his favorite hangout about to be torn down, he realizes that his entire world has fallen apart.

THE LAST LAUREL
Writer: Rod Serling. Director: Daryl Duke. Guest Cast: Jack Cassidy.
A paralyzed man, who can raise his spirit from his body through the art of levitation, decides to use this power to avenge himself on his supposedly unfaithful wife. His plans of murder, however, go awry.

Second Season: 1971

THE BOY WHO PREDICTED EARTHQUAKES
Writer: Rod Serling. Director: John M. Badham. Guest Cast: Clint Howard.
A ten-year old boy, whose predictions are always proved true, suddenly and mysteriously stops predicting.

MISS LOVECRAFT SENT ME
Writer: Jack Laird. Director: Gene Kearney. Guest Cast: Sue Lyon, Joseph Campanella.
A blonde, gum-chewing babysitter reports for an evening's work at the home of a vampiric gentleman.

THE HAND OF BORGUS WEEMS
Writer: Alvin Sapinsley. Director: John M. Lucas. Guest Cast: Ray Milland, George Maharis.
A man begs a surgeon to remove his hand, which he claims possesses a murderous mind of its own.

PHANTOM OF WHAT OPERA?
Writer: Gene Kearney. Director: Gene Kearney. Guest Cast: Leslie Nielsen, Mary Ann Beck.
A masked phantom kidnaps a beautiful young girl with a startling secret of her own.

A FEAR OF SPIDERS
Writer: Rod Serling. Director: John Astin. Guest Cast: Kim Stanley, Patrick O'Neal.
A woman vows that a man, who had cruelly rejected her, one day will need her desperately.

CLASS OF '99
Writer: Rod Serling. Director: Jeannot Szwarc. Guest Cast: Vincent Price, Brandon de Wilde.

"Since Aunt Ada Came to Stay"

"How to Cure the Common Vampire"

"The Caterpillar"

In a classroom of the future, an instructor in bigotry addresses a most unusual graduating class.

JUNIOR
Writer: Gene Kearney. **Director:** Theodore Flicker. **Guest Cast:** Wally Cox, Barbara Flicker.

Parents debate about whose turn it is to get up in middle of the night and give junior a glass of water.

SINCE AUNT ADA CAME TO STAY
Writer: Alvin Sapinsley. **Director:** William Hale. **Guest Cast:** Jeanette Nolan, James Farentino, Michele Lee, Jonathan Harris.

Aunt Ada, a witch, is looking for a younger body to inhabit.

A DEATH IN THE FAMILY
Writer: Rod Serling. **Director:** Jeannot Szwarc. **Guest Cast:** E.G. Marshall, Desi Arnaz, Jr.

When a wounded man fleeing the law meets up with a strange mortician, his troubles really start.

SATISFACTION GUARANTEED
Writer: Jack Laird. **Director:** Jeannot Szwarc. **Guest Cast:** Victor Buono, Cathleen Cordell.

A gentleman rejects several beautiful job applicants before selecting a less attractive but fully-packed young lady—to devour!

THE FLIP SIDE OF SATAN
Writers: Malcolm Marmorstein, Gerald Sanford. **Director:** Jerrold Freedman. **Guest Cast:** Arte Johnson.

A ruthless disc jockey gets his just deserts when he encounters the occult.

THE DIFFERENT ONES
Writer: Rod Serling. **Director:** John M. Lucas. **Guest Cast:** Dana Andrews.

In accordance with the Federal Conformity Act of 1993, a man must send his misfit son to another planet.

HELL'S BELLS
Writer: Theodore Flicker. **Director:** Theodore Flicker. **Guest Cast:** John Astin.

A car crash victim winds up in a very personal Hell.

KEEP IN TOUCH—WE'LL THINK OF SOMETHING
Writer: Gene Kearney. **Director:** Gene Kearney. **Guest Cast:** Alex Cord, Joanna Pettet.

To find the girl in his dreams, a man gives her description to the police on a trumped-up charge.

THE MERCIFUL
Writer: Jack Laird. **Director:** Jeannot Szwarc. **Guest Cast:** Imogene Coca, King Donovan.

A couple that takes marriage very seriously agrees to a most unusual marital pact.

WITH APOLOGIES TO MR. HYDE
Writer: Jack Laird. **Director:** Jeannot Szwarc. **Guest Cast:** Adam West.

Dr. Jekyll agrees to sample an unusual potion prepared by his assistant.

WITCHES' FEAST
Writer: Gene Kearney. **Director:** Jerrold Freedman. **Guest Cast:** Agnes Moorhead, Ruth Buzzi, Fran Ryan.

A trio of cackling hags prepares dinner.

DR. STRINGFELLOW'S REJUVENATOR
Writer: Rod Serling. **Director:** Jerrold Freedman. **Guest Cast:** Forrest Tucker.

A con artist in medicine man's clothing tries to trick the citizens of a small western town with a "miracle" drug.

THE DIARY
Writer: Rod Serling. **Director:** William Hale. **Guest Cast:** Patty Duke, Virginia Mayo, David Wayne.

A cruel gossip columnist drives an aging ex-star to suicide—then receives a mysterious diary from the deceased.

THE BIG SURPRISE
Writer: Richard Matheson. **Director:** Jeannot Szwarc. **Guest Cast:** John Carradine.

An eccentric farmer tells three curious youngsters where to dig for a very special prize.

PROFESSOR PEABODY'S LAST LECTURE
Writer: Jack Laird. **Director:** Jerrold Freedman. **Guest Cast:** Carl Reiner.

A college professor makes the mistake of defunking Lovecraftian gods, despite protests from students Robert Bloch and August Derleth!

THE MIRACLE AT CAMAFEO
Writer: Rod Serling. **Director:** Ralph Senensky. **Guest Cast:** Harry Guardino, Julie Adams, Ray Danton.

Tracing a couple to a Mexican town famous for its faith healing, an insurance investigator suspects a man has fraudulently collected $500,000 for an accident from which he plans to "miraculously" recover.

A MATTER OF SEMANTICS
Writer: Gene Kearney. **Director:** Jack Laird. **Guest Cast:** Cesar Romero, E.J. Peaker.

A vampire checks in at a local blood bank—and demands a withdrawal.

AN ACT OF CHIVALRY
Writer: Jack Laird. **Director:** Jack Laird. **Guest Cast:** Ron Stein, Deidre Hudson, Jimmy Cross.

A ghost is trapped in an elevator with some suspicious characters.

A MIDNIGHT VISIT TO THE BLOOD BANK
Writer: Jack Laird. **Director:** William Hale. **Guest Cast:** Victor Buono.

Another vampire and another blood bank.

THE PHANTOM FARMHOUSE
Writer: Halsted Welles. **Director:** Jeann Szwarc. **Guest Cast:** David McCallum, Linc Marsh, David Carradine.

When a patient missing from a priva hospital turns up murdered, the man who ru the hospital decides to do a little investigating his own.

SILENT SNOW, SECRET SNOW
Writer: Gene Kearney. **Director:** Gene Kea ney. **Guest Cast:** Radames Pera, Lisabe Husk, Lonny Chapman. Narrated by Orso Welles.

A twelve-year-old boy becomes engulfed his own fantasy world where it never stop snowing.

A QUESTION OF FEAR
Writer: Theodore Flicker. **Director:** Jack Lair **Guest Cast:** Leslie Nielsen, Fritz Weaver, Jac Bannon.

A former Army officer bets he can survive night in a supposedly haunted house.

THE DEVIL IS NOT MOCKED
Writer: Gene Kearney. **Director:** Gene Kea ney. **Guest Cast:** Helmut Dantine, Franc Lederer.

A vampire makes things difficult for a to Nazi General and his men.

STOP KILLING ME
Writer: Jack Laird. **Director:** Jeannot Szwar **Guest Cast:** Geraldine Page, James Gregor

A woman, who is convinced her husband trying to scare her to death, seeks help from police sergeant.

THE TUNE IN DAN'S CAFE
Writer: Gerald Sanford. **Director:** David Ra fael. **Guest Cast:** Pernell Roberts, Susan Olive

As a couple discusses their marital problem in a cafe, the juke box plays only one recor which seems linked to a tragic romanti triangle of the past.

MARMALADE WINE
Writer: Jerrold Freedman. **Director:** Jerrol Freedman. **Guest Cast:** Robert Morse, Rud Vallee.

Seeking refuge from a storm, a dim-witte young man encounters trouble when h dodges into the home of a retired, and highl mysterious, surgeon.

A FEAST OF BLOOD
Writer: Stanford Whitmore. **Director:** Jeann Szwarc. **Guest Cast:** Norman Lloyd, Sandr Locke, Jill Ireland.

A calculating and beautiful woman is pre sented with a strange gift—a small, mouselik brooch.

"Green Fingers"

"Return of the Sorcerer"

"The Girl with the Hungry Eyes"

PICKMAN'S MODEL
Writer: Alvin Sapinsley. Director: Jack Laird. Guest Cast: Bradford Dillman, Louise Sorel.

Based on a classic H.P. Lovecraft tale, the story concerns a young girl at the turn of the century who is drawn to a gloomy artist whose canvases are filled with visions of monsters.

THE DEAR DEPARTED
Writer: Rod Serling. Director: Jeff Corey. Guest Cast: Steve Lawrence, Harvey Lembeck, Maureen Arthur, Patricia Donahue.

A phony spiritualist who runs a successful operation decides to change partners.

ROOM FOR ONE LESS
Writer: Jack Laird. Director: Jeannot Szwarc. Guest Cast:

A vignette about elevator manners.

COOL AIR
Writer: Rod Serling. Director: Jeannot Szwarc. Guest Cast: Barbara Rush, Henry Darrow, Beatrice Kay.

Based on a classic H.P. Lovecraft tale, the story concerns a mysterious doctor who sought to come to grips with death by prolonging his existence through a strange refrigeration apparatus.

CAMERA OBSCURA
Writer: Rod Serling. Director: John M. Badham. Guest Cast: Ross Martin, Rene Auberonois.

A heartless money-lender receives his just payment when he is hurled through time by a most unusual camera.

DELIVERIES IN THE REAR
Writer: Rod Serling. Director: Jeff Corey. Guest Cast: Cornel Wilde, Rosemary Forsyth.

A turn-of-the-century surgeon hires shady characters to provide cadavers for his medical school, but learns too late the terrible price for

Barbara Anderson in "Fright Night"

asking no questions about where the bodies came from.

THERE AREN'T ANY MORE MacBANES
Writer: Alvin Sapinsley. Director: John Newland. Guest Cast: Joel Grey, Howard Duff.

A student of witchcraft zaps his uncle when the latter threatens to disinherit him, but soon learns that occult forces are more easily stirred than stopped.

I'LL NEVER LEAVE YOU—EVER
Writer: Jack Laird. Director: Daniel Haller. Guest Cast: John Saxon, Lois Nettleton, Royal Dano.

A woman calls upon an old witch to hasten the death of her ailing husband.

THE WAITING ROOM
Writer: Rod Serling. Director: Jeannot Szwarc. Guest Cast: Buddy Ebsen, Gilbert Roland, Steve Forrest, Albert Salmi, Jim Davis, Lex Barker.

After riding past a ominous hanging figure, a gunfighter enters the town saloon where everyone seems to know all about his past, present and future.

HOUSE—WITH GHOST
Writer: Gene Kearney. Director: Gene Kearney. Guest Cast: Bob Crane, Jo Anne Worley.

To get rid of his wife, a man leases a house with most unusual furnishings.

QUOTH THE RAVEN
Writer: Jack Laird. Director: Jeff Corey. Guest Cast: Marty Allen.

While writing his famous poem, Edgar Allen Poe is pestered by a noisy bird.

THE MESSIAH OF MOTT STREET
Writer: Rod Serling. Director: Don Taylor. Guest Cast: Edward G. Robinson, Tony Roberts, Yaphet Kotto.

Critically ill, an impoverished, seventy-seven-year-old Jew is anxious to stay alive to look after his nine-year-old grandson. Realizing that his abiding faith in the coming of the Messiah is another reason for his grandfather's living, the boy goes in search of Him.

THE PAINTED MIRROR
Writer: Gene Kearney. Director: Gene Kearney. Guest Cast: Zsa Zsa Gabor, Arthur O'Connell, Rosemary de Camp.

Owners of a shop dealing in secondhand merchandise buy a mirror reflecting a strange, prehistoric landscape—that is alarmingly alive!

LOGODA'S HEADS
Writer: Robert Bloch. Director: Robert Bloch. Guest Cast: Patrick MacNee, Brock Peters, Tim Matheson, Denise Nichols.

Witch doctors and Voodoo figure prominently in this vest-pocket revenge story.

HOW TO CURE THE COMMON VAMPIRE
Writer: Jack Laird. Director: Jack Laird. Guest Cast: George Carlin, Richard Deacon.

Fearless vampire exterminators provide a lesson in stake driving.

THE CATERPILLAR
Writer: Rod Serling. Director: Jeannot Szwarc. Guest Cast: Laurence Harvey, Joanna Pettet, John Williams, Tom Helmore.

A man schemes to murder the husband of a beautiful woman in Borneo by slipping him a deadly insect known as an "earwig." His scheme backfires rather horribly for him.

LITTLE GIRL LOST
Writer: Stanford Whitmore. Director: Timothy Golfas. Guest Cast: William Windom, Ed Nelson.

A brilliant scientist maintains touch with reality by pretending his accidentally-killed daughter is still alive.

LINDEMANN'S CATCH
Writer: Rod Serling. Director: Jeff Corey. Guest Cast: Stuart Whitman, Dana Andrews, Anabel Garth.

To keep the mermaid he has captured—and has fallen in love with—a sea captain recruits the aid of a dabbler in the occult.

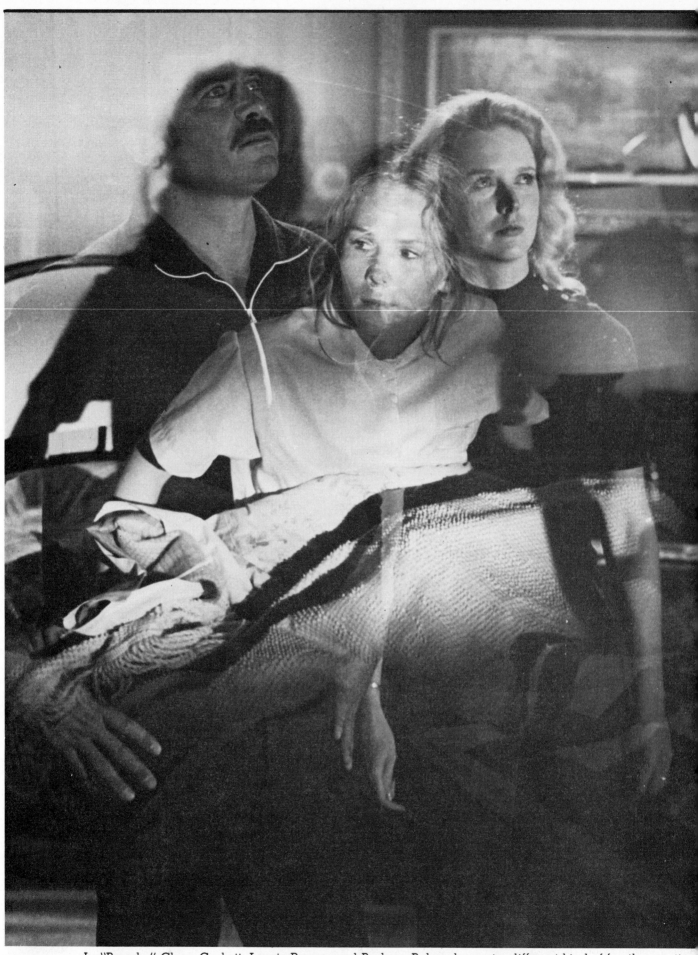

In "Brenda," Glenn Corbett, Laurie Prange and Barbara Babcock spent a different kind of family vacation

"The Ring with the Red Velvet Ropes"

"Fright Night"

"Spectre in Tap Shoes"

TELL DAVID
Writer: Gerald Sanford. **Director:** Jeff Corey. **Guest Cast:** Sandra Dee.

Lost while driving, a girl receives instructions for the right road from an unusual couple, and soon begins to suspect that she has had a glimpse into the future.

MIDNIGHT NEVER ENDS
Writer: Rod Serling. **Director:** Jeannot Szwarc. **Guest Cast:** Susan Strasberg, Robert F. Lyons.

A girl picks up a hitchhiking marine and the two experience a bizarre case of deja vous.

THE DARK BOY
Writer: Halsted Welles. **Director:** John Astin. **Guest Cast:** Elizabeth Hartman, Gale Sondergaard.

Based on a classic August Derleth tale, the story concerns a new schoolteacher in a small, rural community who has visions of a tragic-looking little boy who has been dead for many years.

GREEN FINGERS
Writer: Rod Serling. **Director:** John M. Badham. **Guest Cast:** Elsa Lanchester, Cameron Mitchell.

The "green thumb" of a murdered woman spells doom for the cruel man responsible for her death.

BRENDA
Writer: Matthew Howard. **Director:** Allen Reisner. **Guest Cast:** Glenn Corbett, Laurie Prange.

On her summer vacation, an eleven-year-old girl meets and befriends "The Thing," a weird-looking monster.

THE GHOST OF SORWORTH PLACE
Writer: Alvin Sapinsley. **Director:** Ralph Senensky. **Guest Cast:** Richard Kiley, Jill Ireland.

An American traveler is drawn to a mysterious mansion in Scotland, whose occupant implores him to help rid the place of her late husband's ghost.

THE SINS OF THE FATHERS
Writer: Halsted Welles. **Director:** Jeannot Szwarc. **Guest Cast:** Geraldine Page, Michael Dunn, Barbara Steele, Richard Thomas.

An unusually strong cast in this tense drama of sin-eating and depravity in nineteenth-century Wales.

YOU CAN'T GET HELP LIKE THAT ANYMORE
Writer: Rod Serling. **Director:** Jeff Corey. **Guest Cast:** Broderick Crawford, Cloris Leachman, Lana Wood.

Outraged, the head of the Robot-Aids Agency warns a sadistic couple about abusing the help.

Third Season: 1972

THE RETURN OF THE SORCERER
Writer: Halsted Welles. **Director:** Jeannot Szwarc. **Guest Cast:** Bill Bixby, Vincent Price, Patricia Sterling.

A sinister sorcerer hires a man to translate an ancient Arabic manuscript which is said to possess the secret of great power.

THE GIRL WITH THE HUNGRY EYES
Writer: Robert Malcolm Young. **Director:** John Badham. **Guest Cast:** Joanna Pettet, James Farentino, John Astin.

When a struggling young photographer finds the ideal model for an advertising campaign, he is warned never to follow her or see her outside the studio. His curiosity leads to a terrifying conclusion.

FRIGHT NIGHT
Writer: Robert Malcolm Young. **Director:** Jeff Corey. **Guest Cast:** Stuart Whitman, Barbara Anderson.

After moving into an inherited farmhouse, a writer and his wife are told never to move or open a strange trunk in the attic.

THE RING WITH THE RED VELVET ROPES
Writer: Robert Malcolm Young. **Director:** Jeannot Szwarc. **Guest Cast:** Gary Lockwood, Joan Van Ark, Chuck Connors.

The new, self-assured heavyweight champion of the world faces a strange match in an even stranger world.

RARE OBJECTS
Writer: Rod Serling. **Director:** Jeannot Szwarc. **Guest Cast:** Mickey Rooney, Raymond Massey, Fay Spain.

Though he fears a doublecross, the world's most feared gangster takes refuge in his girl friend's apartment when he is critically injured.

YOU CAN COME UP NOW, MRS. MILLIKAN
Writer: Rod Serling. **Director:** John Badham. **Guest Cast:** Ozzie and Harriet Nelson.

The wife of a wacky, unsuccessful inventor agrees to become the subject of his latest, most dangerous experiment.

WHISPER
Writer: David Rayfael. **Director:** Jeannot Szwarc. **Guest Cast:** Sally Field, Dean Stockwell, Kent Smith.

When a girl visiting an old English country house starts hearing voices of the dead, her companion fears she may be losing her mind, or worse—the voices might be real!

THE DOLL OF DEATH
Writer: Jack Guss. **Director:** John Badham.
Guest Cast: Susan Strasberg, Alejandro Rey, Murray Matheson, Barry Atwater.

An Englishman enlists the power of Voodoo to foil the faithless activities of the girl he was intending to marry.

DEATH ON A BARGE
Writer: Halsted Welles. **Director:** Leonard Nimoy. **Guest Cast:** Lesley Warren, Lou Antonio, Brooke Bundy, Robert Pratt.

An unusual vampire tale, about a lonely young man who falls in love with a mysterious girl who lives on a barge but forbids him to come aboard.

SHE'LL BE COMPANY FOR YOU
Writer: David Ray Field. **Director:** Gerald Perry Finnerman. **Guest Cast:** Jack Oakie, Leonard Nimoy, Lorraine Gary, Kathryn Hays.

A widower, relieved at his wife's death, is given a cat to keep him company by his late wife's friend. The feline turns out to be more foe than friend.

SPECTRE IN TAP SHOES
Writer: Gene Kearney. **Director:** Jeannot Szwarc. **Guest Cast:** Sandra Dee, Dane Clark, Christopher Connelly.

A girl returns to her New England home to find her sister dead—hanging from a noose. She then begins to see and hear evidence of her sister's continued presence.

SOMETHING IN THE WOODWORK
Writer: Rod Serling. **Director:** Edmund M. Abrams. **Guest Cast:** Geraldine Page, Leif Erickson.

An alcoholic is convinced that a convict, killed in her house years earlier, lives as a ghost in the attic.

FINNEGAN'S FLIGHT
Writer: Rod Serling. **Director:** Gene Kearney. **Guest Cast:** Burgess Meredith. Cameron Mitchell, Barry Sullivan.

Through hypnosis, a convict relieves some of the anxieties of a fellow convict serving a life sentence. Unexpected side effects, however, lead to a bizarre conclusion.

THE OTHER WAY OUT
Writer: Gene Kearney. **Director:** Gene Kearney. **Guest Cast:** Burl Ives, Ross Martin.

A straight suspense thriller, involving murder, blackmail and the unexpected.

HATRED UNTO DEATH
Writer: Halsted Welles. **Director:** Gerald Perry Finnerman. **Guest Cast:** Dina Merrill, Stephen Forrest, Fernando Lamas.

The capture of a strange, almost human gorilla spells terror for a husband and wife writing team who capitalize on their African adventures.

KOLCHAK: THE NIGHT STALKER

Kolchak really isn't a pure horror show, although it deals with man-killing monsters and creatures every week. The simple fact is you can't do a legitimate "horror show" on network time, as the sponsors don't want to scare people out of their pants. So we decided to titillate, not terrify, to have fun with it.

—Darren McGavin
Actor, Co-producer

The premise of *Kolchak: The Night Stalker* is that ancient, fabled monsters stalk twentieth-century America. In the dark corners of our nation's cities, in alleyways and abandoned buildings, in scientific research centers, on college campuses, aboard luxury liners, within sewers, sports arenas, high-rise buildings and hospitals, they lurk, waiting to pounce on their next unsuspecting victim.

Enter Carl Kolchak, a hard-bitten, down-at-the-heels newspaperman with a gift for snappy patter and a nose for supernatural news. Though ulcer-ridden Tony Vincenzo (Simon Oakland), Kolchak's editor, respects or at least tolerates his *enfant terrible,* the cops and political hacks despise him for his smart-aleck manner and unorthodox methods. He works alone, trusts no one; he has many contacts but few friends. The world be damned, camera and tape recorder are sufficient companions for our modern-day Dr. Van Helsing who is dedicated to the defense of the human race in spite of itself. After hours, in the solitude of his office, Kolchak jabs the *Record* button and sardonically discusses the day's assignment with his tape recorder. Though he will get his monster eventually, the reward for his diligence and canniness—the big scoop—always eludes him since the authorities are determined to keep the public ignorant and will put a lid on the story.

The Kolchak character is a pastiche of old newspaperman cliches created by Jeff Rice in his 1970 novel, *The Kolchak Papers.* It sat around the ABC offices for years until producer Dan Curtis of daytime television's *Dark Shadows* dusted it off and handed it to Richard Matheson to adapt as a TV movie. Matheson fleshed out the character but Darren McGavin brought it to life. McGavin comments:

This guy, I've got him in my mind, see, he's fired from the *New York Journal* in 1955. That day, the day he was fired, he was wearing a seersucker suit, a black string tie and a white shirt with a button-down collar. So, he's still wearing 'em. He hasn't bought a suit of clothes since he was fired.... The truth of the matter is I love Kolchak. He's terrific. What he's saying to the world is beautiful— the heck with you, brother, I'll get my story anyway. He's a man in a million.

Kolchak in *The Night Stalker.*

In *The Night Stalker,* a TV movie that gave birth to the series, Kolchak pursued Janos Skorzeny (Barry Atwater), a vampire that terrorized Las Vegas.

The feature they made was entitled *The Night Stalker,* and when it went on the air on March 17, 1972, it broke all ratings records. It was the most popular telefilm ever broadcast at that time. In it, Carl Kolchak pieced together the mystery of Janos Skorzeny (Barry Atwater). Las Vegas was being terrorized by a killer who stalked his victims—young, attractive women—late at night. Each victim sports a neck wound and has been drained of blood. The coroner's report states that the wounds contain human saliva. The authorities, as usual, are dumbfounded, but this information piques Kolchak's interest and then his prepared mind picks up a second clue—the hospital was burglarized and blood plasma is missing. Kolchak is now convinced that he is dealing with a vampire and that it can

Going after the vampire to drive a wooden stake into it's heart.

only be Janos Skorzeny. He stalks Skorzeny to his lair armed only with a silver cross—which vampires find very unsettling—and a wooden stake. When he finds his vampire, he drives the stake home and rids Las Vegas of its menace. His scoop, however, is suppressed by thankless authorities, and Carl Kolchak is pinned with a murder rap and drummed out of town.

The author of the original novel, Jeff Rice, says that he had always wanted to write a vampire story and drive a stake into the seedy heart of Las Vegas:

A vampire could easily live in Las Vegas, and nobody would think anything was odd—they wouldn't suspect he was a vampire. Men who never come out in the daytime make up about twenty-five percent of the town's work force. Working the "graveyard shift," if you'll pardon the expression.

Though a critical and popular success, *Kolchak* was a bit of an embarrassment to ABC because of the violence it portrayed. Additionally, the network was ashamed that this lowbrow monster movie garnered the highest rating of ABC's season. Nevertheless, a year later *Kolchak* returned in a second TV movie, *The Night Strangler,* written by Matheson. Dr. Malcolm Richards (Richard Anderson, late of the *Six Million Dollar Man*) is an old alchemist who must murder women periodically in order to maintain his youthful appearance. The final thrilling scenes in which Kolchak prowls Anderson's gaslit world beneath the streets of Seattle is fantasy scripting at its best. "It was like another world down there, a world of yesterday," narrates Kolchak. "Sidewalks and storefronts just as they'd been left after the fire of 1889. Windows built to admit the light, admitting only darkness, now. Ground floors of office buildings, now the unused cellars of those buildings. The tomb of Old Seattle. . . ."

The fascinating concept is actually based on fact. Matheson and his family had often gone camping in the Seattle area and had gone on the tour of "The City Under-

In "The Ripper," the premiere episode of the series, Jack the Ripper turns up in Chicago.

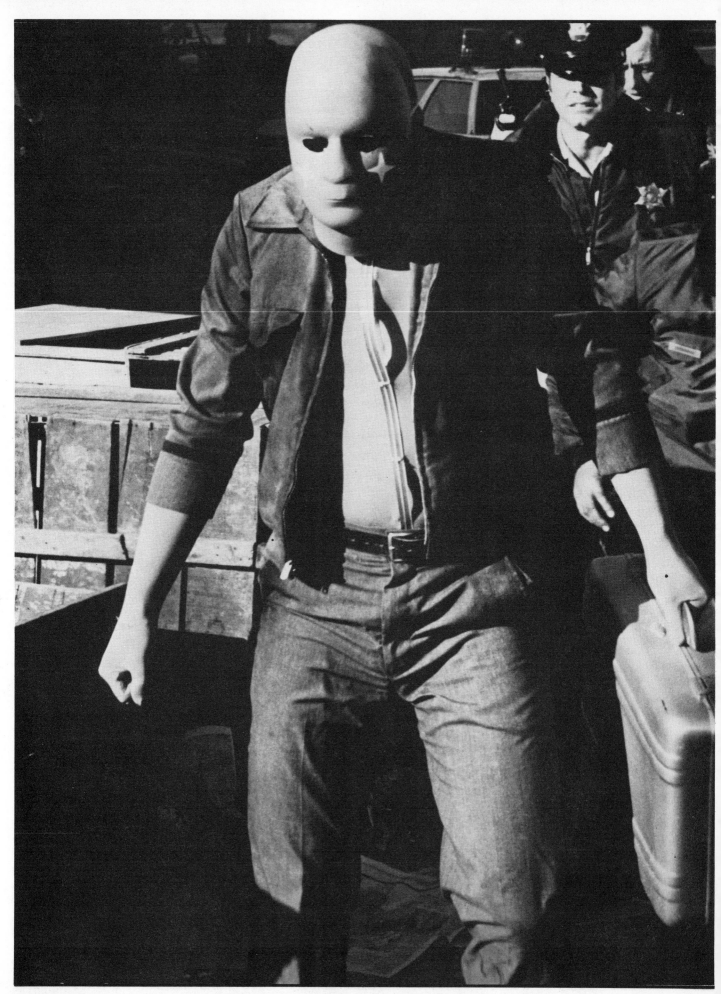

neath Seattle," where the old storefronts and streets still do, in fact, exist.

Convinced that the rumpled reporter was an excellent series prospect, McGavin decided to coproduce a weekly program for ABC with his own company, Francy Productions. The series was filmed at Universal Studios, and each episode featured a different monster to challenge Kolchak's detective journalism. Simon Oakland was recruited from the feature films to continue his role of Vincenzo, though now they worked for a wire service. The other regulars were co-workers—prissy, sarcastic Ron Updyke (Jack Grinnage) and sweet little old Emily Cowles (Ruth McDevitt), the only person in the world our hard-nosed hero loves and trusts. McGavin adapted the same successful formula that had been used in the features right down to Kolchak's pulse-quickening narration. In *The Night Strangler*, Matheson had added some touches of humor and had made the monster-hunting newshawk a richer and more eccentric personality. McGavin liked this approach, since it increased the fun and took the edge off some of those goose-pimply sequences that might have caused trouble with the network censors. (Even so, when the show went into summer repeats at prime time, moments considered too intense for family viewing were snipped.)

In order to cut costs, McGavin let Matheson go and hired less accomplished writers. Their scripts, while lively, lacked Matheson's special knack for pacing and character conflict. Jimmy Sangster's tribute to H. P. Lovecraft, "Horror in the Heights," did come close, however. The monster in this story was a Rakshasah which, according to legend, has power over the mind and can lure its victims to their deaths by appearing to them as someone they trust: to an elderly Jew, it appears as a rabbi; to a rookie cop, his sargeant; to Carl Kolchak, Miss Emily—the only person he trusts. It is not, of course, Miss Emily, but the advance scout of a race of monsters that is waiting to invade earth and devour all humanity. Aided by a fellow monster-tracker played by Abraham Sofear, Kolchak tracks the Rakshasah and puts an arrow through it, saving the human race for the nonce.

Taking a tip from the better horror movies, McGavin kept his monsters in the shadows, preferring suggestive horror to the explicit stuff. Prolonged closeups and well-lit scenes were replaced by quick cuts and hazy hand-held photography. The photographer also helped to convey the documentary look of actual news coverage. And McGavin barred all publicity shots of the monsters themselves:

I didn't want our viewers thinking we were some sort of "monster-of-the-week" thing. I happen to have a terrible sense of reality, and when I look at a guy in a rubber mask I say, "There's a guy in a rubber mask." That bores me. It's much more frightening if the lights suddenly go out in the house and something starts scratching at the door and you don't know what the hell it is. You open the door and there's nothing there. You shut the door and pretty soon it starts again. Now *that's* scary.

Unfortunately, the show went through an entire season of twenty episodes almost completely unnoticed—not even graced with a Cleveland Amory review in *TV Guide*. Compounding the lack of response, the show was then sued by Jeff Rice, who claimed that he had never given permission to spin off his creation into a weekly series.

OPPOSITE: In "Mr. R.I.N.G." Kolchak's prey was a rampaging robot.

When ABC's new programming boss Fred Silverman took over, the demise of *Kolchak* was inevitable. Silverman had a reputation for disliking fantasy sci-fi shows, not to mention those with legal problems and low ratings. After bravely defending the human race against all sorts of monsters, Carl Kolchak, underpaid newshawk, and Darren McGavin, talented but unappreciated actor, were axed by the network.

INDEX
OF
EPISODES

KOLCHAK: THE NIGHT STALKER

1974—one season/20 episodes
ABC/Francy Productions for Universal TV
60 minutes/color

Regular Cast: Darren McGavin (Carl Kolchak), Simon Oakland (Tony Vincenzo), Jack Grinnage (Ron Updyke), Ruth McDevitt (Emily Cowles).

Executive Producer: Darren McGavin. **Producer:** Paul Playton, Cy Chermak. **Creator:** Jeff Rice. **Story Consultant:** David Chase. **Music:** Gil Melle.

THE RIPPER

Writer: Rudolph Borchert. **Director:** Allen Baron. **Guest Cast:** Beatrice Colan, Ruth McDevitt.

The original Jack the Ripper is responsible for a series of brutal slayings in modern-day Chicago.

THE ZOMBIE

Writer: Zekial Markel. **Director:** Alex Grasshoff. **Guest Cast:** Joe Sirola, Charles Aidman, Val Bisoglio.

Key figures in Chicago's underworld are being killed off by an unstoppable, zombielike creature.

U.F.O.

Writer: Rudolph Borchert. **Director:** Allen Baron. **Guest Cast:** James Gregory, Mary Wickes, Dick Van Patten.

The bone marrow from animals and humans is being drained by an invisible space force.

THE VAMPIRE

Writer: David Chase. **Director:** Don Weiss. **Guest Cast:** Jan Murray, Kathleen Nolan, William Daniels.

The female victim of a vampire Carl Kolchak destroyed in Las Vegas emerges from the grave.

THE WEREWOLF

Writers: David Chase, Paul Playdon. **Director:** Don Weiss. **Guest Cast:** Eric Breadan, Henry Jones, Bob Hastings.

While on a pleasure cruise, Carl Kolchak is stalked by a blood-lusting werewolf.

FIRE-FALL

Writer: Bill S. Ballinger. **Director:** Don Weiss. **Guest Cast:** Fred Beir, Philip Carey, Madlyn Rhue.

A famous pianist is tormented by a strange, diabolical alter-ego.

THE DEVIL'S PLATFORM

Writer: Donn Mullally. **Director:** Allen Baron. **Guest Cast:** Tom Skerritt, Ellen Weston, Julie Gregg.

A crafty young politician, in league with Satan, transforms himself into a murderous "hound from Hell' to do away with the competition.

BAD MEDICINE

Writer: L. Ford Neale. **Director:** Alex Grasshoff. **Guest Cast:** Richard Kiel, Ramon Bieri, Alice Ghostley, Victor Jory.

A creature from American Indian folklore, capable of changing into the forms of different animals, threatens modern-day Chicago.

THE SPANISH MOSS MURDERS

Writer: Al Friedman. **Director:** Gordon Hessler. **Guest Cast:** Keenan Wynn, Severn Darden, Randy Boone, Johnny Silver.

A legendary swamp monster is "dreamed" into reality by a patient at an experimental research center.

THE ENERGY EATER

Writers: Arthur Rowe, Rudolph Borchert. **Director:** Alex Grasshoff. **Guest Cast:** William Smith, Michael Strong, John Alvin.

A new hospital is plagued with mysterious disasters caused by an invisible creature that thrives on electrical energy.

HORROR IN THE HEIGHTS

Writer: Jimmy Sangster. **Director:** Michael T. Caffey. **Guest Cast:** Phil Silvers.

Elderly residents of a ghetto neighborhood in Chicago are being gnawed to death by a monster which appears to its victims as someone they trust.

MR. R.I.N.G.

Writer: L. Ford Neale. **Director:** Gene Levitt. **Guest Cast:** Julie Adams, Corrine Michaels.

A rampaging robot escapes from a scientific institute.

THE PRIMAL SCREAM

Writers: Bill S. Ballinger, David Chase. **Director:** Robert Scherer. **Guest Cast:** Pat Harrington, Katherine Woodville, Lindsay Workman.

Million-year-old oil cells from the Arctic grow into a prehistoric, apelike creature.

THE TREVI COLLECTION

Writer: Rudolph Borchert. **Director:** Don Weiss. **Guest Cast:** Nina Foch, Lara Parker.

Wooden mannequins come to life at the command of a beautiful witch.

CHOPPER

Writers: Steve Fisher, David Chase. **Director:** Bruce Kessler. **Guest Cast:** Larry Linville, Jim Backus, Sharon Farrell.

Members of a hoodlum gang are being killed by a headless corpse on a motorcycle.

DEMON IN LACE

Writers: Stephen Lord, David Chase. **Director:** Michael Kozoll. **Guest Cast:** Andrew Prine, Keenan Wynn.

"Succubus," a demon in female form, preys on her admiring young students on a college campus.

LEGACY OF TERROR

Writer: Arthur Rowe. **Director:** Don McDougall. **Guest Cast:** Ramon Bieri, Pippa Scott, Sorrell Booke, Victor Campos.

Aztec sun worshippers murderously acquire fresh human hearts to resurrect a centuries-old mummy.

THE KNIGHTLY MURDERS

Writers: Michael Kozoll, David Chase. **Director:** Vincent McEveety. **Guest Cast:** John Dehner, Hans Conried, Robert Emhart, Jeff Donnell.

A twelfth-century knight menaces Chicago.

THE YOUTH KILLER

Writer: Rudolph Borchert. **Director:** Don McDougall. **Guest Cast:** Cathy Lee Crosby, Dwayne Hickman.

Young men—perfect physical specimens—suddenly die from rapid aging.

THE SENTRY

Writers: L. Ford Neale, John Huff. **Director:** Seymour Robbie. **Guest Cast:** Kathie Brown (Mrs. McGavin), Tom Bosley.

A lizardlike creature threatens an underground installation when scientists take away its eggs.

The monsters and demons on the show were rarely photographed or seen in full light. In this rare shot from "Demon in Lace," one of the creatures peers over Kolchak's shoulder.

The biggest problem with Space: 1999 *(first season) was the characters weren't "human." One aspect of our new stories is greater depths in the relationships the Alphans. We want audiences to live the situations with them. It is important that they are likable, believable people.*
— Fred Freiberger
Producer (second season)

Executive producer Gerry Anderson and producer Sylvia Anderson, his wife, made SPACE: 1999 in Great Britain with the intention of selling it in the U.S., but the American networks balked. Not wanting their efforts to collect dust, the Andersons sold the show for syndication and it has consistently garnered high ratings since it's been on the air. The first show was aired in 1975.

From the beginning *Space: 1999* has been determined to pull free of *Star Trek*'s gravitational field, but has ended up orbiting it. Whether or not fans and people connected with the show like it, the program is almost always compared to *Star Trek* rather than criticized on its own merits. One viewer says, "The major difference I can see between *Star Trek* and *Space: 1999* is philosophy. In *Star Trek* all life forms are to be treated as intelligent. In a recent episode of *Space: 1999* there was a monster, and all they could think of doing was killing it." Martin Landau, the star of the show, criticizes *Star Trek* as being too "macho" because their ship packs heavy artillery, whereas he claims *Space: 1999* is not macho presumably because the Alphans are helpless. Other critical reactions to the show are divided and tend to get passionate. Comments range from "spectacular" and "the most impressive television production in the history of the medium," to "this show is dumb," and "abysmal beyond belief." These antithetical appraisals are reactions to the erratic character of the shows.

The premise of the series is actually interesting. Man in the year 1999 had been using the dark side of the moon as a dump for nuclear waste. A self-maintaining scientific installation, Moonbase Alpha, is a kind of eternal night watchman at the dump, but also has the less routine job of preparing for extensive space exploration. Lo and behold, a new planet called Meta wanders into the solar system and, as a result of the mounting pressure to explore it, Commander John Koenig, clearly the best man for the job, is put in charge of Alpha.

Curious disasters begin to occur. Some astronauts on the moon begin dropping like flies, while others, their eyes turning bright green, go insane. Koenig's top officers, Professor Victor Bergman (Barry Morse) and Dr. Helena Russell (Barbara Bain), are baffled, but while they attempt to solve the mystery, Koenig is pressured to prepare the Meta flight by his visiting superior officer, unsympathetic,

"Breakaway" was the premiere episode wherein Dr. Russell (Barbara Bain), Commander Koenig (Martin Landau) and Dr. Bergman (Barry Morse) began their strange odyssey.

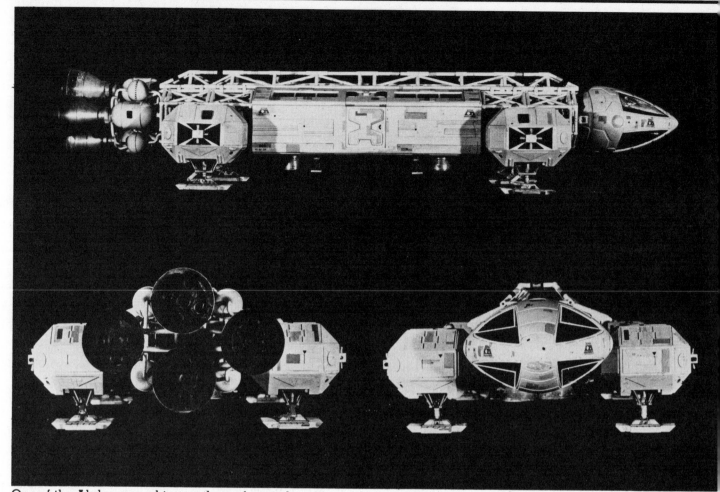

One of the Alpha spaceships as shown from side, rear, and front, is determinedly different from *Star Trek's* Enterprise.

hard-driving Commissioner Simmonds (Roy Dotrice). The cause of the disasters is finally discovered to be magnetic radiation, but before any action can be taken, it causes the nuclear wastes to explode, hurtling the moon out of its orbit into the vastness of the galaxy. So the odyssey begins with the moon and its three hundred eleven reluctant passengers from Alpha careering in space.

What does Alpha encounter on its unexpected trek? Trouble! Ultraintelligent and usually snobbish alien life

Commissioner Simmonds (Roy Dotrice) delivers an order to Commander Koenig.

forms tell the pilgrims to get lost whenever they propose to land and stay somewhere for awhile. The attitude here is the opposite of *Star Trek's* "optimism factor": there can be no brotherhood among beings from different planets, only distrust, fear and hatred.

The show works best on a purely visual level. Its special effects and scenic design are breathtaking. Brian Johnson, the director of special effects, was one of the designers for Stanley Kubrick's film classic, *2001: A Space Odyssey.* "We're working on a different scale here," he explains, "yet we're paying just as much attention to detail and perspective." Probably Johnson's most important creations for the show are the *Eagle* spaceships that take the crew to and from the planets they are asked to leave. Three separate models were built for shooting the spaceships' exteriors; the largest is four feet long. All *Space: 1999* special effects shots are filmed in miniature scale settings, using photo cutouts for backgrounds with a tabletop base.

As a result of the special effects, the best episodes depict visits to planets with bizarre environments, weird physical laws and inhabitants, or interplanetary wars fought by sleek spaceships whose weapons cause spectacular Fourth of July explosions.

Obviously, any TV series that even approaches the beauty of Kubrick's *2001* would be a joy to behold, and those who are enthusiastic about the show must be responding on a purely visual level as *Space: 1999* has no real drama to redeem it. On the plot level, the stories are unintelligible or, even worse, have abandoned intelligence. In the first place, the plots display a swaggering

ABOVE: The Eagle defends Moonbase Alpha in a spectacular battle sequence.
BELOW: Special effects wizard Brian Johnson puts the final touches on a miniature set.

disregard for scientific accuracy. Isaac Asimov, the prolific and admired science fiction writer and scientist, claims that the show is scientifically preposterous. He says that neither the moon nor the Earth could survive an explosion of the magnitude required to send the Earth's only satellite on a wild junket into space. Even if the moon were to survive this first catastrophe, it would take lifetimes for it to run into another inhabited planet—*if* it were aimed. Since the Alphans are on an accidental course, it would take longer. Those of us prudent enough to remain here on Earth would have to wait millenia for the next episode—though perhaps many would prefer it that way. *Star Trek* solved the same problem with an imaginary "warp drive," not a perfect solution, but at least the problem was not ignored.

The series has other scientific problems as well. The moon is supposedly drifting in a sunless void, yet it is always illuminated brightly. How are the inhabitants of Moonbase Alpha fed? These are not quibbles about detail. In the fifties, or earlier, when all space adventure *was* fiction and the layman had little scientific knowledge, it was possible for the creators of science fiction to ignore the importance of consistency with scientific fact. Modern viewers, even young ones, have witnessed *actual* space travel. They are sophisticated and like their science fiction with large dollops of science.

Abandoning science has not been *Space: 1999's* only flaw; to a great degree, it has abandoned reason, as well: the stories often cannot be understood. "The Black Sun" is a good example of the kind of unintelligible plots offered up. In this episode, the hapless moon is being drawn toward what the writers call a "black sun." In fact, it must be what

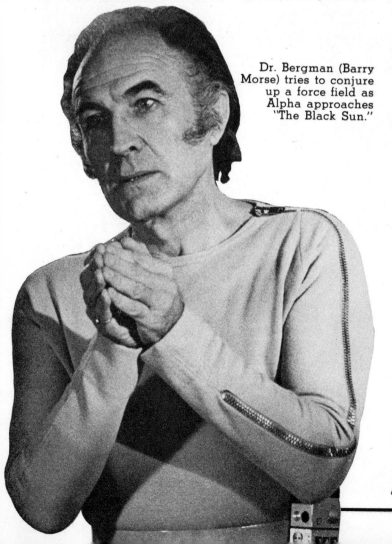

Dr. Bergman (Barry Morse) tries to conjure up a force field as Alpha approaches "The Black Sun."

scientists today call a black hole—an area of such great mass and with such a powerful gravitational field that it can destroy everything in its vicinity. The crew builds a force field hoping to save Alpha from destruction—to no avail. Koenig and Bergman finally send the rest of the crew off into space as they remain on Alpha to "go down with the ship." As they draw close to the "black sun" they become transparent, then all sound stops. In seconds, they age eons and hear a disembodied, childlike voice (God's? Kubrick's?) proclaiming itself as the prime mover of the universe. The voice stops, and Koenig and Bergman return to normal. They conclude that the force field they had built to stave off destruction had worked after all, and that they had simply fallen through the black sun. This story is so filled with holes it's no wonder that they fell through. For one, sound stops in a vacuum, something as dense as a black hole would *increase* its transmission, not smother it. And, if sound stopped, how did they hear the strange voice? If their force field had worked, how is it that they got sucked into the black sun anyway? Most importantly, what did the whole experience *mean*? Great dramatic emphasis is placed on it but no follow-up or explanation is ever offered. It is pure phantasmagoria. Unfortunately, "The Black Sun" is not unique in its flaws; many of the other stories are equally fatuous.

In addition to the inane story lines, the show's characters are heroic, but wooden. For instance, Bain and

Catherine Schell joined regulars Bain and Landau as Moonbase Alpha's resident alien, Maya, during the second season.

Landau play people who are romantically involved but act like business partners. By contrast, in *Star Trek* the interplay among the different characters animated each of the stories, whereas here each character could have been a clone from Mr. Spock. The attempt to make the Alphans larger-than-life heroes, although conceptually interesting, does not work as it did on shows like *Batman* or *Mission Impossible* (the latter, another Bain-Landau costar venture). On the former the approach was "high camp" and viewers accepted—even expected—the characters to be stilted and predictable. On *Mission Impossible* the viewer was so involved with the intense, cleverly designed plots that the individual personalities of the characters automatically were subordinated. It was necessary that they act like machines; emotional displays would subvert the missions. On *1999*, though, the approach is serious, not camp, and the missions are much too hazy to carry the show on their own without the backup of strong personalities.

Although pleased by the show's widespread popular success, the executive producer Gerry Anderson was all too aware of its flaws and wanted to make any changes necessary for it to comply with the laws of nature and make its characters believable. During its first year on the air, Anderson's wife left his bed, board and show. Anderson then hired Fred Freiberger, who had produced Star Trek's third season, to take over. Freiberger vowed to make the principals more believable, starting by adding fire to the

love affair between the characters played by Bain and Landau. He also wanted to add new characters, most significantly an alien named Maya who would serve as Alpha's science officer. In handling the editorial side of things, Freiberger also called for scripts containing "more honest adventure," as an effort to get away from the confused, metaphysical claptrap they had been accused of airing.

Freiberger was successful in the humanization of the first season regulars. The introduction of Maya however was not the wisest move. Audiences looked upon her as a gimmick—a Mr. Spock rip-off, a token, rather than a resident, alien.

As the end of the second season approached, the series had actually slipped in popularity and was dying out on both coasts. In New York, they resorted to using *Star Trek* reruns as a lead-in to *Space*.

The stories no longer had the absurd aspects they displayed in the first season, but they became silly Saturday morning action adventure rather than serious science fiction. Industry rumors said that if the series continued at all, it will be without Freiberger at the helm. It all leaves one to wonder whether with all its flaws, *Space* should have left well enough alone—*Space: 1999* became *Cancelled: 1977*.

INDEX
OF
EPISODES

SPACE: 1999
1975-1977
Syndicated/an I.T.C. Production
60 minutes/color

Regular Cast: Martin Landau (John Koenig), Barbara Bain (Helena Russell), Barry Morse (Victor Bergman—first season only), Nick Tate (Alan Carter), Catherine Schell (Maya—beginning second season), Tony Anholt (Tony Verdeschi—beginning second season).

Executive Producer: Gerry Anderson. **Producer:** Sylvia Anderson (first season), Fred Freiberger (second season). **Creators:** Gerry and Sylvia Anderson. **Special Effects:** Brian Johnson. **Costumes:** Rudi Gernreich. **Music:** Barry Gray.

First Season: 1975-1976

BREAKAWAY
Writer: George Bellak. **Director:** Lee H. Katzin. **Guest Cast:** Roy Dotrice, Philip Madoc, Lou Satton, Eric Carte.

In this initial adventure a chain reaction of thermonuclear explosions blasts the moon out of Earth's orbit and sends it hurling into space. On the barren sphere, the three hundred and eleven men and women of Moonbase Alpha, a self-sustaining scientific installation, survive.

EARTHBOUND
Writer: Anthony Terpiloff. **Director:** Charles Crichton. **Guest Cast:** Christopher Lee, Roy Dotrice.

Commissioner Simmonds, who was visiting Moonbase Alpha when the moon was blasted out of orbit, sees an unexpected chance to return home when an alien spaceship en route to Earth encounters the Alphans and crashlands near their base.

DRAGON'S DOMAIN
Writer: Christopher Penfold. **Director:** Charles Crichton. **Guest Cast:** Gianni Garko, Douglas Wilmer, Barbara Kellerman, Michael Sheard, Susan Jameson.

Astronaut Tony Cellini baffles everyone with a story the experts refuse to believe—of a group of stationary spaceships, a space graveyard, with a terrifying monster guarding the entrance.

DEATH'S OTHER DOMINION
Writer: Anthony Terpiloff. **Director:** Charles Crichton. **Guest Cast:** Brian Blessed, John Shrapnel, Mary Miller.

The Alphans are invited to share a lost paradise and immortality on the frozen planet Ultima Thule with members of a space expedition from Earth launched in 1986.

THE TESTAMENT OF ARKADIA
Writer: Johnny Byrne. **Director:** David Tomblin. **Guest Cast:** Orso Maria Guerrini, Lisa Harrow.

Commander Koenig must free Moonbase Alpha from the power-draining influence of the desolate planet of Arkadia. Complicating matters are two specialists who are determined to renew civilization on the dead world.

THE TROUBLED SPIRIT
Writer: Johnny Byrne. **Director:** Ray Austin. **Guest Cast:** Giancarlo Prette, Hillary Dwyer, Anthony Nicholls.

When a botanist is forbidden to continue a series of experiments on plants, the Alphans are terrorized by his murderous, vengeful spirit—a spectre that seeks retribution for the man's death before it occurs.

MATTER OF LIFE AND DEATH
Writer: Art Wallace. **Director:** Charles Crichton. **Guest Cast:** Richard Johnson, Stuart Damon.

The discovery of Dr. Russell's husband, lost in space years earlier, nearly leads to disaster when the Alphans realize that he is composed of anti-matter, and that living on his planet would mean violent death for humans.

FORCE OF LIFE
Writer: Johnny Byrne. **Director:** David Tomblin. **Guest Cast:** Ian McShane, Gay Hamilton, John Hamill, Eva Rueberstaier.

Commander Koenig and his crew must stop one of the Moonbase technicians, whose sudden, consuming need for heat threatens Alpha with doom.

ALPHA CHILD
Writer: Christopher Penfold. **Director:** Ray Austin. **Guest Cast:** Julian Glover, Cyd Hayman, Wayne Brooks.

When an Alphan woman gives birth, she unwittingly becomes part of an attempt by aliens to avoid their civilization's extinction by taking over the bodies of Moonbase personnel.

ANOTHER TIME, ANOTHER PLACE
Writer: Johnny Byrne. **Director:** David Tomblin. **Guest Cast:** Judy Geeson.

A weird space phenomenon which creates duplicates of the Moonbase and its inhabitants leads to the death of a young woman—who had already envisioned the disaster.

THE BLACK SUN
Writer: David Weir. **Director:** Lee H. Katzin. **Guest Cast:** Paul Jones, Jon Laurimore.

Commander Koenig must bank all hope for survival on Professor Bergman's plan to create a new force field when the Moonbase is drawn into a deadly "black sun."

GUARDIAN OF PIRI
Writer: Christopher Penfold. **Director:** Charles

Crichton. **Guest Cast:** Catherine Schell, Michael Culver.

Only Commander Koenig sees through a seductive woman's entreaties to join her on the planet Piri for a blissful, machine-controlled existence.

THE LAST SUNSET
Writers: Christopher Penford, Charles Crichton. **Director:** Charles Crichton. **Guest Cast:** None.

The Alphans must determine whether the planet Ariel, which closely resembles Earth, is really the hope for their future that it appears to be.

THE LAST ENEMY
Writer: Bob Kellett. **Director:** Bob Kellett. **Guest Cast:** Caroline Mortimer, Maxine Audley, Kevin Stoney, Carolyn Courage.

Commander Koenig must negotiate a cease-fire between two warring planets whose battling threatens to destroy the Moonbase.

END OF ETERNITY
Writer: Johnny Byrne. **Director:** Ray Austin. **Guest Cast:** Peter Bowles, Jim Smilie.

Commander Koenig must risk his own life in order to destroy a psychopathic alien.

SPACE BRAIN
Writer: Christopher Penfold. **Director:** Charles Crichton. **Guest Cast:** Shane Rimmer, Carla Romanelli, Derek Anders.

Moonbase Alpha faces danger on a collision course with a gossamerlike organism that has annihilated an Eagle craft and crew and taken possession of the mind of another crew member.

VOYAGER'S RETURN
Writer: Johnny Byrne. **Director:** Bob Kellett. **Guest Cast:** Jeremy Kemp, Barry Stokes, Alex Scott, Lawrence Trimble.

A scientist hurries to retrieve valuable research information from an Earth-launched spacecraft before the Alphans destroy it. Unknown to them, he is responsible for the malfunction that turned the ship into a deadly killer.

WAR GAMES
Writer: Christopher Penfold. **Director:** Charles Crichton. **Guest Cast:** Anthony Valentine, Isla Blair.

A planet's attack on Moonbase Alpha leaves the Alphans no alternative but to relocate on the planet. But the aliens who inhabit it warn them that humans would be destructive to their civilization—and they will protect themselves at any cost.

THE INFERNAL MACHINE
Writers: Anthony Terpiloff, Elizabeth Barrows. **Director:** David Tomblin. **Guest Cast:** Leo McKern.

Dr. Russell and Commander Koenig must free themselves from a powerful man-machine that plans to keep them as its human companions until the day they die.

THE FULL CIRCLE
Writers: Jesse Lasky, Jr., Pat Silver. **Director:** Bob Kellett. **Guest Cast:** Oliver Cotton.

When two Alpha reconnaissance flights pass through a time warp, the crews find themselves sharing an existence with their Cro-Magnon counterparts.

MISSING LINK
Writer: Edward Di Lorenzo. **Director:** Ray Austin. **Guest Cast:** Peter Cushing, Joanna Dunham.

A scientist from a planet millions of years in the future abducts Commander Koenig for his studies of a "missing link."

RING AROUND THE MOON
Writer: Edward Di Lorenzo. **Director:** Ray Austin. **Guest Cast:** Max Faulkner.

The Alphans must destroy a mission from a dead planet that is absorbing Moonbase information and destroying personnel as part of a plan to attack Earth.

COLLISION COURSE
Writer: Anthony Terpiloff. **Director:** Ray Austin. **Guest Cast:** Margaret Leighton.

The Alphans plan to use explosives to avoid a collision course with another planet, but an alien woman convinces Koenig that destiny would be better served if their planets did collide.

MISSION OF THE DARIANS
Writer: Johnny Byrne. **Director:** Ray Austin. **Guest Cast:** Joan Collins, Aubrey Morris, Dennis Burgess, Paul Antrim, Robert Russell.

A landing party travels to a huge spaceship, where the fourteen remaining survivors of a dead planet stay alive by cannibalism.

Second Season: 1976-1977

THE METAMORPH
Writer: Johnny Byrne. **Director:** Charles Crichton. **Guest Cast:** Brian Blessed, Anoushka Hempel.

This first episode of the season, produced by Fred Freiberger, introduces Maya to the regular cast. On the planet Psychon, an evil-minded alien named Mentor captures the Alphans and tries to drain their minds. His daughter Maya who is capable of transforming herself into any form, helps the Earth people escape.

ALL THAT GLISTERS
Writer: Keith Miles. **Director:** Ray Austin. **Guest Cast:** Patrick Mower.

Moonbase Alpha is invaded by hostile living rocks. The strange alien life forms can com-

municate, transport themselves and attack unsuspecting Alphans with deadly rays.

THE EXILES
Writer: Donald James. **Director:** Ray Austin. **Guest Cast:** Peter Duncan, Stacy Dorning, Margaret Inglis.

The Alphans rescue two innocent-looking young aliens who turn out to be psychopathic killers.

JOURNEY TO WHERE
Writer: Donald James. **Director:** Tom Clegg.

Guest Cast: Freddie Jones, Isla Blair, Roger Bizley, Laurence Harrington, Jeffrey Kissoon.

Koenig, Dr. Russell and Alan Carter are transported back to the planet Earth as it was in 1339 during the Black Plague.

THE MARK OF ARCHANON
Writer: Lew Schwartz. **Director:** Charles Crichton. **Guest Cast:** John Standing, Michael Gallagher.

Two aliens are released from suspended animation. They then begin to infect the Alphans with a mysterious disease.

Catherine Schell's Maya was intended to increase the show's ratings, but audience response to her was only lukewarm.

ONE MOMENT OF HUMANITY
Writer: Tony Barwick. **Director:** Charles Crichton. **Guest Cast:** Billie Whitelaw, Leigh Lawson.

Helena and Tony Verdeshi are kidnapped by a lovely female alien, who hopes to use the Earthlings as emotional blueprints for her heartless android masters.

THE RULES OF LUTON
Writer: Charles Woodgrove. **Director:** Val Guest. **Guest Cast:** David Jackson, Godfrey James, Roy Marsden.

Maya and John Koenig are spirited to a strange planet where they are pitted against three horrifying aliens.

THE TAYBOR
Writer: Thom Keyes. **Director:** Bob Brooks. **Guest Cast:** Willoughby Goddard.

An interstellar slave trader offers the Alphans a ride home in exchange for Maya.

THE BETA CLOUD
Writer: Charles Woodgrove. **Director:** Robert Lynn. **Guest Cast:** None.

A space cloud containing a horrifying creature attacks Moonbase Alpha.

BRIAN THE BRAIN
Writer: Jack Ronder. **Director:** Kevin Connor. **Guest Cast:** Bernard Cribbins.

A super-robot, originally from Earth, kidnaps Koenig and Dr. Russell and threatens Moonbase Alpha with gravitational disturbance.

THE CHRYSALIS A-B-C
Writer: Tony Barwick. **Director:** Val Guest. **Guest Cast:** Ina Skriver, Sarah Douglas.

A planet protected by powerful energy beams rattles Alpha before Commander Koenig and his team can investigate.

CATACOMBS OF THE MOON
Writer: Anthony Terpiloff. **Director:** Robert Lynn. **Guest Cast:** James Laurenson, Pamela Stephenson.

Weird visions of destruction haunt an underground miner as his critically ill wife fights for her life.

SEEDS OF DESTRUCTION
Writer: John Goldstone. **Director:** Kevin Connor. **Guest Cast:** None.

In a cavern within an asteroid, strange alien crystals create an evil duplicate of Koenig.

SPACE WARP
Writer: Charles Woodgrove. **Director:** Peter Medak. **Guest Cast:** None.

Caught in a strange space warp, Moonbase Alpha inhabitants are afflicted by sudden madness.

NEW ADAM, NEW EVE
Writer: Terence Feely. **Director:** Val Guest. **Guest Cast:** Guy Rolfe.

A space being who calls himself "God" offers the Alphans a new planet Earth to colonize.

A MATTER OF BALANCE
Writers: Pip and Jane Baker. **Director:** Charles Crichton. **Guest Cast:** Lynn Frederick, Stuart Wilson.

The keeper of an alien temple intends to substitute the Alphans with his dying race.

BELOW: In "Seeds of Destruction," Koenig found himself ensnared in an alien force field.

THE BRINGERS OF WONDER
Writer: Terence Feely. **Director:** Tom Clegg. **Guest Cast:** Stuart Damon, Patrick Westwood.

In this two-part episode, a spaceship from Earth lands on Moonbase Alpha, but only John Koenig sees the visitors as the horrifying aliens they really are.

THE LAMBDA FACTOR
Writer: Terence Dicks. **Director:** Charles Crichton. **Guest Cast:** Debra Fallander, Jess Conrad.

A cosmic cloud transforms one of Moonbase Alpha's women into a megalomaniac with strange super powers.

DEVIL'S MOON
Writer: Michael Winder. **Director:** Tom Clegg. **Guest Cast:** Hildegarde Neil.

Commander Koenig is captured and held prisoner by a race of cat women.

DORZAK
Writers: Pip and Jean Baker. **Director:** Charles Crichton. **Guest Cast:** Lee Montague, Jill Townsend.

An evil space criminal from Maya's home planet Psychon threatens the Alphans.

SEANCE SPECTRE
Writer: Donald James. **Director:** Peter Medak. **Guest Cast:** Ken Hutchinson, Carolyn Seymour.

Moonbase Alpha finds itself on a collision course with another planet.

Note: As of this writing, the final two episodes of this season were in production and information on them was unavailable.

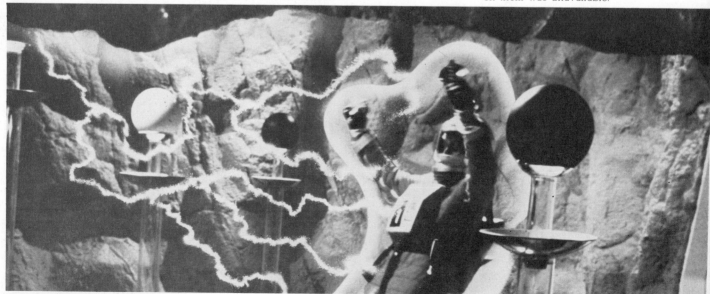

FANTASTIC TELEVISION
FANTASTIC TELEVISION
FANTASTIC TELEVISION
FANTASTIC TELEVISION

PART 2: THE FULL PICTURE

So many science fiction and fantasy shows have appeared on television that to highlight all of them as in "Fine Tuning" would be impossible. "The Full Picture" is a mini-encyclopedia containing capsule descriptions and critiques of all of these other shows.

"American Telefantasy" is a compendium of American sci-fi and fantasy series, spanning *Inner Sanctum* and *Out of This World, Buck Rogers* and *Wonder Woman, Captain Video* and *Captain Nice* and many, many more.

"British Telefantasy" focuses on the most interesting sci-fi appearing on the "telly," from *Quatermass,* which has been running practically since television began in Britain, to *The Avengers,* which has enjoyed as much popularity in the United States as it has in the United Kingdom.

Almost all children's programming is fantasy, and it would require volumes to list every show. For "Kid Stuff," only the best have been selected. Interestingly, quite a few have been imported. From Japan have come such memorable cartoon shows as *Ultra Man* and *Astro Boy.* England has produced *Captain Scarlet and the Mysterons* and *The Thunderbirds.* These last two were filmed using a technique called supermarionation, where the stars of the show are actually puppets that are controlled both by wires and electronically. There have been, of course, innumerable American children's shows. Among those selected for "Kid Stuff" are Hanna-Barbera's popular cartoon families, the Stone-Age Flintstones and the Space-Age Jetsons, as well as an excellent animated *Star Trek* featuring the voices of William Shatner, Leonard Nimoy, et al.

Made-for-TV movies are a relatively recent phenomenon, but many fantasy and science fiction movies have already hit the home screen. These have ranged from *Frankenstein—The True Story,* written by Christopher Isherwood, not Mary Shelley, to *The Night That Panicked America,* which dramatized Orson Welles's legendary broadcast that convinced many Americans that Martians were invading New Jersey. Sometimes a made-for-TV movie is actually a pilot for a regular series. Listed here are examples such as *Kung Fu,* which made it, and Irwin Allen's *City Beneath the Sea,* which did not.

All in all, "The Full Picture" is the most comprehensive treatment of telefantasy on earth...or anywhere else.

AMERICAN TELEFANTASY

THE ADDAMS FAMILY (1964, ABC) starred Caroline Jones as Morticia, John Astin as Gomez, her husband, Jackie Coogan as Uncle Fester and Ted Cassidy as Lurch, the family butler. This was the video version of Charles Addams's *New Yorker* cartoons pitting the family against regular folks. It ran for two years, then left network television, though it can still be found on local stations.

ALFRED HITCHCOCK PRESENTS (1955-62, CBS) and **THE ALFRED HITCHCOCK HOUR** (1962-64, CBS; 1964-65, NBC) both began with the strains of "Funeral March of the Marionette," and the corpulent profile of Alfred Hitchcock. Most of the shows were crime dramas in which the villain got away with murder. Perhaps the most famous was "Lamb to the Slaughter," starring Barbara Bel Geddes as the wife of the chief of police. She bludgeons her husband to death with a frozen leg of lamb and serves the incriminating weapon to the investigating detectives.

Alfred Hitchcock's somber "good ev-e-ning" opened each of his shows.

In one of the supernatural tales that Hitchcock aired, "Banquo's Chair," a police inspector, played by John Williams, tries to trick a woman's murderer into confessing by hiring an actress to play the dead woman's ghost. Confronted with the "ghost," the killer confesses. At the same moment, the actress arrives apologizing for being detained. "Where the Woodbine Twineth" and "The Glass Eye" are supernatural tales that are classic Hitchcock. They share the premise of inanimate things taking over people. "The Glass Eye" concerned a ventriloquist whose dummy had a mind of its own. "Woodbine" dealt with prejudice as well as with fantasy. In it, a little girl changes places with the black doll she stores in a box. Hitchcock was on the air for seven years in his role as host, director and producer. Straddling his crime stories with their ironic conclusions were Mr. Hitchcock's sardonic introductory and closing remarks which demonstrated that one can see through water but one still swallows it, or something.

ATOM SQUAD (1953, NBC) was one of TV's earliest sci-fi offerings. In these daily fifteen-minute cliff-hangers accentuating scientific terms and bunsen burners, Bob Courtleigh and Bob Hastings helped to keep our planet in orbit during the early '50s.

BEWITCHED (1964, ABC) co-starred Dick York (later Dick Sargent played the part) as Darren Stevens, Elizabeth Montgomery as Sam(antha) his wife and Agnes Moorehead as Endora, his mother-in-law. Samantha and her mother are witches. Darren is an advertising man who tries to make Sam give up witchcraft for him. Endora pulls Sam in the other direction. A twitch of the nose, and Sam could do anything. The show was extremely popular and ran for eight years—long enough for Darren and Samantha to produce two children who also had the powers. Paul Lynde and Maurice Evans each made frequent guest appearances as Samantha's warlock uncle and father.

In 1976, the pilot film for a series called *Tabitha* was aired. It was meant to treat fans of the *Bewitched* series to Samantha's daughter Tabitha—all grown up and on her own. So far, no one's bought it.

THE BIONIC WOMAN (1976, ABC), a spinoff of the *Six Million Dollar Man*, stars Lindsay Wagner as Jaime Sommers, former sweetheart of Steve Austin, who got herself patched up bionically after a sky-diving accident. She leads a double life as a school teacher—one who keeps kids in line by ripping phone books in half—and as an undercover agent for the Office of Scientific Investigation. Oscar Goldman, head of OSI in *The Six Million Dollar Man*, played by Richard Anderson, moonlights in the series. To Ms. Wagner's credit, her acting serves to enliven the series and makes it truly fun to watch.

ABOVE: Endora (Agnes Moorehead) and Samantha (Elizabeth Montgomery), the mother and·daughter witches of *Bewitched.* RIGHT: The Addams Family. BELOW: Jaime Sommers (Lindsay Wagner) is checked while Col. Steve Austin (Lee Majors) and Oscar Goldman (Richard Anderson) look on in a scene from *The Bionic Woman.*

BUCK ROGERS (1950, ABC) starred Ken Dibbs as Buck, Lou Prentis as Lt. Wilma Deering, Harry Sothern as Dr. Huer and Harry Kingston as Black Barney. This crude, video-tape adaptation of the popular comic strip was filmed live in New York. Set in the distant future, it followed the intergalactic adventures of Buck and his friends, who were based in a small scientific complex in a cave behind Niagara Falls.

CAPTAIN NICE (1966, NBC) was a satirical sitcom inspired by the success of *Batman*. It ran for one season and followed the forgettable exploits of a mild-mannered chemist played by William Daniel who discovered a formula that transformed him into a super-powered crime fighter. Ann Prentis was Daniel's policewoman-girl friend, Candy Cane.

CAPTAIN VIDEO (1949, DuMont) first starred Richard Coogan and later Al Hodge in the title role with Don Hastings as the Video Ranger. The Captain was an "electronic wizard, master of time and space and guardian of the safety of the world" (no less), who created incredible weapons like the Cosmic Vibrator, which could jangle a man to death, and his main weapon, the Opticon Scillometer, which enabled him to see through solid objects. Woe to the world should these devices fall into the wrong hands. The chief possessor of those wrong hands was Dr. Pauli, himself the noted inventor of the "sound barrier," which made all sound cease, enabling the evil doctor to sneak up to Captain Video's secret mountain top headquarters. This was TV's first blast-off to the stars.

CAPTAIN Z-RO (1955, syndicated) was written by and starred Roy Steffens. The mustachioed and goateed hero held the patent on a device which allowed him to travel through time and space. He showed up in a different time and place for each episode, always decked out in a space suit emblazoned with Zs and what looked like a stethoscope coming out of the ear flaps of his hook-topped beanie.

COMMANDO CODY (1955, NBC) was a space opera that starred Judd Holdren as Cody, Sky Marshal of the Universe, and Aline Tower as his assistant, Joan. Together the masked hero and his frumpy aide fought that evil alien genius, "The Ruler." If you took away his ray gun, and gave him a bow and arrow, Cody would look ready to do battle with cruel King John. This was a series with one foot in the future, the other in its mouth.

DARK SHADOWS (1966, NBC) made one critic exclaim, "It's Halloween, five days a week!" As television's first soap opera cum horror show, it stood out among the usual romantic sudsers. Originally intended as an atmosphere-drenched gothic romance, the show was dangerously close to cancellation when a new character was intro-

DARK SHADOWS

duced. Craggy-faced vampire Barnabas Collins (Jonathan Frid) turned it into a hit and quickly became a cult hero. Gothic romance switched to gothic horror—tailored, of course, for daytime audiences—and was surprisingly effective on its own peculiar terms. Regulars were Joan Bennett, Alexandra Moltke, Grayson Hall, Lara Parker (a witch), David Selby (a werewolf), Kathryn Leigh Scott, Louis Edmonds, Nancy Barrett, Anthony George, David Hennessey, Joel Crothers, David Ford, Roger Davis and Jerry Lacy. Because of its five-days-a-week format, DARK SHADOWS has the distinction of having more episodes aired than any other fantasy series—one thousand.

ESP (1958, ABC) was a kind of quiz show with actual inconclusive tests of telepathy, clairvoyance and precognition presented live on the air. The contestants were called "sensitives." Vincent Price was the host.

THE EVIL TOUCH (1973, syndicated) offered one season's worth of a bizarre and unintentionally campy horror-fantasy-sci-fi anthology produced in Canada on a shoestring budget. It featured well-known American actors like Kim Hunter and Darren McGavin in decidedly morbid teleplays. Host Anthony Quayle always looked somewhat embarrassed as he delivered the framework narration posed within a fog of what appeared to be cigar smoke.

FANTASTIC JOURNEY (1977, NBC) stars Jared Martin as Zarian, an Earthling from the 23rd century, Ike Eisenmann as 13-year-old Scotty who is skilled in ESP and Carl Franklin as a medical expert. The three form a team that is lost in The Devil's Triangle, where the past, present and future converge and provide strange perils in the form of alien creatures, parallel worlds and supernatural forces. Roddy McDowell joined the regular cast after the third episode.

FLASH GORDON (1951, DuMont) was a refugee from the comics which starred Steve Holland (Buster Crabbe

starred in the movies) as the legendary superhero. Irene Champlin was Dale and Joe Nash played Dr. Zarkov. This Flash had trouble on many different planets, including Earth: the low-budget sci-fi hash it offered was universally panned.

THE FLYING NUN (1967, ABC) cast Sally Field as Sister Bertrille, a nun in the habit of hang gliding because of the peculiar aerodynamics of her cornette. For spice, the convent was in Puerto Rico and it was filled out with Madeleine Sherwood, Marge Redmond, Linda Dangcil and Shelley Morrison, some of whom were amused, some not, by Sister Bertrille's high jinks. The series was based on a book by a woman named Tere Rios. Despite an initial reluctance on the part of the network, fearing they might insult the Catholic Church, the show was approved and enjoyed a nice, solid and profitable three-year run.

GEMINI MAN (1976, NBC) stars Ben Murphy a researcher Sam Casey, Katherine Crawford as his gir friend and colleague Dr. Abby Lawrence and Williar Sylvester as his no-nonsense boss, Leonard Driscoll. It' basically a slightly different twist on the old invisible ma idea. Casey was caught in a radioactive explosion tha affected his body's cellular structure; since then, he's bee: able to make himself invisible (although only for fiftee: minutes a day) by flicking on a device he wears on his wris' The government decides to turn him into their new "secre weapon." If it all sounds a bit like *The Six Million Dolla Man*, it should—both shows are produced by Harv Bennett.

GET SMART! (1965, NBC) was a spoof of the covey c James Bond-like spy shows that jammed the airwaves. Do: Adams played Maxwell Smart, Agent 86, and Barbar: Feldon played Agent 99 for the course of the show's five year run. This pair worked for the secret governmen agency CONTROL which sought to stamp out the crimina activity of that outlaw organization KAOS. Though outfitte: with the latest in crazy gismos, Smart always got his mar despite this technology. His native stupidity, incompetenc and lack of physical prowess did the trick. Two of Smart' catch phrases caught on with the public: "Sorry about tha Chief," and "Would you believe...?" Edward Pla' appeared as the Chief and Dick Gautier appeared often a Hymie the robot.

THE GHOST AND MRS. MUIR (1968, NBC) feature: Edward Mulhare and Hope Lange in the movie roles mad: famous by Rex Harrison and Gene Tierney. Captain Danie Gregg used to own, but now haunts, Gull Cottage on th: New England coast. Widow Muir bought the place outraging the captain, who could not tolerate the notion of : mere slip of a woman moving into his home. He rattle: chains and did whatever else a ghost could to frighten Mrs Muir, but the sensible lady was scarcely annoyed. / romance. In supporting roles were Reta Shaw as Gul Cottage's housekeeper, Charles Nelson Reilly as Captair Gregg's surviving relative, and Harlan Carraher an: Kellie Flanagan as Mrs. Muir's children.

GHOST STORY (1972, NBC), which ran for just one year was an attempt to be droll and yet scary, like a ride on : roller coaster that makes you scream and laugh at the sam: time. Initially, Sebastian Cabot played the host, Winstor Essex, a mysterious rich man who wandered in at the beginning of each show fondling a brandy snifter introduced the proceedings and wandered back in at the end to help us compose ourselves. Where he went in between must have been far more interesting than the dramas. Cabot, the format and the title were all dropped after thirteen episodes. It continued on NBC as *Circle o. Fear* for the balance of the year.

THE GIRL FROM U.N.C.L.E. (1966, NBC) was a spinoff o the *Man* from the same organization. Stefanie Power: played April Dancer, a filly who could keep the world safe from THRUSH as well as any man. But not as long; the show lasted just one year, never achieving the magic of it: parent.

THE GIRL WITH SOMETHING EXTRA (1973, NBC) wa: a sitcom starring a defrocked Sally Field as Sally Burton and the something extra was ESP. Husband John, played by John Davidson, brother-in-law Jack Sheldon and bes'

ABOVE: Don Adams and Barbara Feldon in *Get Smart!*
BELOW: The cast of *The Ghost and Mrs. Muir.*

friend Zohra Lampert all found it discomfiting having their private thoughts revealed. There was little to hold it together besides Sally Field looking cute, and it disappeared after one year.

GOOD HEAVENS! (1975, ABC) was an entry that lasted just one season. It starred Carl Reiner as Mr. Angel, a kind soul who helped troubled mortals find happiness. This was an offbeat fantasy sitcom which was more down to earth (pardon the pun) than most, concentrating on the people helped by the good-natured spirit rather than on Mr. Angel himself. An interesting failure.

GREAT GHOST TALES (1961, NBC) appeared as a summer replacement for Tennessee Ernie Ford's show and was an anthology of thrillers. It was far from great and made a quick exit by the middle of the next season.

THE GREEN HORNET (1966, ABC) starred Van Williams as Britt Reid, editor and publisher of the *Daily Sentinel* by day, and the Green Hornet by night. Bruce Lee played his trusted manservant Kato. Together they fought to clean up organized crime—in the show's old radio days, crime was disorganized—with feats of derring-do.

April Dancer (Stephanie Powers) was *The Girl from U.N.C.L.E.*

HOLMES AND YO-YO (1976, ABC) stars Richard B. Shull as Alexander Holmes, a not very bright cop, and John Shuck as Gregory "Yoyo" Yoyonovich, his not-much-brighter partner—who's also a robot! Wacky comedy from producer Leonard Stern, formerly of *Get Smart*.

LEFT: Barbara Eden was TV's genie, Jeannie. ABOVE: The hero of Kung Fu was played by David Carradine. BELOW (left to right): Joe E. Ross, Imogene Coca, Frank Aletter and Jack Mullaney, regulars on *It's About Time*.

DREAM OF JEANNIE (1965, NBC) starred Larry Hagman as astronaut Tony Nelson and Barbara Eden as Jeannie. Shipwrecked Tony pulls the cork out of a bottle one day and out pops Jeannie ready to do her new master's bidding. The trouble is that she misunderstands just about everything he orders and her presence is awkward to explain to people like his boss, a NASA psychiatrist played by Hayden Rourke. Bill Daley as Tony's goofy pal was in on the secret, but not much help. The show had a five-year stint during which the whereabouts of Barbara Eden's navel—her midriff was bare—became the source of much speculation during the show's run (and reruns). Was the network keeping it covered or was she not in possession of one?

THE IMMORTAL (1970, ABC) was on the air for one season. It starred Christopher George as Ben Richards, a man with a unique blood condition which made him immune to all diseases as well as the normal aging process. A transfusion of his blood was tonic to the sick and dying; and there was one particularly unscrupulous billionaire in need of Ben's corpuscles who stopped at nothing to get him on tap. The blood-craving villain forces Richards to become a fugitive and get into a new scrape every week.

INNER SANCTUM (1951, syndicated) was a radio suspense show that turned to television and kept its famous creaking door. It was one of the first television shows to experiment with special visual effects.

THE INVISIBLE MAN (1975, NBC) featured David McCallum as an updated invisible hero. Our modern invisible man, Dr. Daniel Weston, was lucky enough to have a friend who made a lookalike life mask for him to wear whenever he wanted to travel cognito. His situation forced him to become a fugitive in order to bring justice to society. Jackie Cooper played Carlson, his boss, for the pilot; Craig Stevens played the role on the series. Wife Kate was played by Melinda Fee in both the pilot and the series. The show was meant to compete with the *Six Million Dollar Man* but, although it had the benefit of likeable performers and good special effects, it lacked the oomph of that series. Invisible Dr. Weston disappeared completely at the end of the 1975-76 season.

IT'S ABOUT TIME (1966, CBS) was a sitcom which took us back to the Stone Age where two astronauts named Hector and Mac—Jack Mullaney and Frank Aletter—travel back in time and run into a cave family made up of Imogene Coca as Shad, Joe E. Ross as Gronk, Mary Grace as Mlor and Par Cardi as Breer. Also around were Cliff Norton as Boss and Mike Mazurki as Clon. Bumblers all.

JET JACKSON, FLYING COMMANDO (1955, syndicated) starred Richard Webb as Jet and Sid Melton as his sidekick (everyone had a sidekick then). In some precincts, the sci-fi crime show was known as *Captain Midnight*. This was one of TV's early forays into sci-fi. Then it had some allure for the littlest children, but a look at it today reveals plots, costumes and "scientific" equipment that even preschoolers would laugh at.

KUNG FU (1972, ABC) starred David Carradine as Caine, an oriental priest, skilled in the martial arts, who was chased through the old west by his own people in this odd mixture of several genres. The mystical aspects of Chinese religion and philosophy provided some bizarre moments, and the striking photography (slow motion was used

prominently) helped create the proper mood. For that quick pick-me-up, Caine would get into a trance-like state and commune with a spiritual ancestor. The star's more immediate ancestors, father John Carradine and brother Keith, occasionally appeared on the show. David Carradine became something of a cult hero as the show cashed in on the popularity of the oriental martial arts until the end of its last season in 1975. Keye Luke appeared regularly as Master Po.

LIGHTS OUT (1949, NBC) was a primordial emigre from radio specializing in supernatural horror. The live half-hour melodramas were hosted for the first part of the run by movie bad guy Jack La Rue, later by Frank Gallop. There was an unsuccessful attempt to resurrect it as a new series in 1972. A modern hour-long occult chiller was aired under the series' title, but the thrills it promised were nonexistent.

THE MAN AND THE CHALLENGE (1959, NBC) starred George Nader as Glenn Barton, athlete, former Marine and medical expert, whose job was to test and ascertain the limits of human physical and mental endurance. The viewer's patience was put to the greatest test of all.

THE MAN FROM U.N.C.L.E. (1964, NBC) made heroes of Robert Vaughan and David McCallum. As U.N.C.L.E. (United Network Command for Law Enforcement) agents Napoleon Solo and Illya Kuraykin, they fought world-wide crime—especially as organized by THRUSH, a secret criminal organization dedicated to taking over the world. Leo G. Carroll was Alexander Waverly, head of U.N.C.L.E. This was one of the many spy thrillers spawned at the time. Its setting was futuristic, its weaponry fantastic and clever, its mood tongue-in-cheek. An extremely popular show, particularly with college audiences, it ran for four years.

MEN INTO SPACE (1959, CBS) starred William Lundigan as a spaceman who got into and out of scrapes and natural disasters—like moonquakes—each episode for a couple of seasons.

MISTER ED (1960, CBS) was a horse of another caliber: he could talk, but only to owner and co-star Wilbur Post (played by Alan Young). The series had an astonishingly long run (six years) and survived several dilemmas, including Young's growing dissatisfaction with playing second banana to a nag and the disappearance of regulars Larry Keating and Edna Skinner after seventy-nine shows. Also co-starring were Connie Hines (as Wilbur's wife), Leon Ames and Florence MacMichael.

MR. TERRIFIC (1966, CBS) was a high-flying nebbish created to cash in on Batmania. Service station owner Stanley Beamish, played by Stephen Strimpell, became a super hero when he downed a "power pill" developed by the government. Like Captain Nice, it lasted only a season. The principal difference between Beamish and Captain Nice was that Stanley flapped his arms when he flew, while the captain glided.

THE MUNSTERS (1964, CBS) were a close-knit family of suburban ghouls. Fred Gwynne was Herman Munster, a dead ringer for Frankenstein, Yvonne deCarlo was his wife Lily. Al Lewis as Grandpa Munster looked like a blood relation to Dracula, but was really a sweetheart. Pointed-eared Eddie Munster, played by Butch Patrick, had very little childlike appeal. The only normal one around was niece Marilyn, played first by Beverly Owen, then by Pat Priest. Marilyn never saw anything odd about her relatives, but the residents of 43 Mockingbird Lane had trouble making it with everyone else during its two years on the air.

MY FAVORITE MARTIAN (1963, CBS), which co-starred Ray Walston as Uncle Martin the Martian and Bill Bixby as newspaperman Tim O'Hara, delighted audiences until it ended in 1965. A Martian anthropologist with a vast array of powers was stranded on Earth—in Las Vegas, no less—and O'Hara took him under his wing, passing him off as his uncle. Keeping Uncle Martin's identity secret and his antennae under his hat became the source of fun in this sitcom.

MY LIVING DOLL (1964, CBS) was a short-lived comedy starring Julie Newmar as Rhoda the robot and Bob Cummings as a psychiatrist entrusted with her and hell-bent for turning her into the perfect woman. Fellow shrink Jack Mullaney fell head over heels for Rhoda, while Cummings's sister (Doris Dowling) wanted to see her permanently disconnected. After one season, she got her wish.

MY MOTHER, THE CAR (1965, NBC) explored the scant comic possibilities of reinCARnation. David Crabtree, played by Jerry Van Dyke (Dick's brother), discovered that his mother's spirit (the voice of Ann Sothern) inhabited the radio of his 1928 Porter automobile. The short-lived farce had Crabtree in a continual battle with his wife and children who wanted to scrap the Porter for a station wagon. After a one-season run, Crabtree joined his mother.

MY WORLD AND WELCOME TO IT (1969, NBC) ran for one season and starred William Windom as John Monroe and Joan Hotchkis as his wife. This sitcom was based as loosely as the skin on a bassett hound on the life and work of James Thurber. Monroe was a cartoonist and writer whose equanimity was imperiled at every turn by his loving spouse, his bright daughter (Lisa Gerritsen, who now plays Cloris Leachman's daughter on the *Phyllis* show), his gruff editor (Harold J. Stone) and his two dogs (Christabel and Irving). His only solace was his imagination, which was illustrated in odd animated sequences and wild daydreams.

NANNY AND THE PROFESSOR (1970, ABC) was a sitcom starring Juliet Mills as Phoebe Figalilly the Nanny and Richard Long as Professor Harold Everett, father of three (no mama). Phoebe was practical, pretty and psychic. For three years Everett and oldest son Hal (David Doremus) tolerated her shenanigans while Butch (Trent Lehman) and Prudence (Kim Richards) adored them.

THE NEW PEOPLE (1959, ABC) involved a bunch of young people, each a different sterotype—a militant black, a college dropout, etc.—stranded on a remote Pacific island after their plane crashes. Since there was scant hope of rescue, they worked out the problems of civilization in microcosm—a bone thrown to that visionary generation that they quickly threw out after one season.

LEFT: Ray Walston was everyone's favorite Martian.
ABOVE: *My Living Doll* starred Julie Newmar as Rhoda the Robot and Bob Cummings as her psychiatrist owner.
BELOW: Two members of the Munster family, Grandpa (Al Lewis) and Herman (Fred Gwynne).

ABOVE: That's Cliff Robertson sporting the goldfish bowl in the title role of *Rod Brown of the Rocket Rangers.*
BELOW: Truman Bradley, host of *Science Fiction Theatre,* and friend.

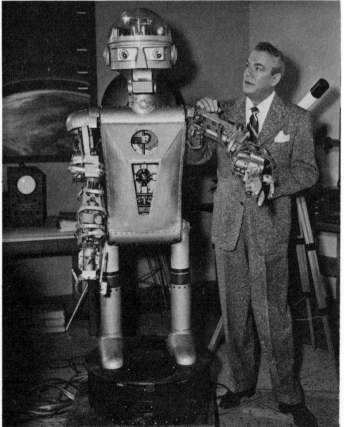

PLANET OF THE APES (1974, CBS) was a one-season series based on the popular *Apes* movies. Starring in simian roles were Roddy McDowall as Galen, Booth Coleman as wily Dr. Zaius and Mark Lenard as the militaristic Urko. James Naughton and Ron Harper played human astronauts Burke and Virdon. The year was 2000 and the apes ruled the earth and wanted to destroy the human trouble-makers whom Galen befriended.

ROCKY JONES, SPACE RANGER (1953, syndicated) was a space adventure show for kids which starred Richard Crane in striped pants, baseball cap, tee-shirt and a grave expression on his mug. His team was always behind but never lost. By the end of 1954, audience interest waned completely and the show went off the air.

ROD BROWN OF THE ROCKET RANGERS (1953, CBS) starred Cliff Robertson in the title role. The series was set in the 22nd century and the Rocket Rangers, operating off Omega Base, battled interplanetary evil in the course of exploring the cosmos. John Boruff played Commander Swift of the Ranger force, while Bruce Hall as Ranger Frank Boyle and Jack Weston as Ranger Wilbur "Wormsey" Wormser rounded out the crew.

SCIENCE FICTION THEATRE (1956, syndicated) was a sci-fi anthology hosted by Truman Bradley, who each week opened the show by demonstrating the invention or scientific principle upon which the evening's show was based. Like its longer-running and more successful cousin, *One Step Beyond, Science Fiction Theatre* tried very hard to present all of its bizarre melodramas in a matter-of-fact, credible way—almost journalistic in its approach—and always avoided any kind of trick ending. It was an interesting attempt which still runs in syndication on local stations across the country, even though its original appearance merited only two year's worth of shows.

THE SECOND HUNDRED YEARS (1967, NBC) starred Monte Markham as Luke Carpenter, an Alaskan gold prospector who was frozen into a glacier in 1900 at the age of thirty-three and thawed out in 1967. He emerged a still-youthful thirty-three, but found his son Edwin (Arthur O'Connell) was sixty-seven and that his thirty-three-year-old grandson (also played by Markham) looked just like him. So it was—three generations and grandpappy Luke practically a kid. After one season, no one was interested and the series retired.

THE SIX MILLION DOLLAR MAN (1973, ABC) stars Lee Majors as Steve Austin who, after barely surviving a jet crash, has some capital improvements made on him by a secret government agency: he now has two bionic legs, one bionic arm and a bionic eye. He can't run faster than a speeding bullet but can easily do sixty. The series is based on a novel by Michael Caidan, and at this writing is still a prime-time feature that shows no signs of losing its popularity. In the Fall of 1976, the Bionic Boy, played by Vincent Van Patten, made his appearance. If he gets a series of his own, bionic people will soon reign supreme on television.

THE SIXTH SENSE (1972, ABC) attempted to explore the chilling potential of ESP and telepathic phenomena as experienced by psychic investigator Michael Rhodes, played by Gary Collins. Most of the entries were traditional murder mysteries with rather haphazardly placed ESP gimmicks. The series was a flop. In 1974, each of the show's hour installments (25 in all) was condensed to half an hour and syndicated as part of Night Gallery.

THE SMOTHERS BROTHERS SHOW (1965, CBS) was a one-season sitcom starring Tommy Smothers as a hapless angel who flew on wings and good intentions. Tommy returned to Earth to help his quick brother Dick out of "jams and stuff," but seemed more to get him *into* "jams and stuff."

SPACE PATROL (1951, ABC) starred Ed Kemmer as Commander Buzz Corry and Lyn Osborn as Space Cadet Happy, both of whom spent their video lives with their heads stuck in goldfish bowls and punching up villains. This series has immeasurably enriched the language with such phrases as "He's lost his rockets" and "Smoking Rockets!"

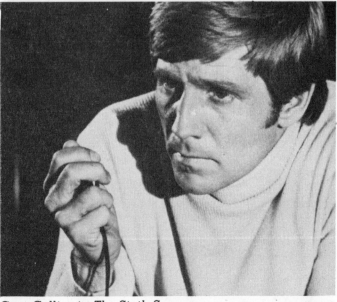

Gary Collins in *The Sixth Sense*.

THE ALIEN ORO - "STARLOST"

STARLOST (1973, syndicated) was a Canadian video-taped sci-fi series featuring Keir Dullea. It was so bad that its creator, Harlan Ellison, disowned it and signed the pilot with his pen name, Cordwainer Bird. The premise was that the survivors of the destroyed planet Earth are traveling on an endless journey through space in a huge spaceship. This endless voyage came to an abrupt end after one season.

STRANGE PARADISE (1969, Metromedia) was a fortunately short-lived Canadian soap opera that never did well in this country. The paradise was an island, the strange element was voodoo. Colin Fox starred in a dual role as an industrial tycoon possessed by witchcraft and voodoo on a Caribbean island, and the tycoon's own French ancestor of 300 years ago.

TALES OF THE UNEXPECTED (1977, NBC) is a suspense anthology featuring stories in the O. Henry tradition, with the occult a frequent subject. Produced by Quinn (*The Invaders*) Martin, the show made its debut in the Spring of 1977 with William Conrad as host.

TALES OF TOMORROW (1951, ABC), a futuristic anthology series, featured lots of creatures visiting from other planets. Some fine work was done, including an adaptation of Jules Verne's *20,000 Leagues Under the Sea*, which starred Thomas Mitchell as Captain Nemo and Leslie Nielson and Bethel Leslie in supporting roles.

TOM CORBETT, SPACE CADET (1950, syndicated) was a space opera which starred Frankie Thomas as Corbett the adventurer from the year 2335. His wardrobe was limited to a jumpsuit, polka-dotted at the cuffs, and a bib with metal studs.

TOPPER (1953, CBS) pitted Leo G. Carroll as staid banker Cosmo Topper against fun-loving ghosts George and Marion Kirby (played by Robert Sterling and Anne Jeffreys). The Kirbys, along with their alcoholic St. Bernard Neil, had been killed in an avalanche in the Swiss Alps, but took the first boat back to haunt Topper, who had moved into their former home. This sitcom was characterized by Topper's attempts to make his own unkempt, ghost-ridden reality jibe with his wife's (Lee Patrick) and everyone else's who, unlike Cosmo, didn't see or hear George, Marion or Neil.

Topper had the distinction of having appeared on all three national networks during its run. In 1974, Roddy McDowall and Stefanie Powers starred in a pilot for NBC called *Topper Returns*. Topper, however, did not and has not returned except as reruns on local stations.

WAY OUT (1961, CBS) was a supernatural horror anthology hosted by fantasy writer Roald Dahl. What distinguished this chiller were its especially morbid stories and incredible monster make-ups by Dick (*The Exorcist*) Smith. The show was strategically slotted right after *Twilight Zone* on Friday evenings, but this didn't help the terrible ratings—it was cancelled after only one month!

THE WILD, WILD WEST (1965, CBS) starred Robert Conrad as James West and Ross Martin as his sidekick Artemis Gordon, two 1870s underground agents for President Grant stationed in the American West. The show had an extremely successful four-year run. Its magic formula was a combination of strange and often kinky, but fascinating, villains and sophisticated technology somehow made plausible in the show's nineteenth-century setting.

WONDER WOMAN (1975, ABC) debuted as a made-for-TV feature movie starring Cathy Lee Crosby. When it failed to win over an audience, the network recast the title role making Lynda Carter its new superperson. This time, it caught on and continues to appear as a semi-regular series in the 1976-1977 season. The show's creators opted for an action format in order to avoid the campiness of the old *Batman* series. Hard as they try, the camp aspect does creep in from time to time. But the show is all good fun and Ms. Carter has some gutsy women's movement speeches. Wonder Woman's sweetheart, Major Steve Trevor, is well played by Lyle Waggoner. Beatrice Colen appears as Etta Candy and Richard Eastham is General Blankenship. In the Fall of 1976, Wonder Girl, played by Debra Winger, joined the superheroine.

WORLD OF GIANTS (1959, syndicated) starred Marshall Thompson and Arthur Franz. Using the outsized props of Universal's "The Incredible Shrinking Man," this short-lived sci-fi adventure followed the exploits of its six-inch tall hero, who worked as the government's most resourceful espionage agent.

TOP: Robert Conrad as James West of *The Wild, Wild West* goes after his man. BOTTOM: Burgess Meredith was one of the kinky villains featured on *The Wild, Wild West*. RIGHT: Lynda Carter is TV's *Wonder Woman*.

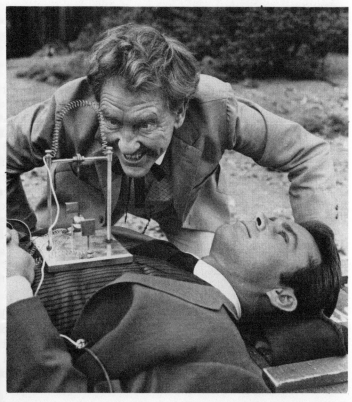

BRITISH TELEFANTASY

A FOR ANDROMEDA and **THE ANDROMEDA BREAKTHROUGH** were both British series written by novelist and cosmologist Fred Hoyle. Each concerns a beautiful female android that was created by mysterious beings from the Andromeda constellation. The stars were Mary Morris and Julie Christie.

BBC copyright photograph

Film star Julie Christie appeared as Andromeda in the final episode of *A for Andromeda*.

THE AVENGERS is a popular British fantasy-adventure series that has undergone many changes in character since it first appeared in the early 1960s. Originally debonair secret agent John Steed, played by Patrick MacNee, had two male partners. These were soon replaced by Honor Blackman, who had wowed moviegoers in *Goldfinger*. By 1965, Blackman got tired of the role and in stepped Diana Rigg as Mrs. Emma Peel. The combination of beauty and karate-chopping along with the wit and sophistication of her relationship with Steed made the show and its stars international favorites. Bizarre criminals and strange, futuristic weaponry added to the excitement and fun. Particularly enjoyable was a continually returning troupe of robots called the Cybernauts. After three years Rigg left the show and was replaced by Linda Thorson as Tara King. The series was cancelled soon after this but revived again in 1976. In its most recent incarnation, MacNee is still at the helm as Steed and his assistant is played by Joanna Lumley. American audiences have had the opportunity to see only the versions with Rigg and Thorson.

THE CHAMPIONS were a team of superhuman agents who received their unearthly physical and mental powers from a lost race of people in Tibet. Despite the comic-book premise, some episodes of this short-lived British-made adventure series were fairly well done. It starred Stuart Damon, Alexandra Bastedo and William Gaunt. The first ten of its thirty filmed episodes were shown in America in 1968 on NBC.

Alexandra Bastedo, Stuart Damon and William Gaunt, in *The Champions*.

Fine acting, witty scripts and a host of bizarre criminals combined to make *The Avengers* one of the most popular TV shows both in Britain and the United States. BELOW: Diana Rigg as Mrs. Emma Peel, one of television's most exciting heroines. TOP RIGHT: Honor Blackman was Patrick MacNee's first female partner. BOTTOM RIGHT: Patrick MacNee as the ever-cool and debonair John Steed.

ABC copyright photograph

Eccentric scientist Dr. Who has been played by both Tom Baker (opposite above) and John Pertwee (above). Among the creatures he encountered were Daleks (opposite, above), Cybermen (opposite, bottom left) and Styggrom, leader of the Kreals (opposite, bottom right). BELOW: A scene from "The Deadly Assassin."

BBC copyright photograph

DR. WHO is an eccentric scientist-adventurer who travels in time and space at the speed of light to combat some of the strangest alien invaders ever squeezed out of the tube. This whimsical, though hopelessly lowbrow, sci-fi serial has been keeping British youngsters glued to their TV sets for over a generation. Several actors have played Who through the years, and two feature-length movies were based on him. For the record, Time-Life has up for offer thirteen color *Who* adventures made in 1970 and starring John Pertwee for TV syndication in the U.S.

THE INVISIBLE MAN was produced in London and followed the adventures of Dr. Peter Brady, a young scientist whose experiments misfired, leaving him irrevocably invisible. Forces of good and evil opposed each other for his talents, but the good won and Brady elected to use his unique situation for the betterment of mankind. Of course, he had to fight the bad guys every step of the way, which gave the show its *raison d'etre*. Some noteworthy British actors guested on the show, but the identity of the actor who played the invisible Brady has not been revealed to this day.

This series had a successful American run beginning in 1958 on CBS. The American-made version, which premiered in 1975, did not share the success of its parent show.

JOURNEY TO THE UNKNOWN was a trip, not through outer space and time warps, but through inner space and warped minds. This British-made anthology series dealt with everyday situations and people thrown out of joint by twisted psyches. In America, the trip lasted only one season on ABC. This series was also known as *Out of the Unknown*.

MOONBASE 3 appeared in 1973 and was a six-episode mini-series about life on a European moonbase. Donald Houston played David Caulder, the Director of the whole operation. The setting was 30 years in the future.

MY PARTNER, THE GHOST was an offbeat British adventure series starring Mike Pratt and Kenneth Coper as a pair of private detectives. Only thing is, one of them was a ghost. He came back to help his partner after being killed on a case. Featured was Annette Andre. The series was titled *Randall and Hopkirk (Deceased)* in some places.

ORSON WELLES'S GREAT MYSTERIES, hosted by Welles, was a collection of original and classic stories from famous mystery writers and was produced in Britain. Among the better adaptations was "The Monkey's Paw," featuring Patrick Magee. The series appeared on American television during 1973 in syndication.

OUT OF THE UNKNOWN was another popular British science-fiction anthology series. Plots usually involved earthlings making contact—both friendly and unfriendly—with extraterrestials. The series should not be confused with its similarly-named cousins, *Journey to the Unknown, Out of This World,* both of which were also British sci-fi series. The others were also shown in America, while *Out of the Unknown* was not.

OUT OF THIS WORLD was a British sci-fi anthology hosted by veteran film actor Boris Karloff. An ambitious production, it contained five series of thirteen plays each, adapted from short stories by John Wyndham, Isaac Asimov, Rog Phillips and other masters of the genre. American audiences were able to see this series in 1963.

QUATERMASS has been on British television since the early 1950s. Nigel Kneale created the intrepid Dr. Bernard Quatermass. The original plot dealt with a returning space traveler who metamorphoses into a giant menacing vegetable. The second stage of the good doctor's evolution in series form has him accidentally discover enemy aliens who mean to take over the Earth by infiltrating human bodies and brains. The latest series plot deals with the possible insect origins of mankind. The entire Quatermass series is important because of its attempt to revolutionize traditional conceptions of horror. It replaces the run-of-the-mill monsters with more interesting, intelligent kinds of creatures, and the resulting horrors are even more disturbing.

UFO was a British show that made its first appearance in 1970. It has a lot in common with the children's puppet show *Captain Scarlet and the Mysterons;* both are produced by Gerry and Sylvia Anderson, both feature a team of futuristic heroes combating deadly alien invaders and both contain excellent special effects. It is not surprising, then, that the acting in the live-action UFO has been termed "wooden"; Commander Straker (Ed Bishop) and his group of intrepid alien-fighters (George Sewell, Peter Gordeno and Gabrielle Drake) defend the world with a maximum of courage and a minimum of expressions. It's the same problem that plagued the first year of the Anderson's most recent space opera, *Space: 1999.*

TOP: *Moonbase 3* is a European installation, set 30 years in the future. CENTER: "The Monkey's Paw," on *Orson Welles's Great Mysteries,* starred Patrick Magee. LEFT: A humanoid of *Out of the Unknown.*

ABOVE: Attending to an explosion in the rocket. BELOW: A Martian. RIGHT: The regulars of *Quatermass and the Pit* during a break in filming (left to right): Prof. Quatermass (Andre Morell), Barbara Judd (Christine Finn), Dr. Roney (Cec Linder).

BBC copyright photograph

British Telefantasy/173

KID STUFF

THE AMAZING THREE (1967, syndicated) was an unsuccessful, but interesting, cartoon series. In it three outer space observers disguised themselves as animals and came to Earth to decide whether or not to destroy it. In the course of their mission they met Kenny—a human child—and befriended him.

ARK II (1976, CBS) is an exciting live-action adventure show set 500 years in the future. Danger and fascinating discoveries await a group of young people sent to a world where civilization as they knew it no longer exists.

ASTRO BOY (1963, syndicated) was an imaginative import from Japan, the first of many sci-fi/fantasy/adventure cartoon shows to be developed there for the American market. Dr. Astro created the show's hero in the year 2000 shortly after his own son perished in an auto crash. Astro Boy used his remarkable powers to combat outer space monsters and mad scientists. Limited animation was contrasted by clever storylines and engaging characters.

CAPTAIN SCARLET AND THE MYSTERONS (1967, syndicated) was created by Gerry and Sylvia Anderson, who would later be known for *Space: 1999*. Filmed in Super Marionation, this British-made show was several notches above any of the earlier attempts that used the process. Captain Scarlet headed the international organization Spectra—Earth's defense force working against hostile aliens. The Mysterons came from Mars and were his deadly enemies.

EIGHTH MAN (1965, syndicated) was a Japanese cartoon serial that imitated American comic strips. Tobor, a robot crime-fighter, battled monsters and super-villains in his battle against a mysterious society known as Intercrime.

THE FANTASTIC FOUR (1967, NBC) were the original superheroes that launched Stan Lee's Marvel Comics Group. Unfortunately, this cartoon adaptation was poorly animated and never achieved any popularity with the kids. For the record, the teammates were Mr. Fantastic, who could stretch his body into any shape, the Human Torch, Invisible Girl and the Thing, a powerful but lovable monster.

FIREBALL XL-5 (1962, syndicated) was a children's sci-fi adventure with a catchy theme song. Steve Zodiac and his valiant crew faced startling intergalactic perils. Filmed in Super Marionation.

THE FLINTSTONES (1960, ABC), created by Hanna-Barbera, was a phenomenally successful series that ran for five years after its debut and still can be seen in reruns. The Flintstones and their neighbors the Rubbles were cartoon families of stoneage suburbanites. Adapting modern technology in a prehistoric setting was a gimmick that eventually wore thin, but the characters never did. The Emmy-award-winning show was the *Honeymooners* in cartoon form and audiences of all ages loved it.

FRANKENSTEIN, JR. (1966, CBS) was a lovable monster robot, thirty feet tall and phenomenally strong. Kids loved the animated version, but Boris Karloff fans were horrified.

GIGANTOR (1966, syndicated) was the world's "mightiest robot," controlled by twelve-year-old Jimmy Sparks. The year was 2000. This import from Japan was, on the whole, unimpressive.

THE HERCULOIDS (1967, CBS) were an assortment of futuristic animals featured in this offbeat animated series. Strong and invincible, the main function of the Herculoids was to protect King Zender and his family as well as all the other inhabitants of their utopian planet against invasion from evil aliens.

ISIS (1975, CBS) is a live-action adventure show starring JoAnna Cameron as a schoolteacher who can turn herself into a superheroine. She uses her brains and no small amount of brawn to capture lawbreakers and help misguided youngsters. This show quickly rose to the status of most popular Saturday morning kids' show in 1975.

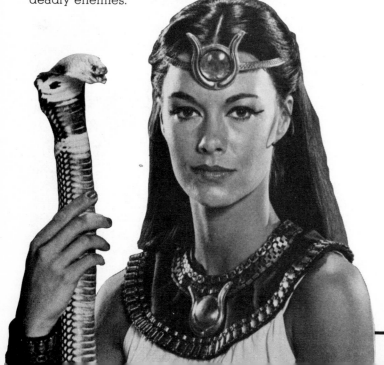

LEFT: JoAnna Cameron as *Isis*.

RIGHT: The lovable *Franken-stein, Jr.* BELOW (clockwise from top left): The Flintstones ran for five years playing to both juveniles and adult audience: *The Herculoids; Astro Boy* was a Japanese import and *Captain Scarlet and the Mysterons* came from England.

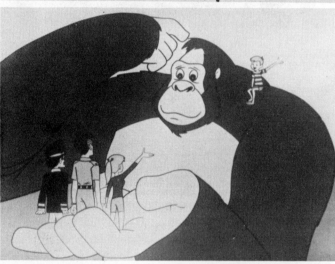

TOP TO BOTTOM: The space-age *Jetsons* were not successful as their ancestors, the Flintstones; *King Kong* became a hero in the kids' version, and Jim Malinda played the title role in *Korg: 70,000 B.C.*

THE JETSONS (1962, ABC) featured the voices of George O'Hanlon, Penny Singleton, Daws Butler and Janet Waldo in this cousin to *The Flintstones* set far in the future. The animated series followed the wild and wacky adventures of a "typical" space-age family. Another victory for Hanna-Barbera.

JOE 90 (1968, syndicated) was another Gerry and Sylvia Anderson offering in Super Marionation. A nine-year-old boy inherited the skills of an adult and became a secret agent in his spare time.

JONNY QUEST (1964, ABC) was the juvenile hero of this well-made sci-fi cartoon series that started out as a prime-time show. Exciting, semi-adult entertainment from the team that made *The Flintstones* and *The Jetsons*. Jonny explored time and space, dealt with monsters, mad scientists and the lot.

KING KONG (1966, ABC) turned the movie monster into a hero and in the transition the mighty creature became the adorable pet of the Bonds, a family dedicated to fighting injustice. It ran for three years and had a rather snazzy theme song.

KORG: 70,000 B.C. (1974, ABC) was a live action drama about a cave family's struggle for survival. The American Museum of Natural History and the Los Angeles County Museum of Natural History were research consultants for this excellent educational adventure series. Narration was by Burgess Meredith.

THE KROFFT SUPER SHOW (1976, ABC) is one of the newest and most popular Saturday morning kid shows. The live-action antics star Captain Kool and the Kongs, a group of kinky-haired, glittered and oddly-attired young men and women—all members of a rock and roll band. They perform in between the adventure stories featuring Wonder Bug—an old broken down heap of a car that can transform into a heroic crimefighting vehicle, evil Dr. Shrinker and the amazing superheroines Electra Woman and Dyna Girl. In the words of Dyna Girl, "Electrafantastic!"

DynaGirl and ElectraWoman of *The Krofft Super Show*.

LAND OF THE LOST (1974, NBC) is another live-action adventure show about a modern family who find themselves marooned in a prehistoric world. Special dinosaur effects were accomplished with the use of a stop-motion animation. Former *Star Trek* scriptwriters D.C. Fontana and David Gerrold contributed many scripts.

THE LOST SAUCER (1975, ABC) is inhabited by Ruth Buzzi and Jim Nabors, humanoids who are in charge of a space ship that is carting human children around the solar system in an effort to get them home. The general wackiness is further augmented by a creature that belongs to the humanoids called a *dorse* (a cross between a horse and a dog).

MARINE BOY (1965, syndicated) was a pint-sized hero who performed his feats of strength to save the world from monsters and madmen beneath the sea. An uninspired export from Japan.

MARVEL SUPER HEROES (1966, syndicated) was the TV version of the adventures of Captain America, the Incredible Hulk, Iron Man, Submariner and Mighty Thor. While the animation was limited, the storylines stuck pretty close to the originals.

RETURN TO THE PLANET OF THE APES (1975, NBC) was a not very exciting animated version of the short-lived CBS live-action series. Simplistic artwork and plots followed the adventures of human astronauts stranded on a planet run by apes.

SHAZAM! (1975, CBS) brought the famous comic book hero Captain Marvel to television. This version is loosely based on the original with an emphasis on good citzenship. John Bostwick played the Captain for the first season, John Davey took over thereafter.

SPACE ANGEL (1964, syndicated) was the second animated adventure (an adventure series called *Clutch Cargo* was the first) produced in Syncro-Vox, a patented technique that made the cartoon characters look like they had real lips. The show's gimmick was asinine but the premise had merit: Scott McCloud—alias Space Angel—was an agent for the Interplanetary Space Force, an organization that worked for the security and welfare of the solar system. Each half-hour show featured five adventures.

SPACE GHOST (1966, CBS) was a superior sci-fi cartoon. Space Ghost was an interplanetary crimefighter who was assisted by two teen-age wards and Blip, a space monkey. The creators of the show also did *The Flintstones* and *The Jetsons*.

SPACE GIANTS (1969, syndicated) were a whole troupe of marauding monsters from Japan. Among them was Rodaka, a red-haired devil from outer space bent on conquering Earth. He used his vast army of prehistoric creatures, synthetic men, strange dwarfs and other horrors to achieve his evil ends. Protecting Earth was Goldar, a fifty-foot golden robot, and his mighty space family. Altogether it was outrageous live-action nonsense.

SPIDERMAN (1967, ABC) was an adaptation of the adventures of the popular comic book hero. Peter Parker, typical college freshman, became the wall-crawling, web-spinning Spiderman whenever supervillains threatened New York.

STINGRAY (1965, syndicated) was a Super Marionation series set in the year 2000. A fantastic submarine and its crew encountered deadly dangers beneath the sea.

STAR TREK (1973, NBC) was an animated version of the regular show that featured the voices of William Shatner, Leonard Nimoy, DeForest Kelley, James Doohan, Majel Barrett, Nichelle Nichols and George Takei in the roles they played on the live action version. It was done in limited animation and based on stories written by many of the regular show's writers. In all, this was head and shoulders above the usual Saturday morning drivel.

SUPERCAR (1962, Syndicated) was an incredible device that could fly, swim and fight crime in this Super Marionation adventure from England. The puppet regulars included Mike Mercury, Supercar's pilot, Dr. Beeker, a brilliant but wacky scientist, Mike's teenage ward Jimmy, and Mitch, their pet monkey.

THUNDERBIRDS (1966, syndicated) was another creation of Gerry and Sylvia Anderson (*Space:1999*) and still stands as a crowning achievement in the world of puppet-fantasy series. Filmed in Super Marionation, the setting was the 21st century and featured the adventures of spaceage heroes. The format was a 30-minute cliffhanger followed by a half-hour solution.

ULTRA MAN (1966, syndicated) was a ludicrous live-action series from Japan. A scientific investigation squad of the future explored and combatted dangerous outer space phenomena. The hero of the title is a team member who can transform into a karate-chopping superhero whenever necessary. Interestingly, the series creator was Eiji Tsuburaya, the special effects wizard who gave the world Godzilla.

MADE-FOR-TV MOVIES

THE AQUARIANS (1970, Universal, NBC). Operating from a futuristic undersea complex called "The Deep Lab," a team of intrepid explorers investigates pollution caused by nerve gas leaking from a sunken freighter. Produced by Ivan Tors (*Science Fiction Theater*), directed by Don McDougall; with Ricardo Montalban, Jose Ferrer, Leslie Nielson, Kate Woodville.

BAFFLED (1972, ITC, NBC). Leonard Nimoy, *Star Trek's* pointy-eared Mr. Spock, plays an American race driver with flashes of ESP in this silly but enjoyable suspense yarn, filmed in England. Directed by Phillip Leacock; with Nimoy, Susan Hampshire, Vera Miles, Rachel Roberts, Christopher Benjamin.

BLACK NOON (1971, Screen Gems, CBS). A traveling preacher and his young bride unwittingly settle in a town run by devil worshippers. Standard slow-motion dream sequences and photography tricks prove more cliched than creepy. Directed by Bernard Kowalski; with Roy Thinnes, Yvette Mimieux, Gloria Grahame, Lynn Loring, Ray Milland, Henry Silva.

CAT CREATURE, THE (1973, Screen Gems, ABC). This was Robert Bloch's (author of the book on which *Psycho* was based) homage to old style horror movies. The curse of an Egyptian cat goddess brings death and destruction to twentieth-century mortals. A standout is veteran screen villianess Gale Sondergaard as the cat queen. Directed by Curtis Harrington; with Sondergaard, David Hedison, Stuart Whitman, Merideth Baxter, Keye Luke, John Carradine.

CITY BENEATH THE SEA (1970, Twentieth Century-Fox, NBC). An ambitious pilot from Irwin Allen that didn't make it as a regular series. In 2050 A.D., colonists in the world's first underwater city face dangers from without: meteors, deep sea monsters, and within: personal squabbles. There were excellent special effects and a so-so plot. Directed by Allen; with Robert Wagner, Stuart Whitman, Rosemary Forsyth, Joseph Cotten, Richard Basehart, James Darren.

COLD NIGHT'S DEATH, A (1973, Spelling-Goldberg, ABC). A ponderous, talky horror story set in an arctic wasteland research laboratory. Two quarrelsome scientists, sent to replace a dead predecessor, find themselves the unwitting subjects of a bizarre experiment conducted by monkeys! Directed by Jerrold Freedman; with Robert Culp, Eli Wallach, Michael C. Gwynne.

CROWHAVEN FARM (1970, Aaron Spelling-Paramount, ABC). Witchcraft, reincarnation and Hope Lange are set in the middle of a corny horror story. Despite much contrivance, this movie manages a few really effective scare sequences. Directed by Walter Grauman; with Lange, Paul Burke, Lloyd Bochner, John Carradine, Patricia Barry, Cyril Delevanti.

DAUGHTER OF THE MIND (1969, Twentieth Century-Fox, ABC). Based on a Paul Gallico story, this supernatural suspense thriller concerns a noted American scientist who is haunted by the ghost of his little girl. The "phenomenon" is finally revealed as a clever plot to get the scientist to defect to an enemy country. Directed by Walter Grauman; with Ray Milland, Gene Tierney, Don Murray, Pamelyn Ferdin, George Macready, Edward Asner.

THE DEAD DON'T DIE (1974, Douglas Cramer, NBC). In 1934 Chicago, Varek, a crazed zombie master, launches an insidious plot to rule the world with his army of living dead. This formula thriller is reminiscent of creaking grade-C horror movies of the forties, although the zombie makeups are pretty hair-raising. Directed by Curtis Harrington; with George Hamilton, Ray Milland, Linda Cristal, Joan Blondell, Ralph Meeker, Reggie Nalder.

THE DEADLY DREAM (1971, Universal, ABC). This is a confusing melodrama about a man whose nightmares are real. Directed by Alf Kjellin; with Lloyd Bridges, Carl Betz, Don Stroud, Richard Jaeckel, Phillip Pine.

DEATH TAKES A HOLIDAY (1971, Universal, ABC). This movie was a poor remake of the 1934 Fredric March fantasy classic. Death, played by Monte Markham, comes to Earth to discover why human beings cling so to life, and ends up falling in love with a beautiful woman. Slick direction by Robert Butler; with Markham, Myrna Loy, Yvette Mimieux, Melvyn Douglas, Maureen Reagan.

THE DEVIL AND MISS SARAH (1971, Universal, ABC). An evil outlaw places the weak-willed bride of a farmer under his demonic control. The film's Old West setting doesn't rescue this undistinguished chiller from the deadly spell of boredom. Directed by Michael Caffey; with Gene Barry, James Drury, Janice Rule, Logan Ramsey, Charles McGraw.

DEVIL'S DAUGHTER, THE (1972, Paramount, ABC). In this mild reworking of the *Rosemary's Baby* premise, a woman is hounded by a coven of Satanists determined to possess her soul. Slick and unconvincing, the film wastes a competent cast. Directed by Jeannot Szwarc; with Shelley Winters, Belinda Montgomery, Robert Foxworth, Jonathan Frid, Joseph Cotten.

DON'T BE AFRAID OF THE DARK (1973, Lorimar Productions, ABC). After moving into a mansion she has inherited, a young woman is terrorized by gnomelike

ABOVE: Monte Markham and Yvette Mimieux in *Death Takes A Holiday*.
ABOVE RIGHT: Leonard Nimoy in *Baffled*.
RIGHT: Robert Culp in *A Cold Night's Death*.
BELOW: (left to right): Ray Milland, Joan Blondell and George Hamilton in *The Dead Don't Die*.

creatures. Some gruesome monster make-up and an eerie score by Billy Goldenberg are the only interesting elements of this tame shocker. Directed by John Newland; with Kim Darby, Jim Hutton, Pedro Armendariz, Jr., Barbara Anderson, Lesley Woods.

DRACULA (1975, Dan Curtis, CBS). Jack Palance's overplayed Count Dracula is long on meaningless dialogue and short on conviction, coming across more like a love-starved Barnabas Collins (*Dark Shadow's* resident ghoul) than Bram Stoker's classic vampire. Although it was only shown on TV here, the movie was filmed in Europe and released in England as a theatrical movie. Screenplay by Richard Matheson; produced and directed by Dan Curtis; with Jack Palance, Simon Ward.

Jack Palance made a successful switch from playing movie heavies to portraying classic ghouls on TV, with starring roles in *Dracula* and, here, in *The Strange Case of Dr. Jekyll and Mr. Hyde.*

DUEL (1971, Universal, ABC). Despite some hokey symbolism, this offbeat man-vs.-machine story packs quite a punch. A man, driving home from a business trip, tangles with a monster truck in a duel to the death. Written by Richard Matheson, from his short story; directed by Steven ("Jaws") Spielberg; with Dennis Weaver, Tim Herbert, Charles Peel, Eddie Firestone.

EARTH II (1971, MGM, ABC). Forgettable dramatics mar this otherwise interesting sci-fi story about a self-contained space station orbiting the Earth. Directed by Tom Gries; with Hari Rhodes, Gary Lockwood, Tony Franciosa, Lew Ayres, Scott Hylands.

THE EYES OF CHARLES SAND (1972, Warner Bros., ABC). A man inherits "the sight," a peculiar gift that enables him to peek into the future. Unfortunately, his unique power is wasted in this contrived murder mystery, which was a pilot for a never-launched series. Directed by Reza Badiyi; with Peter Haskell, Barbara Rush, Sharon Farrell, Bradford Dillman, Adam West.

FEAR NO EVIL (1969, Universal, NBC). This is the first—and the best—made-for-television occult chiller. A young woman sees visions of her dead fiance in a grotesque antique mirror; it's up to psychiatrist David Sorel to save her soul from possession. This was actually a pilot for the never-launched *Bedevilled* series. It also spawned a sequel, *Ritual of Evil.* Directed by Paul Wendkos; with Louis Jourdan, Lynda Day (George), Bradford Dillman, Carroll O'Connor, Wilfred Hyde-White.

FRANKENSTEIN—THE TRUE STORY (1974, Universal, NBC). This epic adaptation, filmed in England, has very little to do with the "true story" of Mary Shelley's Frankenstein, but is a brilliantly written variation of the central theme. According to Christopher Isherwood's screenplay, Frankenstein's assistant had the burning desire to create life from the dead. A surgeon, played robustly by James Mason, pieced together a bride for the monster. Despite the changes, this ambitious production is one of the best horror films ever made. Directed by Jack Smight; Michael Sarrazin, Leonard Whiting, David McCallum, James Mason, Sir Ralph Richardson, Margaret Leighton.

ABOVE and LEFT: Leonard Whiting as Dr. Frankenstein and Michael Sarrazin as the monster he created. BELOW: Louis Jourdan chats with Wilfred Hyde-White in *Fear No Evil*. In the same movie Bradford Dillman found himself in a less comfortable situation.

GARGOYLES (1972, Metromedia, CBS). A prehistoric race of half-human, half-reptilian creatures plan to wipe out mankind in this mediocre movie. However there were excellent makeup and costumes by Ellis Berman and Ross Wheat, who won Emmys for their work. Directed by B.W.L. Norton; with Cornel Wilde, Jennifer Salt, Bernie Casey, Grayson Hall.

GEMINI MAN, THE (1975, Universal, NBC). This pilot for the weekly series is actually a reworking of David McCallum's unsuccessful *Invisible Man* series. In this new version, Ben Murphy plays an undersea researcher who can remain invisible for only a few hours at a stretch. It is a fair adventure, created by the producers of the *Six Million Dollar Man.* Directed by Allan Levi; with Katherine Crawford, Richard Dysart, Dana Elcar.

GENESIS II (1973, Paramount, CBS). Producer Gene Roddenberry evidently hoped for another *Star Trek* in this pedestrian sci-fi flick about a twentieth-century scientist who, preserved in suspended animation for a few centuries, thaws out in a strange, hostile world. Remade the following year as *Planet Earth,* the film was directed by John Llewellyn Moxey; with Alex Cord, Mariette Hartley, Lynn Marta, Percy Rodrigues, Harvey Jason, Ted Cassidy.

HAUNTS OF THE VERY RICH (1972, Lillian Gallo, ABC). Seven people, vacationing on a mysterious tropical island, lose touch with reality in this bizarre but uneven reworking of the *Outward Bound* premise. Some nice touches in direction by Paul Wendkos; with Lloyd Bridges, Cloris Leachman, Edward Asner, Tony Bill, Anne Francis.

HAUSER'S MEMORY (1970, Universal, NBC). A effective science-fiction spy thriller, this feature concerns scientist involved in a dangerous experiment in which simple chemical transfer can transmit one person memory to another. His assistant injects the serum into hi own arm and embarks on a trip of terror, encountering th enemies in the other man's past. Directed by Boris Saga with David McCallum, Susan Strasberg, Lilli Palmer, Lesli Nielsen.

HORROR AT 37,000 FEET, THE (1973, Anthony Wilson CBS). This feature had an interesting premise, but wa botched by overly conventional handling. Occult force are at work when an unseen power in a 747's cargo hol produces strange voices, freezing cold and a bizarr headwind that holds a plane motionless in the sky. Directe by David Lowell Rich; with William Shatner, Roy Thinnes Buddy Ebsen, Tammy Grimes, Lynn Loring.

HOUND OF THE BASKERVILLES, THE (1972, Univer sal, ABC). This tedious remake of the Sherlock Holme classic was the pilot for a never-launched series to b called *Great Detectives* in which Conan Doyle's famou sleuth was to rotate with Nick Carter, Charlie Chan and other notables. The major error of this feature was casting Stewart Granger as Holmes. He was too congenial a fellow without a trace of the arrogance so necessary to the role Directed by Barry Crane; with Granger, William Shatner Bernard Fox, John Williams, Anthony Zerbe.

THE HOUSE THAT WOULDN'T DIE (1970, Aaron Spelling-Paramount, ABC). The house, of course, is haunted. Its restless spirits possess a few of its inhabitant before they manage to unlock its secret and exorcise the place. Directed by John Llewellyn Moxey; with Barbara Stanwyck, Katherine Winn, Richard Egan, Michae Anderson, Jr.

THE IMMORTAL (1969, Paramount, ABC). This was the pilot for the short-lived series of the same name. After ar accident, test driver Ben Richards discovers that his peculiar blood type makes him immune to all diseases, as well as to the aging process. Ben is forced to flee when a billionaire decides to capture him and turn him into a private "fountain of youth." Directed by Joseph Sargent with Christopher George, Jessica Walter, Barry Sullivan, Carol Lynley, Ralph Bellamy.

INVISIBLE MAN, THE (1975, Universal, NBC). When a brilliant scientist discovers a way to make himself invisible, he is faced with keeping his secret formula from falling into the wrong hands. This passable pilot for the short-lived TV series of the same name benefits from likable lead players and top-notch special effects. Directed by Robert M. Lewis; with David McCallum, Henry Darrow, Melinda Fee, Jackie Cooper.

KILLDOZER (1972, Universal, ABC). Based on a famous science-fiction story by Theodore Sturgeon and probably inspired by the success of *Duel,* this well-made man-vs.-machine thriller pits a small band of construction workers against a murderous bulldozer. The machine is actually possessed by an alien intelligence, but why it chooses to kill everyone in sight is never established. Taut direction by Jerry London; with Clint Walker, Carl Betz, Neville Brand, James Wainwright, Robert Ulrich.

Two of the all time great ladies of the movies, Gloria Swanson in *Killer Bees* and Bette Davis as *Madam Sin.*

KILLER BEES (1974, R.S.O. Films, ABC). Gloria Swanson, in her television acting debut, plays the bizarre matriarch of a weathy bee-farming family who is secretly a human Queen Bee. This silly concept was treated more imaginatively in Freddie Francis's *The Deadly Bees* (1967) and *The Outer Limits'* "ZZZZZ." Directed by Curtis Harrington; with Swanson, Edward Albert, Kate Jackson, Craig Stevens.

KUNG FU (1971, Warner Bros., ABC). This was the pilot to TV's popular western-adventure series. Directed by Jerry Thorpe; with David Carradine, Barry Sullivan, Keith Carradine, Keye Luke.

THE LAST CHILD (1971, Aaron Spelling, ABC). Population control is the villain of this chase drama set in 1994. In it a pair of young people commit an unpardonable crime—they have a second child. The issues and problems explored in this reasonably effective film are actually far more intriguing than the results. Edward Asner is excellent as a guilt-ridden population inspector. Directed by John Llewellyn Moxey; with Michael Cole, Janet Margolin, Van Heflin, Harry Guardino.

THE LEGEND OF LIZZIE BORDEN (1975, Paramount, ABC). Director Paul Wendkos's daring and morbid account of the 1892 Lizzie Borden murder case. In the fascinating title role, a gaunt, expressionless Elizabeth Montgomery sheds the last vestiges of her *Bewitched* image and is properly bizarre. Directed by Paul Wendkos; with Fionnuala Flanagan, Ed Flanders, Katherine Helmond, Don Porter, Fritz Weaver, Helen Craig, John Beal.

LOOK WHAT'S HAPPENED TO ROSEMARY'S BABY (1976, Paramount, ABC) took up where the feature film starring Mia Farrow left off. The infant of dubious parentage grows up before our eyes and everything hinges on his 21st birthday when it will be known once and for all whether the experiment worked and if he is indeed the child of Satan. There's one good chill in the midst of this rather poor movie when Patty Duke Astin as the child's mother is whisked away in a speeding bus—without a driver. Directed by Sam O'Steen; with Stephen McHattie as Rosemary's offspring, Ruth Gordon (recreating her earlier movie role), Patty Duke Astin, Ray Milland, George Maharis, Tina Louise, Broderick Crawford and Lloyd Haines.

THE LOVE WAR (1970, Aaron Spelling-Paramount, ABC). Creatures from warring planets Argon and Zinan take human form to fight it out, using Earth as the neutral territory. Kyle, one of the Argonian soldiers, jeopardizes his mission by falling in love with an Earthling, Sandy, who is actually a Zinan spy. More a chase-action melodrama than a science-fiction tale, but the final shot of Sandy in her true alien form is haunting. Directed by George McCowan; with Lloyd Bridges, Angie Dickinson, Harry Basch.

MADAM SIN (1971, Universal, ABC). Bette Davis as a female "Dr. No" who plans to control the world with the help of a C.I.A. agent. Not quite bad enough to be camp, but close. Directed by David Green; with Davis, Robert Wagner, Paul Maxwell.

ABOVE: Burl Ives was *The Man Who Wanted to Live Forever.*
BELOW: Moon of the Wolf featured a werewolf, stock-in-trade of horror flicks since film-making began.

THE MAN WHO WANTED TO LIVE FOREVER (1970, Palomar, ABC). The new head of a heart research center in the Canadian wilderness begins to suspect a terrible truth about his institute. Unpleasant science-fiction story originally titled *The Heart Farm*. Directed by John Trent with Burl Ives, Stuart Whitman, Sandy Dennis.

MOON OF THE WOLF (1972, Filmways, ABC). This telefeature is about werewolves in modern-day Louisiana and a host of red herrings. Directed by Daniel Petrie; with David Janssen, Barbara Rush, Bradford Dillman, John Bernadino.

THE NEW ADVENTURES OF THE INVISIBLE MAN
See: **THE INVISIBLE MAN.**

THE NEW, ORIGINAL WONDER WOMAN (1975, Warner Bros., ABC). Stanley Ralph Ross, of *Batman* fame, scripted this spirited adaptation of the comic book favorite that juggles both camp and serious elements. As WW, the anatomically perfect Lynda Carter is a real eyeful, and Lyle Waggoner is equally well cast as her war hero sweetheart Steve Trevor. Directed by Leonard Horn; with Stella Stevens, Red Buttons, John Randolph, Cloris Leachman, Henry Gibson, Kenneth Mars, Eric Braedan, Fannie Flagg.

NIGHT GALLERY (1969, Universal, NBC). Actually a series pilot, these three tales of terror were hosted by Rod Serling. In the first, directed by Boris Sagal, a scheming nephew murders his uncle and lives to suffer the bizarre consequences. The second, directed by Steven (*Jaws*) Spielberg, features Joan Crawford as an evil blind woman with a passion to see: she steals the sight of another for a few hours, but is foiled by a power blackout. The concluding segment, handled by Barry Shear, concerns the terrible punishment awaiting a Nazi war criminal obsessed with a painting in a museum. In this uneven bag of shudders, Spielberg's segment fares best. With Roddy McDowell, Ossie Davis, George Macready (first story); Crawford, Barry Sullivan, Tom Bosley (second story); Richard Kiley, Sam Jaffe (third story).

NIGHT SLAVES (1970, Warner Bros., ABC). This is a science-fiction tale disguised as a mystery. Stopping at a small town, our hero, a man with a metal plate in his head-watches as hypnotized townspeople awaken in the middle of the night and go off to a nearby field to work on a disabled spaceship. Offbeat and interesting. Directed by Ted Post; with James Franciscus, Lee Grant, Scott Marlowe, Andrew Prine, Tisha Sterling, Leslie Nielsen.

THE NIGHT STALKER (1971, Dan Curtis, ABC). Carl Kolchak's classic adventure. A series of unusual slayings convince the disheveled reporter that a vampire is stalking Las Vegas. The teleplay was written by Richard Matheson from a story by Jeff Rice. Directed by John Llewellyn Moxey; with Darren McGavin, Carol Lynley, Simon Oakland, Ralph Meeker, Claude Akins, Kent Smith, Barry Atwater.

THE NIGHT STRANGLER (1972, Dan Curtis, ABC). The sequel to *The Night Stalker*, Richard Matheson's original story and teleplay pits newshawk Kolchak against a murderous alchemist living beneath the streets of Seattle. The best of the Carl Kolchak monster-fests features a marvelous, word-a-second dialog and ingenious pacing. It succeeds both as a satire and as an imaginative, harrowing

The Night That Panicked America was based on Orson Welles's famous radio report of a Martian invasion.

thriller. Directed by Dan Curtis; with Darren McGavin, Jo Ann Pflug, Simon Oakland, Scott Brady, John Carradine, Wally Cox, Margaret Hamilton, Richard Anderson.

THE NIGHT THAT PANICKED AMERICA (1975, Paramount, ABC). Based on a true incident, this film traces the events surrounding Orson Welles's 1938 radio adaptation of H.G. Wells's *War of the Worlds.* (In case you've forgotten, that broadcast convinced many Americans that Martians had actually invaded New Jersey!). On the whole, this is a fine, well-acted pseudo-documentary. Directed by J. Sargent; with Paul Shenar (as Orson Welles), Vic Morrow, Will Geer, Cliff DeYoung, Michael Constantine, Walter McGinn.

THE NORLISS TAPES (1973, Dan Curtis, NBC). Scriptwriter William F. Nolan's entry in the ghost-hunter sweepstakes is a disappointing collection of warmed-over *Night Stalker* scenes. Norliss, a grim reporter investigating rumors of a living dead man, soon finds himself in the clutches of an ancient demon-spirit. Directed by Dan Curtis; with Roy Thinnes, Angie Dickinson.

THE PEOPLE (1971, Metromedia, ABC). "The People" are space visitors who colonized our world years ago but still retain some unearthly powers (i.e., levitation, ESP, etc.). The new wrinkle is that these aliens are peace-loving, old-fashioned folks, almost like extraterrestrial Waltons. A mild yet engaging sci-fi fantasy, directed by John Korty; with Kim Darby, William Shatner, Dan O'Herlihy, Diane Varsi.

THE PHANTOM OF HOLLYWOOD (1974, MGM, CBS). Strange, uneven remake of the *Phantom of the Opera,* switched to a Hollywood setting. Directed by Gene Levitt, starring Ross Martin, Jackie Coogan, Broderick Crawford, Peter Lawford.

The resident phantom of a large movie studio comes back to life in order to frighten the owners out of selling in *The Phantom of Hollywood.*

THE PICTURE OF DORIAN GRAY (1973, Dan Curtis Production, ABC). Shane Briant brought Oscar Wilde' famous character to life. A beautiful young man shows n physical signs of aging or of the dissolute life he leads. hidden portrait, however, does. Directed by Dan Curtis, th movie was presented in two 90-minute parts.

PLANET EARTH (1974, Warner Bros., ABC). A reworkinc of Gene Roddenberry's *Genesis II* concept, as twentieth century scientist Dylan Hunt, revived from suspendec animation in the future, encounters a society ruled b women. Standard sci-fi fare, not up to Roddenberry' earlier work on *Star Trek*. Directed by Marc Daniels; with John Saxon, Janet Margolin, Diana Muldaur, Ted Cassidy

POOR DEVIL (1972, Paramount, NBC). Christopher Lee as Satan is the most interesting element of this silly farce about a lowly assistant in Hell, played by Sammy Davis, Jr. who gets a chance to earn his horns by capturing the sou of a desperate man (Jack Klugman). This pilot for a never launched series was directed by Robert Scheerer; with Davis, Jr., Klugman, Gino Conforti, Adam West, Madlyr Rhue.

THE QUESTOR TAPES (1974, Universal, NBC). A sophisticated android, played by Robert Foxworth, is the star of this latest unsold pilot film produced by Gene (*Star Trek*) Roddenberry. Directed by Richard A. Colla; with Robert Foxworth, Mike Farrell, John Vernon, Lew Ayres Dana Winter, James Shigeta.

RITUAL OF EVIL (1970, Universal, NBC). Psychiatris David Sorel trespasses on the supernatural while investi- gating the death of one of his patients. This sequel to *Fea No Evil* and the second pilot for Universal's unsolc *Bedevilled* series is part psychological character study part occult thriller. The effective score by William Goldenberg was later used as background music for *The Sixth Sense*. Directed by Robert Day; with Louis Jourdan Anne Baxter, Diana Hyland, Wilfred Hyde-White, Belinda Montgomery.

ABOVE: Shane Briant played the title role in *Picture of Dorian Gray,* Oscar Wilde's classic chiller. **BELOW:** An android, played by Mike Farrell, prepares to activate Questor, an ambulatory computer. **BELOW RIGHT:** Anne Baxter in *Ritual of Evil.*

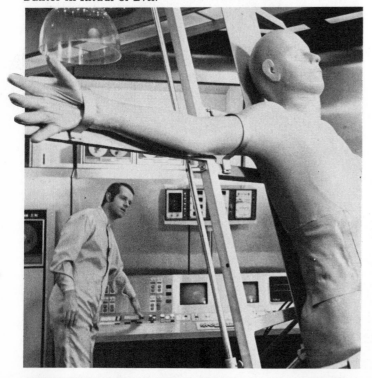

SANDCASTLES (1972, Metromedia, CBS). The old *Ghost and Mrs. Muir* theme is reworked in this love story in which one lover is a ghost. Directed by Ted Post; with Jan-Michael Vincent, Bonnie Bedelia, Hershel Bernardi.

SATAN'S SCHOOL FOR GIRLS (1973, Spelling-Goldberg, ABC). Roy Thinnes, the dean of TV-demon movies, plays Satan in this silly chiller about an outbreak of evil at a fashionable girl's school. Directed by David Lowell Rich; with Thinnes, Pamela Franklin, Kate Jackson, Jo Van Fleet, Lloyd Bochner.

SATAN'S TRIANGLE (1975, Danny Thomas Productions, ABC). Murder and mayhem occur in that infamous area off the Florida coast. Kim Novak is the sole survivor of a bizarre storm that wiped out all the other passengers on a small fishing boat. There are occasional creepy moments in this supernatural sea saga, but mostly melodrama. Written by William Read Woodfield; with Novak, Doug McClure, Alejandro Rey, Jim Davis, Ed Lauter.

SCREAM OF THE WOLF (1974, Dan Curtis, ABC). The hunt is on for a murderous monster, but the terror turns out to be more psychological than supernatural. An effective thriller, from the producer of the *Night Stalker* features. Directed by *Dan Curtis,* with Clint Walker, Peter Graves.

RIGHT: Kim Novak made one her infrequent TV appearances in *Satan's Triangle.* BELOW: Roy Thinnes of the old *Invaders* series in *Satan's School for Girls.*

SEARCH FOR THE GODS (1975, Warner Bros., ABC). One can surely thank the gods that this pilot never made it to the home screen. A team of explorers searches for ancient gods in the Taos, New Mexico area. Directed by Jud Taylor; with Stephen McHattie, Kurt Russell, Victoria Racimo, Raymond St. Jaques, Ralph Bellamy.

ABOVE: Veteran movie actor Lew Ayres (right) and Glenn Corbett in *The Stranger*. BELOW: Barbara Eden gave birth to an extraterrestial child in *The Stranger Within*.

SHADOW ON THE LAND (1968, Screen Gems, ABC). In the not-so-distant future, America becomes a Nazi-like dictatorship challenged by a fearless underground. This pilot had an interesting concept and was very well handled. Directed by Richard Sarafian; with Jackie Cooper, John Forsythe, Carol Lynley, Gene Hackman.

SHE WAITS (1971, Metromedia, CBS). A young woman is haunted by the sound of a music box in this inept tale of ghostly possession. Directed by Delbert Mann; with Patty Duke, David McCallum, Lew Ayres, Dorothy McGuire, Beulah Bondi.

THE SIX MILLION DOLLAR MAN (1973, Universal, ABC). This lively pilot for the popular adventure series explains how Col. Steve Austin, after surviving a near-fatal accident, was "repaired" with bionic limbs and turned into a government secret weapon. Directed by Richard Irving; with Lee Majors, Darren McGavin, Martin Balsam, Barbara Anderson.

SOLE SURVIVOR (1969, Cinema Center 100, CBS). Guilt and retribution mark the discovery of a downed B-52 in the Libyan desert, as the wandering ghosts of its crew wait anxiously for release. Contrived but well-acted drama, directed by Paul Stanley; with Vince Edwards, Richard Basehart, William Shatner, Larry Casey.

SOMETHING EVIL (1970, Bedford Productions, CBS). There are some shuddery moments in this possession tale. Johnnie Whitaker plays a child controlled by a demonic force that strikes with the ferocity of a hurricane. Directed by Steven (*Jaws*) Spielberg; with Sandy Dennis, Darren McGavin, Ralph Bellamy.

THE STRANGER (1972, Bing Crosby Productions, ABC). A man suddenly finds himself on a strange planet, with two moons in its night sky. This was a pilot for a never-launched series, directed by Lee H. Katzin; with Glenn Corbett, Cameron Mitchell, Lew Ayres, and Sharon Acker.

THE STRANGER WITHIN (1974, Lorimar, ABC). Combining elements of *Rosemary's Baby* and *The Exorcist* with science fiction, Richard Matheson's uneven teleplay explores the mystery of a woman who gives birth to an extraterrestrial child. Directed by Lee Phillips; with Barbara Eden, George Grizzard, Joyce Van Patten.

THE STRANGE CASE OF DR. JEKYLL AND MR. HYDE (1974, Dan Curtis Production, ABC). The classic tale of horror penned by Robert Louis Stevenson was brought to life with the split personality hero played by Jack Palance. It told the story of the two warring parts of man's soul, with Dr. Jekyll representing all that is good and Mr. Hyde personifying evil. Directed by Dan Curtis, it was presented on two consecutive nights in 90-minute installments.

SWEET, SWEET RACHEL (1971, Stan Stepner, ABC). This so-so pilot for Universal's *The Sixth Sense* (with different names and characters) concerns a woman tormented by ghoulish ESP images. Alex Drier plays the psychic researcher later replaced by Gary Collins's Dr. Michael Rhodes in the series. Directed by Sutton Roley; with Drier, Stefanie Powers, Pat Hingle, Louise Latham, Steve Ihnat, Brenda Scott.

THE TIME TRAVELERS (1975, Twentieth Century-Fox, ABC). Rod Serling and Irwin Allen joined forces to produce this mediocre story about a group of scientists who travel

backward in time to prevent the Chicago fire. It was a pilot for a never-launched series. Directed by Alex Singer; with Sam Groom, Tom Hallick, Richard Basehart, Trish Stewart.

TRILOGY OF TERROR (1974, ABC Circle, ABC). Three contemporary stories of the bizarre. Actress Karen Black starred in all three. "Millicent and Therese" are rival sisters whose bitter hatred soon turns to murder. "Julie" is a teacher being blackmailed by one of her students for past indiscretions in which she played an unwilling part. Or was it? "Amelia" is a young woman, dominated by her mother, who buys a fetish doll for her new male companion. Soon after, the doll comes to life and embarks on a terrifying campaign of murder. Richard Matheson scripted the last (and best) segment, and all three were based on his short stories. William F. Nolan adapted the first two. Pilot—for a never-launched anthology series to be entitled *Dead of Night*. Directed by Dan Curtis.

THE UFO INCIDENT (1975, Universal, NBC). This superb dramatization of the book *Interrupted Journey* details the strange adventure of real-life couple Betty and Barney Hill. They claimed to have been abducted by pint-sized space creatures who brought them aboard their flying saucer for exhaustive tests. The acting is brilliant, the direction restrained and terrifyingly subtle. One of the best made-for-TV movies. Directed by Richard A. Colla; with James Earl Jones, Estelle Parsons, Bernard Hughes.

WHEN MICHAEL CALLS (1971, Twentieth Century-Fox, ABC). A mother receives phone calls from a voice sounding like her dead son's in this banal, predictable chiller. Directed by Philip Leacock; with Elizabeth Ashley, Ben Gazzara, Michael Douglas.

ABOVE: Karen Black in a tour-de-force set of performances in *Trilogy of Terror*. Clockwise from top left: Amelia, Millicent, Therese and Julie. **BELOW:** James Earl Jones held by alien creatures in *The UFO Incident*.

INDEX